BEING REEM

Joey Essex was born in 1990 in Bermondsey, South London, before moving to Essex. He has starred in nine series of the hit ITV2 show *The Only Way Is Essex*, appeared in the 2013 series of *I'm A Celebrity . . . Get Me Out Of Here!* and has travelled around the world for his own ITV2 show *Educating Joey Essex*. He owns his own shop, Fusey, in Brentwood, Essex. This is his first book.

BEING REEM

Joey Essex

HODDER

First published in Great Britain in 2014 by
Hodder & Stoughton
An Hachette UK company

First published in paperback in 2014

1

A CIP catalogue record for this title is available from the British Library

ISBN 978 1 444 79435 9

Typeset in Sabon MT by Palimpsest Book Production Ltd, Falkirk, Stirlingshire
Printed and bound by CPI Group (UK) Ltd, Croydon, CR0 4YY

Hodder & Stoughton policy is to use papers that are natural, renewable and
recyclable products and made from wood grown in sustainable forests. The
logging and manufacturing processes are expected to conform to the
environmental regulations of the country of origin.

Hodder & Stoughton Ltd
338 Euston Road
London NW1 3BH

www.hodder.co.uk

This book is dedicated to the memory of my beautiful mum, Martine Essex. I'll always miss you. And to my dad, Donald Essex, my hero and the person I'll always look up to.

CONTENTS

PROLOGUE*

KEVIN WYRE
Assistant Head Teacher, West Hatch High School, Chigwell, Essex, 2001–2007

When kids at my school find out I used to teach Joey Essex I always feel like I'm letting them down slightly if I don't tell them, 'Oh he forgot how to walk one day.' But it wasn't like that. When they ask me 'Is he really that stupid?' I always say, 'No'.

He always was a really nice lad with a decent attendance record. He looked smart and although he was never going to set the world on fire academically he wasn't stupid either.

Like many students, Joey found learning difficult and didn't see the value in certain things that he didn't think he needed. However, a lot of kids who think that way go off the rails behaviourally – they battle with teachers because they don't see the relevance of it – but even though Joey didn't find school easy he was happy enough to conform. He got on with everybody and, despite the hardship he suffered when he lost his mum, he always had a huge smile on his face.

Sometimes you hear of past students doing really well and deep down you think, 'Actually you don't deserve that. You were a little so and so at school and now you're driving a car like that.' But of all the teachers who worked with Joey there's not one of us who begrudges him anything.

I haven't seen Joey since he left school but I look at where he is now and I don't think anyone could possibly accuse him of not being a decent role model. He's a young man enjoying what comes his way. He's fallen into a lifestyle that he wouldn't have expected to have when he left school but I don't see him in the papers having drug issues, alcohol issues or doing anything bad. Instead, I see a young man who uses his looks, values his family, knows right from wrong and understands his limitations. There's a refreshing level of honesty in Joey – he says it as he sees it and if there's a consequence of that he will deal with it afterwards.

Joey is a kind-hearted young man and when people meet him they can't help wanting to protect and look after him.

When people ask what he was like I tell them he wasn't crashing from problem to problem because he was 'so thick'. However, if he was suddenly to appear on *Question Time* on a Thursday night? Then I might fear for him . . .!

A prologue? What's that? Is it a professional logger or something?

INTRO:
WHAT AM *I* SAYIN'?

3

When I look at myself on telly, I don't realise I'm such a nutty weirdo. I just like to do things in a different way to normal people.

My mates laugh at me all the time. Diags says he used to sit and try and teach me stuff, like when Gordon Brown was the prime minister but I just got him muddled up with Gordon Ramsay. And I really couldn't get my head around maths. My mate Tom Pearce would sit in the kitchen with me for ages and teach me the same sum over and over again and I'd finally say 'I've got it, I've definitely got it', then he'd leave the room and come back and it would've disappeared from my head. People always try and teach me things but just give up in the end.

Whenever I'm on ITV2's *Celebrity Juice* I'm asked all sorts of questions about the world and stuff. One of them was when Keith Lemon asked me what country bordered Wales and I answered 'Russia'. People always ask me if I really thought that. But it was the first place that came into my head when he asked the question and I thought 'I might as well say something'. As for Richard and Judy creating the world? Well they could've easily done it as well as those other two – Adam and whatshername. When people ask me questions like that I always think I know the answer because I've half paid attention to something and put two things together. It just happens that those two things are completely muddled. Still . . . I know I've heard them somewhere.

Like the time one Bonfire Night when my sister Frankie asked me if I knew the history of Guy Fawkes and I said he was the guy who died on the cross. Turns out that was Jesus.

Diags asked me if I knew what Parliament was the other day. I told him:

'It's that big castle in London. The one that has the flags up to tell people when the Queen is in.'

How was I meant to know that's Buckingham Palace?

While we're on the subject, I think it's a very strange idea to put a flag up to tell people if you're in or out. Or 'bait*' as I like to call it. It's a bit bait the Queen telling people what she's up to. Someone even told me a person broke in once and sat on the end of her bed having a chat. A chat with the Queen! 'Alright Queen. Your duvet looks reem.' (That's not what he said but he should've.)

What if there was a flag on my house saying whether Joey Essex was in or not? It would be a huge great big pole up to the sky. Imagine being asleep and having your window broken into then hearing 'All I want is to have a little chat' . . .!

Weird.

P.S. People who know me know I make up my own words for stuff sometimes. It's like I've got my own language. But it means you might not get what I'm talking about in some parts of this book. So there's a reem* Joey Dictionary at the back for any words that have a * next to them.

P.P.S. I've also been reading a book on the toilet which contains facts that will blow your mind. So I've decided to share some of them with you in the book. They're called Joey's Fascinating Facts and you'll see them dotted about throughout the chapters. I hope you like them. I think they're creepy sick*.

CHAPTER 1
FROGS AND FURBIES

SELF-PORTRAIT: JOEY ESSEX AGED TEN

My hair wasn't quite so fusey* in those days

See that picture of me? I drew it when I was ten. I look like a right bean*.

My whole life I've felt like I was different. Even before I was on TV. I feel like somehow I've had a journey that's been totally 'out there' and unique compared to everyone else.

I found some of my schoolwork the other day. There's a sheet of paper that asks me to write down my favourite and my least favourite part about school. I wrote that I liked swimming (I must've liked swimming a lot because I wrote it twice) and the part I didn't like was 'people being horrible to me'. Maybe that explains why I ended up the way I am. I've learnt to stick up for myself and to be proud of being different. And if it ends up making people laugh then that's fine by me.

I was a proper mummy's boy when I was growing up. I'd follow her about everywhere and snuggle up to her at night on the sofa. She was called Tina and was so pretty. I get upset sometimes because I can't remember as much about her as I want to. I was so young when she died that her memory gets blurry. I know she always had good dress sense, wore expensive Hermès scarves, smelt of Chanel perfume and her and my dad had these massive banana-shaped bendy phones – I really wanted one.

My earliest memory is sitting in the back garden in Bermondsey, South London, where we used to live before we moved to Chigwell. Mum had made macaroni cheese and I sat there with my sister Frankie and our mum just looking at the stars. I used to wonder why the moon glowed and whether it was made of cheese.

If I landed on the moon I really don't know if I'd feel chuffed or not. I don't think I'd feel happy about it because I'd be so scared. Plus that space helmet would make me claustrophobic.

My sister Frankie is three years older than me and used to thin
it was funny to dress me up as a girl. I have flashbacks of her
putting me in these weird old-fashioned clothes like a doll (I
probably made quite a good-looking girl, to be fair). She also
used to wind me up *a lot*. I wet myself once and she taped ten
nappies together and wrapped them all round me. She found it
hilarious. Frankie was a really happy kid like me and we laughed
and joked all the time. She was a bit chubbier when she was
younger but she didn't care about it back then. My dad said she
ended up losing too much weight when she got older. She's about
right now.

Frankie's mates were always at the house when I was growing
up. I fancied some of them but would never dare tell her. Anyway,
I'm too young to think about girls in this part of the book so
we'll move on to that later.

It's weird talking about my sister because I've never had to
describe her before. We sometimes get really aggy* with each
other. If she rings me I'll probably say, 'Frank, for God's sake!
I'm doing something' and she'll be exactly the same with me. I
think that's how you are with family. But I'd do anything for her.
She's one of the best girls I've ever met.

My dad is called Donald and he works as a porter in Billingsgate
Fish Market. He has to start at 3am – which should be an illegal
time to start work. Donald is the name of my dad's dad too and
Don is my middle name. Growing up in Essex no one ever believes
this is our real surname.

'Essex? You're making it up!'

Mum and Dad were in their early twenties when they got together. My dad used to be a boxer so did Mum's brothers Tony and Peter and I think that's how they were introduced. Whenever Dad talks about her now he just says she was the most beautiful girl he'd ever met. He loved her so much. He used to love making her laugh.

My dad is always being silly. He says stupid things which make me crack up. I find him hilarious. When we used to go to Spain on holiday he'd say 'Grassy Arse!' really loudly instead of saying 'Gracias'. I think that must be where I get my sense of humour from. Neither of us like being serious all that much.

I probably take after my mum in how I'm built. My Dad's massive! Mum was really slim and had dark Spanish-looking skin that comes from my granddad's side of the family. I think I've got a quarter Spanish in me, or some portion of Spanish anyway (I'm not very good at maths). I reckon that's why I can say 'hola', 'limon' and 'fresa' (although I pronounce it 'fleshay') which mean hello, lemon and strawberry. See – I'm fluent in it!

Mum was always really fashionable. She'd only wear quirky things though, not the same as everyone else. She made her own trends and I definitely get my style from her. All the other women had those Louis Vuitton bags with prints on, but Mum had a black one which was much classier. She had a Gucci bag, which Frankie still has, and the bit where your arm goes through was made out of bone. Unless its bamboo? I don't think it was actual bone . . . that would be odd. Her hair was dark and cut into a bob, she was so much more glamorous than other people's mums.

Her mum, my nanny Linda, is like that too. She's very well dressed for someone who's quite old. Mum and Nanny Linda were like best mates and they'd always go shopping to the Roman

Road market on a Saturday. I loved staring at all the stalls with all these colourful things for sale.

Christmas was brilliant at our house. Mum always decorated the tree with little gold ribbons and all the presents were wrapped in gold paper. Frankie still does the same thing with the tree at my dad's house every year. I found a DVD of me and Frankie when we were kids the other day, opening our presents. My mum is filming us and there's ripped-up gold paper all over the floor. Mum and Dad spoilt us rotten. In the video Frankie's sitting there, pulling open all these designer clothes – she's got D&G dresses and everything. I'm in the corner squealing in a really high-pitched voice, 'I've just got a Furby!'

Furbies were the nuts. They were like cute fluffy little gremlin things. It was the toy everyone wanted and I had one. I don't think I could ever be that excited again even if someone bought me a Ferrari.

Although if anyone reading this would like to buy me a Ferrari, I would like to point out that I will be very happy. I just won't squeal.

Watching the DVD back, I look like I'm about to wet myself. Then you can hear my mum's voice from behind the camera telling me I've got to share the Furby with Frankie. Talk about ruining the moment.

I'd like a Joey Essex Furby that says 'reem' and 'what are you sayin*'?' in a funny voice. I could call it a JERBY.

11

I went to church dressed as Rudolph once. I don't know why. Reindeers are funny aren't they? I used to get them confused with dolphins. I couldn't remember which it was that Father Christmas drove around in the sky. And I didn't know what the Nativity was until someone told me the other day. I thought it was an activity. I also thought Jesus's mum was called Zesus until Helen Flanagan told me it was Mary (this was in a 'Back to School' quiz on *Celebrity Juice*).

I don't understand much about Easter either. Apparently it's got nothing to do with eggs, chickens or bunnies. I know it's to do with Jesus but I thought the eggs came about because he was born in hay (and you get eggs in hay).

But I loved Christmas. And I loved animals, still do. Not that I was always good to them. We had a pet cat called Tiddles when I was younger and I nearly chopped her tail off. I was closing the patio doors and she suddenly jumped through the air into the house (I forgot she had a tail and slammed it). Suddenly the poor cat was hanging in the air, half inside and half outside the house, making this horrible screechy sound. She was properly sicking out*, scratching my face and my ears. Luckily Mum opened the doors and let her out before her tail came off completely. I think she ran off to live in the pub down the road after that. Tiddles HATED ME.

Tiddles, if you're reading this from cat heaven – I'm sorry. I miss you. You were the cutest cat I'd ever seen and I always looked at you like a grey tiger. And that will never change because you looked like a tiger.

I was usually very kind to animals though. Another Christmas, I went out to the back garden and saw a little bird on a bush to the left of the patio steps. He'd broken his wing. It was so cold outside that I felt sorry for him so I took him into the kitchen and gave him some Christmas dinner. Well, I gave him a few peas then let him go. If I'd given him a sprout he might have blown up.

Sometimes I wonder what goes on in animals' minds. When I watch those David Attenborough nature programmes and they're sat there eating insects I wonder, 'What are they thinking about?' They're probably thinking, 'Why are these people watching us on telly? Leave us alone and let us get on with it.' They must have quite boring lives, the ones in the wild. They can't exactly go clubbing or chat up girls so what have they got to look forward to? Imagine having a life that's just about survival? Not being allowed to go out to dinner or go on holiday. Instead it's, 'We've got ant for breakfast' . . . or 'It's time for some meerkat today'.

At least the dogs in Essex get to wear clothes.

But the animals I loved most in the whole wide world were frogs. Tree frogs to be precise. I was addicted to them. Nanny Linda had a boyfriend who had loads of frogspawn and he'd let me take it home and put it in my pond so I could breed them myself. I used to have a little pot by the back door in Chigwell and I'd put all the spawn in there and sit there and wait for them for hours, desperate for something to happen to them.

My bedroom was covered in frogs. I had frog teddies, a frog

bedspread, frog key rings, frog stickers and a frog lamp. Everyone else in my street had garden gnomes but we had special frog gnomes. I was mad on them. If I could've changed my name to Frog I probably would've.

Frog Essex. Sounds quite reem to be honest.

I even went to a frog museum in Chicago once. It blew my mind. I'd gone there to visit my granddad George. He's my mum's dad but he left when she was only little. America was cool – I liked catching glow flies in jam jars and then pretending they were torches. I moved on to ducks when I got older. Frogs and ducks are just small and pointless and don't do much. A bit like me! I never really realised that until I started writing this book.

DUCKS V FROGS

Frogs	Ducks
Good skin texture	Waterproof feathers
Big eyes	They're born with boots on
Long tongues	Beaks that are made of wood

Other boys were into cars, and wrestling, but I never liked it.

I couldn't see the point of wrestling – you'd sit and watch it on TV and everyone would shout stupid things like 'Yeah! Choke! Slam!' but why would you do that? I knew in my head that it was all a big show-off thing and just couldn't understand why people got so excited about it. My dad took me to a wrestling match once and I could tell they weren't properly hitting each other. And I don't like liars.

Remember when people used to tell you TV gave you square eyes? I always knew that was a lie too. But I did believe if you made a funny face and the wind changed it would stay like it forever. I used to stand there on the street pulling these really odd faces just to see if it would happen. I wanted to look like Jim Carrey in *Ace Ventura*. I loved playing stupid fun things like Power Rangers and Ninja Turtles – I thought they were so cool. Anything too serious and I thought it was pointless.

Mum and Dad split up for a few months when me and Frankie were young. I didn't realise at the time but it was because of my mum's condition. She was seriously ill when I was growing up. She was suffering from depression but I didn't know anything about it until after she died. Looking back I think my dad used to shelter us from what was going on. He must've found it hard to cope.

When they split he didn't want to leave Frankie and me but for about four months he stayed at his brother Greg's house nearby. Dad's got two brothers – Big Greg who's 6ft 8 and normal-sized Doug who's just, well, normal.

I didn't start growing until I was about 17. That's when I had a big spurt (funny word: spurt). It's strange how you're in bed one night and the next minute your bones have grown and you're a giant. I'm 6ft now. Which isn't actually a giant at all.

Big Greg's got a wife called Sally and a daughter called Ferne. I was best man at his wedding but he didn't have a stag do. I found out the other day that this was my fault. Apparently organising the stag is the job of the best man. Sorry Greg. If you're reading this, it's not too late – you, me and my dad can go and large it in Ibiza. Reem.

I heard the other day that 'Reem' is now in the top list of baby names. How weird is that? I've never met a baby called Reem. Calling your kid Reem is pretty odd. I prefer Charlie.

Doug's wife is called Joanne and he's got two kids, Daniel and Heather.

Dad's mum is called Nanny Kipper. Well, her actual name's Rita but she had a dog called Kipper so it stuck. He died ages ago so I don't know why we're still using that name. Nanny Kipper always says the exact same thing to me whenever I see her. I say, 'You alright Nan?' and she'll reply, 'Yeah, just big, fat and lonely.' She's never really cared about fashion, nor has my dad. Fashion sense definitely comes from my mum's side of the family. The only thing I have in common with Dad when it comes to clothes is that we both like shorts. Although mine are much shorter than his!

Nanny Kipper always used to buy me face paint when I went to her house. Sometimes I'd paint weird things like books on my face – who knows, maybe people will face-paint this book on! And she always used to cook me bacon sandwiches in brown bread.

That's making me hungry . . .

Even though my dad's dad was called Donald, I called him Granddad Whiskers. He had loads of wispy bits on his chin, a bit like a beard, but not really. I can't remember him and Nanny Kipper being together. He used to be in the marines, which might explain why they didn't stay together. I reckon they split because he was always underwater. Maybe she couldn't find him down there.

Granddad Whiskers kept loads of antiques. There were mirrors, big wooden things, lamps and all sorts. My dad takes after him like that because he never likes buying anything brand new and he collects old watches. Granddad was well built like my dad and was always laughing and joking.

On my mum's side, there's her brother Peter – he's married to Jackie and has twins called Summer and Scarlett. They're about 16 now.

Imagine if I had a twin Joey Essex. That would annoy the hell out of me. Seeing someone who looked the same would be well confusing. How would I know which one was me?

WHO ARE YOU ??
I'M JOEY ESSEX!
SO AM I!

Mum's other brother is Tony Simms who's married to my aunty Karen. He's Chloe and Charlie's dad. They've got two younger sisters called Frankie and Demi. I think one day the producers of *TOWIE* might find a way to get them on the show. Chloe has a different mum to the others though. Her mum left when she was just a kid. I think that's why we're so close because she knows how it is not to have your mum around.

Charlie is two years younger than me and joined *TOWIE* in series nine. I used to hang out with him loads when we were kids, probably even more than we do now to be honest. We spent loads of time together growing up and I don't know why but I always call him Jake. In my head I just thought 'Jake' meant 'Charlie'. I still get those names confused now!

I sort of remember Chloe changing my nappy once and talking about Marmite. Maybe she meant my nappy looked like it had Marmite in it. And I think she bunked off school at some point and a helicopter followed her. Which is jokes*.

Chloe is eight years older than me. She's also one of the only people I can tell all my secrets. Chloe's got a young daughter called Maddy. She's really cute and she loves me. I spoil her with loads of presents at Christmas and birthdays. A lot of kids love me to be fair. Especially babies. They always look at me funny.

Whenever I walk down the street and happen to pass a baby in a pushchair they always stare at me. I think 'Who are you staring at baby?'

Even though I don't remember too much about my mum and dad splitting up, I was so happy the day they got back together. Dad was wearing a yellow shirt (unless it was me who was dressed in yellow. One of us looked like Bart Simpson anyway) and they were cuddling and crying together. I didn't realise you had emotions like that at the time. But I knew I was so pleased about it.

JOEY'S FASCINATING FACTS:

#1 Kangaroos have three vaginas.
(That's quite incredible.)

CHAPTER 2

FRIENDS AND FIGHTS

You're as useless as you can be
just like a bumblebee
you're as useless as a book
to read just like a little weed
you're as useless as a soul
just like a demons skull
you're as useless as a crum
just like the sun
you're as useless as a drum, just like a
      chewing gum!

JOEY ESSEX
2000, Year 5

There was kid who lived in our street called Frankie Kingshot. There was also a boy called Dean Peach. What with me being called Joey Essex, we must have sounded like something out of a cartoon.

Some of the kids who lived near me in Bermondsey were

properly naughty – one of them tried to shoot me in the face with an air rifle once. Luckily it missed otherwise I might not have had a face. I remember thinking 'Why is someone trying to shoot me?'

But my best friends were – and still are – Tom Pearce, Jake Taylor and Steve Cass (there's also James Bennewith – aka Diags – but I haven't met him in this part of the book so don't worry about him yet!). Tom lived a few doors down from me and is ridiculously clever. He got a first in Economics at Loughborough University. He's also the clumsiest person I know.

I know Tom will read this and say 'Oooi!' but it's true. He breaks <u>everything</u>. If I came back to my house after I'd left him there my pens would all be chewed, my remote control* batteries would all be hanging out and he'd have broken the window. He smashed my chandelier once and an ancient lamp that was worth thousands of pounds.

*I call a remote control a presser. It sounds better.

Still, when we were younger I was the one having accidents. One day I was riding my new bike round the close with Tom and our mate Charlie Skeggs watching on. It was a chrome bike with peg things on the wheels and I thought I was the nuts. I was about to go round a corner and I stuck my arms in the air showing off – 'Look! No hands!' – BANG. As I flew round the bend, the bike started falling over, my face scraping along the side of the pavement. My mouth was pouring with blood and my teeth went right through my lip. The wound was hanging right open. Not reem.

If I smile now I'm sure you can see a bit of my lip hanging lower than the rest.

Tom and Charlie ran back to my house in a panic and got my dad – there was a trail of blood behind me like something out of a cartoon. It didn't look real.

My mum grabbed my head and was wailing, 'His teeth! They've all gone! His beautiful face!' My big left front tooth had snapped in half.

I was rushed to hospital and had to have stitches in my face, which *killed*. I swear I had a big bit of tissue stuck inside my lip for about four years after that because it got sewed up inside by mistake.

The doctor X-rayed my head and I asked him, 'Have I still got a brain left?'

I'm not sure if I did to be honest.

Mum took me to McDonald's afterwards and bought me some chicken nuggets to cheer me up. Except my face was so bruised and swollen I couldn't fit them into my mouth.

If you can believe this, about two days later my cousin Charlie hit me in the head with a golf club. We were playing with a plastic golf bat in the garden and then, for some reason, I decided to use my dad's real one instead. Charlie grabbed it from me and . . . WHAM – he'd swung it across my face. I didn't feel anything to start with. But when I looked at his face he was all wide-eyed with fear. 'It doesn't hurt,' I said, but then I saw blood and went mental.

So it was back to hospital for Joey Essex.

I've never really been into football but my dad is a huge Millwall supporter and used to take me to matches after school. My mum's side of the family supported West Ham so there was always a bit of jokey rivalry between them. Once my dad made me wear a West Ham shirt to a Millwall game for a laugh. I was really nervous thinking 'Am I going to get beaten up??' But he just found it funny.

I used to think Eric Cantona was the name of a football team. My dad would get really frustrated with me. 'Eric Cantona is a football player! He plays for United!' he'd shout. But I didn't believe him. The thing is, even when I got stuff wrong – which was most of the time – I believed I was right. '*Ooh Aaah Eric Cantona!*' That sounded more like a team than a player to me. It still does.

Dad was really into sport too – he was an amazing boxer when he was younger but in later life he got banned from the ring. I tried boxing for a bit but I wasn't very good at it. Even if I boxed for five years my arms would look like sticks compared to my dad. He doesn't want me to say anymore about this in the book in case the book blows up. But one thing he taught me was to always stand up for myself.

Anyway, forget boxing for now because I was a secret ice-skating demon. If you went to Romford ice rink on a Saturday afternoon you'd see me, little Joey Essex, whizzing about like some icy ninja. I can still ice-skate now – I'm one of those blokes who gets on the ice and starts skimming about backwards doing all these fancy shapes (good to impress the ladies). Imagine if

I'd gone on *Dancing on Ice*. I reckon I could easily pull off that Lycra.

I'm also good at long jump and running. I raced against the whole school once and came second (I was beaten by a girl called Verity but I fancied her so I didn't mind). And I'm brilliant at throwing. I've got a really good aim, it's a known secret between my mates. I can hit a pole from miles away with a stone. If I was in the Olympics, I reckon I'd get a gold medal for throwing.

Joey's special skillz:
- ~~writing~~
- ~~Holding a pen~~
- ~~Knowing who footballers are~~
- Backwards ice-skating
- Throwing
- Counting
- Long jump

CHAPTER 3

'WHEN'S MUM COMING BACK?'

I was at Alton Towers when Princess Diana died in 1997 (I didn't remember the date – I had to look it up). It was raining and I was really fed up because it meant we couldn't go on some of the rides. My mum said it was because the angels were crying. Whenever something bad happens in my life it always seems to be raining.

I didn't know that in a few years they'd be crying for my mum too.

My mum was really protective of me and Frankie and would do anything for us. Every night she would help me with my homework and I would always snuggle up to her. But deep down inside she was ill and unhappy.

I was always confused about what was wrong with my mum. She was often in hospital and I never understood why. Dad's told me since that she always thought there was something the matter with her. She was convinced she was sick. Dad would pay for all these doctors to check her over but they'd all say she was fine. She didn't believe them and was in and out of hospital constantly – she really thought there was something physically wrong with her. But it was all in her head.

I visited her in hospital once and she was smoking. I was really angry. I couldn't understand it. Why was she smoking if she was ill? I pulled the cigarette out of her hand and threw it out the window. My dad told me off. I was frustrated and upset . . . and confused. I was only a kid.

Dad would do everything he could to snap Mum out of it. He'd take her to nice places and buy her expensive clothes just to cheer her up. Once he bought her a huge great fur coat that was worth bundles. Dad was constantly trying to make her happy. But she just wasn't.

It must have been so frustrating for Dad because he couldn't do anything to make her better. I think he paid about £5,000 to get her checked out in a private hospital hoping once and for all she would believe him. But she had an illness and there was nothing anyone could do.

I worry I'm like Mum sometimes. My mates tell me to stop worrying about everything because I overthink stuff. But it's part of who I am. I'm not a chilled-out person. I guess I can just handle it a bit more than she could.

The day we found out she'd died me and Frankie were at my uncle Tony's house, I was ten and Frankie was almost thirteen. Chloe's ex-boyfriend Matthew came over to pick us up to take us to Nanny Linda's. We got an ice cream on the way.

It's funny the things you remember.

When I got to the door my dad came running up to me. He was bending down on his knees, crying 'Mummy's died'. I remember running through the house and putting my head into a pillow. I was screaming and Frankie shouted, 'What's happened?' and she started crying.

Everyone was crying.

I knew dying was a bad thing and it was a shock but I didn't get it. No one I knew had ever died before. What did it mean?

'Don't cry anymore, she'll be back soon,' I said to Frankie.

But she didn't stop. She knew something I didn't.

We didn't know Mum had committed suicide for about two years. Dad didn't tell us how it happened to start with; he just said she fell over in an accident. I guess he was trying to protect us and I don't think he wanted to deal with it himself. I was convinced she was staying in a hotel and was coming back.

As I started getting older I began to get pissed off. Where was she? Why wasn't she here anymore? I'd constantly say to Dad, 'Can you please find out where Mummy's gone or how she's died?' He'd say, 'OK son, I'll try.' I wouldn't let it go – 'Phone the police or something. Someone must know!'

I'd forget about it for a few weeks and then a month later I'd ask again, 'Have you found out anything yet, Dad?'

I didn't know what was going on. Was she going to turn up at the door? Was she gone forever?

About a year or two later an evil girl at school said something to Frankie. She went over to her and said, 'I know how your mum died, she hanged herself.' Frankie ran home and confronted my dad and in the end he sat us down, his arms round us on the sofa, and told us the truth.

But I still didn't want to believe it. It took me about five years to realise she wasn't coming back.

I was doing a PA (personal appearance) in a nightclub recently and a little girl came up to me and said the same thing. It was an under-18 event and she must only have been about ten. She was really weird looking and just stared at me and said, 'By the way I know what happened to your mum. Trust me she's looking down at you, I can see things.'

I was freaked right out. I think she thought she was being nice but it really threw me. I didn't like it.

When someone commits suicide there are so many questions you want answered. But how can you know what drives a person to do that?

My nanny Linda thinks Mum's illness was caused by an accident she had. Apparently about two weeks before I was born she was in a cab with Frankie that crashed and she banged her head. Nan thinks that triggered my mum going a bit ill and funny. But I don't think it did. My mum was suffering from depression.

Someone told me committing suicide is a selfish thing to do because you're hurting other people. But how can you say that? You don't know what the person is going through. To commit suicide you've got to be in another level of pain. To actually do something like that it's got to be proper bad. You must be in a state so terrible that you're not even thinking about what it's going to do to other people.

I don't usually like talking about my mum because whenever I do it makes me cry. Blocking it off just seems easier. I'm welling up just thinking about her now. Just the mention of my mum's name 'Tina' on telly or just the thought of her brings tears to my eyes. I don't like showing emotion to my family. I want them to think I'm alright so they don't have to worry about me. But the truth is I don't think I'll ever get over it.

Sometimes I wonder if I'd be able to accept it more if it had happened when I was older. One of my best mates lost his mum to cancer. But she had it for seven years so he knew it was going to happen.

I know I'm not the only one who's gone through a tough time losing a parent and I feel sad speaking about it but I want people who've gone through the same thing to know they're not alone. There's not any easy way of dealing with it. I don't think it ever goes away properly.

But maybe that's good.

You don't ever want to forget who they are.

CHAPTER 4
'WHY ME?'

'Dear granddad, I don't like it at school, I can't do anything right'

I found that written on a note the other day, stuffed in a folder with some old coursework.

I had trouble learning at school from a young age. I was diagnosed with dyslexia when I was at Chigwell Primary and Mum used to take me to this place where they'd give me a special board to spell letters. They'd show me different ways to hold a pen because I couldn't grab it properly. I still can't. But I couldn't focus. I didn't like people telling me what to do. And after Mum died it got even worse. Mum's death happened when I was in between schools, leaving primary and going into secondary. So I started a new school – West Hatch High – as the kid whose business everyone knew. I remember people coming over asking, 'Are you alright?' I'd just shrug and say, 'Yeah, fine.' I still didn't really get it. And I definitely didn't want to discuss it.

Some people reckoned I stopped learning because of what happened to my mum. Almost like I froze in time. I don't know about that but I do remember it hitting me really hard. I just hid it from everyone. I hid it at school and I still hide it now. If anyone mentions it these days I try to brush it off.

I told you earlier I felt like I was different to all the others and having no mum was one of the reasons why. I found it really tough to get my head around the fact that other people at school had mums and I didn't. I'd sit there and think, 'Why am I the only kid in school whose mum has died?' And because of my learning difficulties I usually had a lady helping me in class. My head would be saying, 'Why do I have a woman sitting with me? Is it just because I don't have a mum?' Sometimes I'd be sat in a room on my own and a teacher would ask if I was happy and tell me to draw a picture of me and my mum. I drew a picture of us holding hands with a balloon in the air. I don't know why.

Everyone else had a mum. Everyone else was cleverer than me.

I started to think I'd been picked out as someone special. So instead of letting it upset me, I just accepted I was different.

That's what I mean when I say I feel like I'm unique. I'm not saying I'm better than anyone else, just that I'm not like other people. There are things that have happened to me that I can't explain . . . me having the surname Essex (which some people still don't believe), my mum dying, getting chosen to do all these amazing things on TV, all the products I've launched, being given a book deal (hello teachers – I've got a book deal. How mad is that?!) . It's just weird when I think about it. It's like fate somehow.

Maybe Mum had something to do with it all along . . .

Memories of home around that time are still a bit fuzzy. I can see me and Frankie watching telly in the lounge, hearing Dad in the kitchen crying, 'Why? Why?' over and over. I used to sleep in bed with my dad some nights after my mum died. It feels weird saying that now. But I guess we both needed the company.

Dad had to quit his job at Billingsgate Fish Market just so he could look after us. Every time I think about that now it amazes me what an incredible man he is and how hard it must have been for him. His mum, Nanny Kipper, moved to Chigwell so she could be nearby and help out. And Mum's mum Linda was always there too. Everyone did what they could to try and help.

A lady called Jackie came round to teach my dad how to cook pasta and different meals. Frankie cooked a lot too. I suppose she had to grow up quickly after Mum passed. She used to follow Mum around everywhere, so somehow she learnt what to do with the oven. Frankie's friends would come over and they'd all cook together sometimes. If they were cooking onions they'd wear goggles because they reckoned it would stop them crying. I thought it was funny so I'd put a pair of goggles on as well and start goofing around the house pulling silly faces.

I wonder why onions make you cry. Weird innit? I was chopping onions the other day and I had tears streaming down my face.

Me and my friend Diags sometimes walk into a shop and if we hear a song that's a proper downer* we look at each other and say 'Do you want to cry?' and try and cry for about ten minutes.

It happened in the Chinese restaurant last week. That song from Titanic* *came on. I said to the waiter, 'Mate, please change the song, I'm literally going to start crying my eyes out.'*

So *we started crying our eyes out. I actually had tears coming out of my eyes. Well sort of. I was straining them. But there was a little tear.*

Leonardo DiCaprio looked sick in that film. I well want to watch that again now.

I hardly ever cry in front of my family.

I cried over a remote control petrol car once (I wanted one for my birthday when I was 14). I also remember Mum cooking me spaghetti bolognese and me wailing, 'I'm not eating it unless you let me play outside!' then getting in a strop because she said, 'Well if you don't eat it you're not playing outside.' I stormed upstairs in tears.

This was stupid because it was my favourite dinner.

Imagine if you could only eat one food for the rest of your life every day. One meal. I don't know why but lasagne has just popped into my mind. Steak would be too chewy to have every day. So would chicken.

School would've been easier if I'd had a mum but looking back I don't think I'd have been as strong inside. I quickly learnt not to take shit from anyone. Which meant I ended up in quite a few scrapes . . .

JOEY'S FASCINATING FACTS:

#2 There are 5.9 calories in the glue of a British postage stamp (which means you could get fat if you send too many letters).

CHAPTER 5

JOEY AND THE TWO GEEKS

Games played by young Joey Essex:

- Knock the cock
- River runs
- Garden hopping
- Getting Diags to smash a bus window
- Lighting fires
- Stink-bombing my uncle's birthday

I had a lot of friends at school but for some reason I also had a lot of people wanting to fight me.

I had a fight after sports day when this nutty kid at school banged me with a chair. I threw my chair back at him and he punched me in the face. So I kicked him in the balls. I never liked fighting but my dad always told me to stick up for myself. He hated bullies. He said, 'You have to be strong no matter what.' So even if I was frightened I would never back down. Which meant I had *a lot* of fights.

It also meant I stuck up for anyone else who got bullied.

There were two boys who always got picked on called Yohan and Anthony and I'd hang about with them sometimes because I felt sorry for them. I knew Yohan from primary school – he loved computers and never spoke a word to anyone except me. Anthony joined in about Year 8 or 9 and on his first day I saw him being pushed over. Some big kid threw him to the ground when he was playing basketball. Everyone was laughing so I told him to come and hang round with me and Yohan. So it was Joey Essex and the two geeks!

Tom and my other mates used to ask me what I was doing with them – 'Why are you hanging out with that pair and not us?' – but I liked them. I used to say to Yohan, 'I bet when you leave school you won't speak to me again' and he promised he would.

Hi, Yohan if you're reading this. You need to give me a call. You haven't spoken to me for years. I'm 23 and I'm still waiting!

I hated people having a hard time. I knew how it felt.

To this day it's always me that people want to pick a fight with, I don't really know why. I got into trouble with the hardest kid in Loughton once. This kid was so tough he didn't care about anything, he'd even been in prison – the lot. Everyone in Essex was scared of him. I was with about twelve mates after school and he looked us up and down and glared, 'I'll beat you all up on my own.'

I begged my mates to run away. I knew I'd be the one that got the brunt of it. For once, I left the scene (sometimes you know when it's not worth it!) and as they were all crossing the road to where he was I said to them, 'Please leave it, he's nuts'. I knew he would think it was to do with me. That's one of the problems having a name like 'Joey Essex' – it means no one forgets your name.

I knew I'd get the shit for it once it was over.

The next day I had a phone call, 'That boy is after you.'

'Why?'

'He's saying you beat him up last night.'

I had to hide from him for years after that. I tried to avoid Loughton as much as humanly possible.

There always seemed like there was someone wanting to fight me. The tallest kid in the school started on me once, probably thinking I'd be scared. But it was like a red rag to a bull because instantly my shackles went up and survival mode kicked in (a bit like the animals in those David Attenborough documentaries, except with better shoes). I ran at him with all my might and we fell on the floor, rolling around. I'm pretty sure I beat him.

No matter what I did, I kept getting myself into situations. A guy even pulled a knife out on me once.

Me and my mates used to hang out at the local swimming pool, the David Lloyd Leisure centre in Chigwell. When it first opened it was really exclusive and had expensive fees. We were only young so we'd climb over the gates so we didn't have to pay. Besides, the only reason we were there was to chat up girls in the Jacuzzi. It was pretty silly looking back.

One day I was sitting in the bubbles with my mate and a few girls. This annoying boy kept splashing one of the girls and shouting 'Ha ha' in a really irritating voice. He was with a group of lads and they just kept laughing at her. And of course, when I see someone being horrible I can't let it go . . .

'Stop splashing her,' I said to the boy.

'Or what? What are you gonna do?'

I told you he was annoying.

'Stop being a dickhead,' I said.

'Who are you talking to?' He was getting really aggy.

In the end I got out of the Jacuzzi but just as I turned my head to go I leant back in and splashed him with the biggest wave you've ever seen.

He was fuming. Him and his mates followed after me shouting and swearing. When I got into the changing rooms I realised there were loads more of them than there were of us. That was usually the way with me; I had a habit of being outnumbered.

One of them came up to me and growled, 'You better get out of here.'

'Why?' I replied

He pulled out a knife.

OH.

SHIT.

We were scrambling about in the changing room trying to get our stuff together as quick as possible.

I called my dad. 'Come and get us!' I whispered, 'We're in David Lloyd. A boy's got a knife!'

Dad was there in a shot.

'Let me through please,' he said to the receptionist. 'My son's in there – his name's Joey Essex.'

'Er, we don't have his name down here sir. He hasn't checked in.'

'Someone in there has got a knife!'

Dad rushed into the changing room (I like to think he also jumped over the barrier but I'm not sure what happened . . . I was too busy cowering in the corner in my trunks). The boys were nowhere to be seen. I remember him cursing and swearing all the way home saying he'd come all that way for nothing. It was scary though, looking back I can't believe a 14-year-old would carry a knife around.

It wasn't just boys who picked on me though. Once I nearly got killed by an old man.

I used to play down at the brook nearby. We'd spend hours down there trying to build 'a base' (I loved a base camp). Basically it was like a treehouse except it wasn't in a tree. One day a few of us, including Jake, were hanging about, doing our building thing and we saw this old geezer staring and shouting at us. He looked furious (to be fair we'd probably taken half the branches out of his garden for our camp). All I remember is that he had a pair of Timberlands on. And they were massive.

'What are you doing?' he yelled and we knew he wasn't after an answer. He wanted blood.

He started marching towards us and immediately my mates ran off. I was wearing my new white Nike trainers and didn't want to get them dirty. I wasn't going to run through a river and ruin them.

I didn't know then that one day I'd become 'Hover Man' and be able to walk on water in my special water-repellent trainers (as seen in series 7 of TOWIE).

Jake and the others were ripping through all the muddy water like their lives depended on it. I was limping along behind him trying not to ruin my trainers. The angry man caught up with me, tripped me over and pushed me in the water. I got up again and he shoved me back in. My heart was thumping. I was shitting myself. The man was pushing my head in the water. 'He's going to kill me!' I thought. I felt like I was drowning.

One of the boys started shouting, 'Don't hurt me and my mum and dad will pay you a million quid!' Then he ran off and left me.

Cheers for that.

Somehow I managed to escape – the man was out of sight. I reached for my phone so I could call my dad. It was soaking wet. I didn't know where the man had gone so I shouted to Jake, 'Quick! Call my dad!' I looked down at my arms and they were bleeding. I was properly shaking. It was awful.

All of a sudden the man reappeared. He pulled up next to me in a car. 'Get in NOW,' he bellowed. I was so frightened I nearly did what he said. Thank God I didn't – who knows what could've happened.

'Get away from me!' I screamed.

I picked up a brick and threatened to throw it at him. But he just stared at me and started driving towards me.

He *was* trying to kill me!

Luckily Dad arrived just in time. Then the man got out of his car trying to explain.

What exactly he was trying to explain I don't know . . . 'Er, excuse me sir I was just trying to murder your son.'

I can't remember the rest but let's just say my dad sorted him out.

When we weren't being bothered by angry old men, me and my mates loved playing by the brook. We'd do these things called river runs (I'd make sure I wasn't wearing my favourite trainers then). You'd run through the brook past all the houses, end up soaked in rat piss then have to go home and shower.

I have a lot of showers. I am very clean. I do everything in the shower including brushing my teeth. That way you don't have to spit out the toothpaste, it just dribbles out of your mouth. Also it means I never have it on my face. I've lost count of the amount of times I've met up with one of my mates like Tom or Arg and they've got toothpaste all over their face. I usually brush my teeth about three or four times a day (which means I have a lot of showers!).

We'd play a game called knock the cock too. This meant hiding in the brook, tying a fishing string to someone's door and pulling it back so it would knock. Whoever opened the door wouldn't be able to see who it was. It would really wind them up. It was a pretty silly game but back then it would really make us laugh.

Garden hopping was another good one. You'd have to wait until about four in the morning when the neighbours were asleep. Then you'd put your hood up and jump over as many gardens as possible without getting caught. We'd worked out a route to go through with holes and tunnels.

We got caught.

One night the police came and we told them we were playing football and lost the ball.

'Oh did you young man? Well that must've been some kick because you're twenty doors down from your house.'

I also used to love setting up traps. I thought I was Macaulay Culkin in *Home Alone*. Me and my mate Jake would sit in his bedroom inventing stuff. I attached some string to Jake's bedpost, then to his doorknob and put a coat hanger on it that would hit him in the face as soon as he opened the door. BAM! It never really hurt him but I'd be in stitches.

I'd put books on the top of doors, anything I could find as a booby trap. I had a robot thing from the film *A Bug's Life* that would shout 'Trespassing' whenever anyone came near. That way I knew when to set the trap off.

It wasn't all innocent fun though. I pretty much ruined my uncle Tony's 40th birthday. There was this big family gathering at an Indian restaurant in Woodford. I went there with a hoodie on and decided it would be funny to throw stink bombs and firecrackers into the restaurant. My dad sicked right out and I felt really bad.

41

The mates I had back then are still my closest friends now. But there's one who became like a brother to me thanks to my dad getting into the dating scene.

I met James Bennewith – or Diags as he's known (Diags because he's got a diagonal-shaped mouth) – and his brother Jack when my dad started dating their mum Debbie.

I didn't realise they were boyfriend and girlfriend for ages. I thought they were just mates. When I did finally work it out a couple of years later, I didn't like it. I remember going up to Dad in the kitchen and asking if Debbie was his girlfriend and when he said 'Yes', I shouted back, 'You can't do that!'

I went to bed that night and cried. But I think it was just from the shock. It hadn't even crossed my mind that Dad would want to be with anyone who wasn't my mum. The next day I was fine. Anyway, it meant I had two brothers and that was cool.

Me and Diags would do everything together – shopping, school, sitting on buses. We were best mates. Before we met he was a bit of a geek and was really good at his schoolwork. I soon knocked that out of him.

I was much naughtier than him. I made him jump out of the back of a moving bus once . . .

. . . I'm not sure if I should write this in the book because I don't want people thinking I was a bad kid – don't judge me please . . .

We used to play this game where you had to shatter the back window of the bus with the hammer. By the way I'm pretty sure this is illegal so don't try this at home. Or on a bus! Another time we filled up balloons with water and covered a car with water bombs. And Diags says when he first met me he remembers me setting fire to a bin in a pub toilet. Not good.

Diags says he used to think, 'Oh my God, I've got to hang around with this idiot kid who sets fire to things, jumps out of buses, hops fences and shines lasers in people's eyes.' He loved me really.

I was the one who convinced him to smoke his first fag when he was 12. He'd been go-karting and I remember him coming to see me wearing a red Ferrari tracksuit.

We didn't look very old though. I'm not sure how we got away with it. We'd go to the corner shop with £1.69 in our pocket, looking about six years old, put on our deepest voice and say, 'Oi, mate have you got any fags?'

Most of the time we'd be told to do one.

We couldn't smoke properly anyway. I think that's what stopped us in the end. People would always look at us and say 'You're not taking it back!' As in we weren't inhaling.

Sometimes when we were bored we'd superglue a two-pound coin on to the pavement outside the shop. We'd sit for hours on the bench nearby watching people come and try to pick it up. One man was there for ages, using every tool possible to get it up. When he managed to get it off the ground I told him it was mine so he had to give it back.

Then there were our 'Tesco Trips'. We'd stay up 'til about 3am playing computer games and all of a sudden we'd give each other the look . . .

'Tescos?'

We'd rush over to the 24hr shop in Woodford and play hide and seek in the aisle for hours. If it was a Sunday we'd be really depressed because it would be closed.

My hair range is stocked in Tesco. Can you imagine the first time I saw it there – 'Joey Essex: D'Reem' – sitting on the same shelf I used to hide behind in the middle of the night?! The staff still know me in that branch and whenever I go in now they remind me I used to be such a pest.

When Dad and Debbie split five years later she didn't want Diags to hang around with me. She didn't think I was a good influence. Looking back I probably wasn't, he tells me now I ruined his life (he's joking), but I didn't mean any harm. We were just having fun and Debbie was just looking out for him.

One day he was round at mine and Debbie came over to get him. I remember she was literally dragging him away from me – I was holding one arm and she had the other. It was like a Diags tug of war! I was trying to pull him up the stairs shouting, 'Get off him! He's my mate!' Debbie won the tug and took him home. That was, until I snuck round a few minutes later and picked him up on my Go-Ped. I really was cheeky!

Dad was heartbroken when he broke up with Debbie. He was crying for days. But I realised afterwards that he was mainly crying over their dog. They'd bought a Weimaraner called Mojo and Debbie took it with her. It was like his baby and he couldn't cope without it. So he rang up one of those places that keep dogs without families and luckily they had a Weimaraner called Alfie. He was infatuated with it and the dog didn't leave his side.

Only one day I heard Dad shouting at me.

'Joe! Come here! What's going on?'

Alfie had been running round the garden and had suddenly gone all limp like he couldn't breathe. He'd taken himself to

Dad's room like he'd gone there to die. I started crying my eyes out. Dad rushed him to the vet's in his car. The next day he rang me in tears, 'They've had to put Alfie down.' There had been something wrong with his stomach.

Dad rang the homeless dog place again and said, 'I want another Weimaraner.' But they didn't have any this time (Weimaraners are pretty rare so it's not like they had them knocking about every day). So he bought a Weimaraner puppy instead and called it Ralfie. Now Ralfie sleeps with Dad in his bed.

How can you sleep in bed with your dog?

Dad met his girlfriend Sasha walking Ralfie. She's got a Staffordshire called Hugo. Sasha's lovely – she's definitely the one for him. They really suit each other, they're just always laughing.

JOEY'S FASCINATING FACTS:

#3 Under extreme high pressure diamonds can be made from peanut butter (I've never seen a diamond in peanut butter in my life, unless that's what the crunchy bits are made of? Definitely try this at home if you can!).

CHAPTER 6

THE BEAUTIFUL BLUE-EYED GANG

Some things to remember about girls:

- Be prepared — she will usually dump you before you dump her
- Don't write a rap about her because she might dump you
- Don't date someone who is twice as tall as you
- Sometimes a girl might also snog your mates
- Don't buy a girl a Christmas present if you think she might dump you
- If you only ever speak to each other on MSN it probably won't work out

I might not have been liked by all the boys but for some reason I was quite popular at school with girls. Diags says it's because they liked my eyes.

Me, Tom and Diags have all got blue eyes. Whenever we meet

a girl we tell them we're 'the beautiful blue-eyed boys' and that 'our eyes are powerful and glumptious*'.

I first kissed a girl when I was about four and we were still living in Bermondsey. Frankie was screaming out to my dad and mum, 'Joey's in the toilet kissing!'.

I think the first girl I fancied was a family friend of mine called Rosie. Everyone called her Bud. My dad used to try and encourage me to get together with her because he was mates with her dad but nothing ever happened. She was really pretty – perfect white teeth and tanned skin – basically your typical Essex girl. I've always liked that type of girl. The first thing I look at is a girl's face. I fancy girls with cute little pixie faces – all innocent and sweet looking.

Unlike most of my mates, I never went for girls with big boobs. They're weird really aren't they . . . boobs? What are they made of? They're like bits of jelly . . .

There was a girl called Lara who lived five minutes away from me. We'd invite her to hang out with us in our 'base' down at the bottom of the brook.

See, I knew how to woo the ladies . . .

One day when we were all sat round, I leant in and snogged her. A few minutes after we'd kissed one of my mates piped up, 'Can I have a go?'

She said yes, so she kissed him too! Funny the things we do when we're young isn't it?

Then there was Hannah, who was half German and really tall. People used to go round the school whispering, 'Oh my

47

God! She's half German!' like it was the weirdest thing in the world. To be honest, I didn't think it was the weirdest thing in the world and that didn't stop me asking her out when someone told me she fancied me though.

'Do you want to be my girlfriend?'

She said yes straight away and I shit myself. I don't think we ever actually spoke. In fact, I think we must be still going out with each other because we never ended it.

Hannah if you're reading this . . . sorry, but you're dumped.

I went out with another girl called Chloe Holden for about two months. But we only ever spoke on MSN.

Then there was Sophie. I quite liked her but it was all very innocent.

I wrote a rap about her.

She was sitting on my lap,
we were talking and texting and shit like that.
I'm so sick like a patient,
you better hurry up cos I'm getting impatient

If you have a clue what that was about let me know.

Megan lasted a bit longer, about four months. She did gymnastics and was always flipping and cartwheeling and stuff. We were 15 and although we didn't actually sleep together (I didn't get on to that business until I was 16) we did mess about a bit.

Sorry Megan if you're reading this – but, you know, this is a story about my life.

One day she called me into the changing rooms and said, 'I need to have a word with you.' I looked at Diags and shrugged, 'Fuck knows what this is about.'

When I came out a few minutes later I looked at him with a sad face. She'd dumped me! I was really upset. I'd bought her a Christmas present and everything. I gave it to Frankie instead. But then Megan actually turned up at my house on Christmas Day and my mate opened the door.

'Is Joey here?'

'No.'

'But I've got his presents . . .'

I popped my head round the corner, said 'OK thanks!' – and swiped them from her. Then I slammed the door in her face. I know this seems a bit harsh now but she'd really hurt me when she broke up with me, and I was only young. But before girls started messing with my mind –

. . . yes, I'm talking about you, Sam and Sydney . . .

– it was just about me and the boys. We even made up our own language.

At one point we'd replace letters in a word with 'O' so no one would know what we were talking about.

We called it the 'O language'. We thought it was our secret language but it was so crap. You could easily tell what we were saying. So instead of 'Alright mate, what are you doing today?' it would be 'Alroght mote, whot you doino todo?'

Well, who do you think I am – Einstein?

There's another stupid word we loved which we still use now. I don't even know how to spell it because it's so ridiculous. It's something like '*abalooleelalelin**' which means 'absolutely disgusting'. You can use it to describe anything like your dinner (or a girl!). It can be shortened to 'abalooleelee' and whenever one of us says it we'll all crease up and that'll be all we'll say all night. I tried to slip it into a conversation on *TOWIE* once but the producers cut it out. Can't imagine why!

I like to make new words on Twitter to send to my followers. I haven't made any new words in ages. There was one, 'so so', the other day. Which is a bit like 'say say*', which you say when you've done something good and you're pleased with yourself.

Me and Tom made up another phrase: cheese and onion*. 'No mate, don't go for her. That girl's cheese and onion . . .' And if a girl's alright then you call her 'prawn cocktail*'. There, that's fresh out of the box that one!

CHAPTER 7

WHAT TIME IS IT?

DAILY MAIL: 29 JANUARY 2014

Calling time on the traditional clock? One in seven Britons can only tell the time using a DIGITAL watch

- A poll has discovered that many adults struggle with simple task
- Many parents are not bothering to teach their kids how
- Joey Essex famously highlighted the issue on *I'm A Celeb* . . .

When I admitted I couldn't tell the time on *I'm a Celebrity . . . Get Me Out of Here!* I didn't realise what a big deal it would be. Now, whenever there's a story about telling the time the papers always use a picture of me to illustrate it. It's like I've become this famous 'non-time-teller'.

I had a flashback from when I was at school the other day and there was a lady holding a big white piece of paper with different clocks on it and she was saying to me, 'Do you want to learn how to tell the time?'

I remember staring at the clocks for ages before it hurt my

head. They looked well confusing. So I refused to listen to what she was saying. Because I struggle with things, if it's too difficult then I just stop myself. I give up before I can get it wrong.

Frankie thinks I didn't learn to tell the time because of Mum dying. She says that's when I'd have been taught it and that I had too much else to deal with.

I'm not ashamed to say I don't know things. I'm always honest. As I said, I don't like liars. And it's not like I don't want to learn, I just sometimes find it tough. The funny thing is – I love watches. So does my dad. He gave me my first Rolex when I was about 13. The day he gave it to me he pretended he'd bought me a dictionary instead for a joke (I was not happy). I've got pictures of me at his house wearing this big gold Rolex on my little wrist. It looks huge.

I can tell the time on a digital clock but if people stop me in the street and ask me what the time is I try and change the subject. Then if they ask why I'm not looking at my watch I just say 'It's a long story!'

I started wearing watches round my ankles a couple of years ago just for a laugh. I had to get an extra-large one and sometimes had to sew straps together. Chloe told me it looked like a prison tag. It didn't catch on.

I saw a video of Tom Cruise recently. He was spouting a lot of weird stuff about something called Scientology.

Me and my mate Dan Edgar sit there having mad conversations, talking about things that we believe in. Except I've decided our stuff isn't Scientology, it's 'Fusetology'.

Fusetology is when you believe that life isn't actually real.

The rest of our mates just think we're being stupid. But we're obsessed with it. We sit there and say that life is too perfect to be real. Why do trees give off oxygen and we drive on roads with petrol that can go in cars?

Yep, I'm a total weirdo . . .

Dan read a thing on the internet that says time doesn't actually exist and that we've just decided we need clocks when really we don't. So when you say you're 'late' for something you're only late because someone decided to turn the day into parts of time.

All the clocks in my flat are set to the wrong times.

I'd better stop now before you think you're reading the wrong book. I just like talking about it. It's jokes. Maybe if you come over to my flat you can join in one day.

By the way does coffee make your wee smell? I've just had some and been to the toilet and it's disgusting.

JOEY'S FASCINATING FACTS:

#4 No scientific experiment has ever been done (or can be done) to prove that time exists. (See, I told you I was on to something.)

CHAPTER 8

BACK TO SCHOOL

Things I've learnt to do:

- ~~Blow my nose~~
- ~~Tell the time~~
- Tie my shoelaces
- whistle really loudly

Another thing I never quite worked out was how to blow my nose. I used to stand in front of the mirror for hours staring at my face and holding down different sides of my nostrils. According to Frankie, I made loads of noise doing it but it never quite went the way it should. So now I just do it the Joey Essex way.

. . . which usually means either blowing it midair or just wiping it on a tissue somehow.

I did learn to whistle though. And I didn't stop doing it for about 6 weeks. It drove Frankie mad. Which meant I did it even more. And I learnt to tie shoelaces but I could see why you needed that.

When it came to picking my subjects for GCSE I told my dad, 'School is literally boring the life out of me. I don't want to do Maths – I don't want to be an adder upper. I don't want to do Science because I don't want to spend my life making potions. And I don't want to take Geography and be like David Attenborough because I'm not going to travel the world and look at animals.'

I didn't know then that I would actually end up being sent to Africa by ITV2.

I knew I wasn't clever academically. It's not that I didn't want to learn, it's that I felt like I didn't know how to learn. I had to go to special lessons just so I could catch up with the work everyone else was doing. When I was in class I couldn't concentrate, I got distracted really easily which is why I think I had to have a teacher sitting next to me all the time. I used to get my words muddled up and I couldn't spell – they say dyslexic people write things backwards and see words differently and I definitely saw stuff that no one else did. I learnt how to spell 'because' by remembering the phrase 'Big Elephants Can't Always Use Small Exits'. The clever kids would understand what the teacher was talking about straight away. But often I didn't understand a word the teacher said. It was like it was another language. That's why I usually had someone sat helping me.

The woman who helped me with my lessons was called Mrs

Copper. Our class was really naughty and if we threw something at the teacher I'd tell her not to grass on me, so she had to be on my side because she never did say anything.

She was nice.

Sometimes in that class we'd wait until the teacher turned round to write on the board then we'd throw coins along the floor – there must've been about seven quid there by the end. I hit a teacher in the head with a two-pence piece once – he turned round too quickly and it went 'Bang!'. I got sent to seclusion. Oh and someone locked our teacher in the cupboard.

When Mum was alive she'd sit for ages going over my home-work with me. Dad did try helping a few times but he was just as bad as me. I don't think he was very clever at school himself. He got expelled actually.

He hasn't ever admitted that to me, I just found out.

Dad wanted me to do well at school; he just knew he wasn't the one to get me through it.

Because Tom was so clever Dad would often be on the phone to him instead: 'Tom, come and teach Joey to do his homework will ya, son?' Tom would come over but I'd always end up mucking about. He'd sit there patiently with me trying to show me how to do fractions or something else with a stupid name and he'd think we'd be getting somewhere. Then the next day he'd test me on it and I'd have forgotten.

When I got my GCSE results the first time round I failed pretty much everything.

When I saw my grades my heart sank. My overriding emotion

was fear. I ran home to my dad in tears. My first thought was, 'I can't cope in the outside world. I'm never going to get a job.' It suddenly hit me that I'd have to be an adult. I think that was my dad's concern too. The thought of sending me out to work in the big wide world frightened the hell out of him.

So instead, my dad begged the teacher to put me back a year. He said that I needed a bit more time to grow up and adjust. And because of what had happened to my mum I think they felt sorry for me and gave me a second chance.

So I went back to school. Only this time, I did even worse in my exams than the first time around.

I'd decided to concentrate on Drama. That was the one lesson I loved and was good at. My teacher rated me too – I was actually predicted a B+. I was great at the practical bit – I've still got the DVD of my Drama exam to prove it. I play a guy who starts off poor and then becomes a rich gymnast. My hair's in a bit of a mullet and looks like a carrot . . .

I thought I looked like Zac Efron.

. . . but my acting is actually really good. Sick in fact.

The problem was, I had a massive bit of coursework to do at the end and I just couldn't be bothered. But it didn't matter! There was a boy in my class who'd already done it! I thought I could copy his instead . . . I'd just try not to make it look too obvious . . . I'd cut out a few paragraphs here and there . . .

What I didn't realise was this meant the whole thing made no sense at all . . .

I handed in my work, thinking I'd nailed it.

Then came the bombshell.

Our teacher announced that the exam board had asked to check twelve people's work at random. And guess whose was picked? Mine and the boy's whose work I'd copied.

At the time I wasn't even worried. I honestly thought I'd got away with it.

I got my exam results back and tore open the envelope. All I cared about was Drama. Nothing else mattered because this was what I was going to do. I wanted to be an actor. That was my future.

I got a U.

I was so upset, I cried my eyes out. My Drama teacher came up to me afterwards in shock. 'I don't know what happened!', she said. But I did. I knew what I'd done. It was totally my fault.

Despite wanting to act, I never once wanted to be famous. I just wanted to earn enough money to buy nice clothes and treat the ladies. My mates always said I'd be famous though – they said I made them laugh with my silly ways.

CHAPTER 9

HABITS AND HAIR

Some of my habits:

- Wiggling my foot
- Biting my nails
- Putting my hand down my pants when I talk to people
- Buying jeans too small for me then throwing the receipt away so I can't take them back
- Smelling food before I eat it
- Eating only a bit of a sweet or biscuit then putting it back in the wrapper so I don't put on weight
- Wearing my socks inside out
- Worrying about things too much
- Cleaning my teeth in the shower
- Blowing bubbles to help me think

Someone asked me if I knew what OCD stood for the other day. I thought it was 'over-controlled dilemma'. Turns out it means 'obsessive compulsive disorder', which sounds pretty much the same if you ask me.

I've been told I'm a bit OCD. I do funny things like take a bite out of a sweet then put the rest of it back in the wrapper. I do the same with biscuits. In my head this means I won't get fat but can still have a little taste of everything. But I'll sit there nibbling away at all of them in a tin while my mates only eat two.

I smell food before I eat it sometimes. If I touch something like a banana in a shop I have to sniff my hands afterwards. Then I have to wash my hands. I probably wash my hands about seven times a day.

Joey Essex is a very clean machine.

I'm quite good at cooking but I can't work out timings very well. So when I cook a roast I'll leave it in for 45 minutes even though I know it needs longer. Then I'll just hang around the oven and watch it until I think it's cooked.

I'm convinced I'm fat at the moment. People look at me and think, 'He can eat what he wants.' But if I start eating burgers I put on weight. I'm pinching my stomach and I swear I can see a roll. It's not a ham one either. Luckily I like healthy food. I've just eaten some asparagus which makes your wee green. I'm into porridge too. Or pozzer as I call it.

I'm probably conscious about my weight because I like to look good in clothes. I've always liked fashion. I reckon I got it from my mum.

I never wanted to dress the same as everyone else. People often look at me and say, 'Why are you wearing that?' But a few months later they'll all be dressed in the same thing. I don't mind though. It's flattering.

I wore the 'H' Hermès belts long before everyone else started wearing them. My sister Frankie bought a fake one from Thailand when I was 17 and I nicked it off her. I didn't even know what it stood for, I just thought it was cool. When I joined *TOWIE* I bought myself a real one for £500 and now everyone has them. But I've still got the picture of me wearing it when I was a kid. I was a trendsetter!

Not everything catches on though . . . remember the ankle watch?

I went through a 'rude boy' stage where I'd wear tiny little rucksacks that you couldn't fit anything in. That and a Nike jacket and black Nike trainers. I actually went through a stage of thinking I was a rapper at one point. But my rapping only happened in my bedroom with Diags listening. I was pretty sick at it. I called myself Essex Boy and made a logo for my MSN picture. If I was ever going to make a mix CD, that was going to be on the front cover. So jokes.

Little did I know back then that I would end up getting a record deal. In March 2014 I had a CD out! It was called *Joey Essex Presents Essex Anthems*. It's not me singing though – it's a collection of cool tracks that you can listen to on holiday or pretend you're in a club when you're really just sat at home! I did an interview to promote it with the *Sun* newspaper and joked that I was going to be a rapper next. The following day their headline said 'Joe-Z'. The only rap I know at the moment is, 'Yo, yo, yo, my name is Joe, I don't live in Hackney I don't live in Bow . . .'

Which probably isn't going to set the charts on fire to be fair.

Clothes are a status symbol in Essex so you'd always have to spend a lot of money on your wardrobe. I once splashed out £1,000 on a Louis Vuitton tracksuit then took it up too short. I went back to the shop and asked if they had the fabric to make it longer again. But they didn't. They're three-quarter length now.

I think they're still in the dry cleaners. I asked the man to press them really hard to see if he could stretch them.

My tracksuits got tighter and tighter until they turned into leggings. Or jeggings. Whatever you call them. I don't like to wear my jeans so tight anymore, they hurt my willy. Plus I can't really walk properly.

I've been to PAs before and had my jeans so tight that I had to change my jeans to tracksuit bottoms because I lost circulation in my legs. I thought my legs were going to fall off! The jeans were called 'super skintight' from ASOS and were soooo skinny. I ordered eight pairs all the same size. And they nearly killed me. They should've been called killer jeans.

My shoes were another thing I liked tight. I'm a size 9 but I'd buy size 7 trainers so you didn't get a crease in them when you walked. Only problem was I couldn't really walk at all.

I always wear my socks inside out. I hate wearing them the right way in. I don't like the seams on my foot. It makes the sock twenty times more comfortable if you wear them the way I do. Although now, if I go to a posh public event I put them the right way round so no one knows my secret.

One thing I'll never change is the length of my shorts. They always have to be short shorts. I even take up my swimming trunks to make sure they're short enough. There was one pair of Gucci shorts that Diags called 'fucking ridiculous'. They were beige and were so tight that we walked past some builders once and they started making whistling noises at me. Diags was well embarrassed but I didn't care.

Like everything else in life, I don't see the point in being serious. Why do clothes have to be all sensible and boring?

And I LOVE being brown. I was about 15 when I first discovered sunbeds and I went to Tanners in Chigwell. I hardly go on them at all anymore, I realise how bad they are for you – plus I don't want to get papped walking out of the tanning shop. The problem was that I was claustrophobic and I didn't want to pull the lid of the sunbed down over me and be in the room on my own. So I made the lady who owned the shop sit in there with me while I fried myself. I bet I was the first customer she'd had who was too scared to go in on their own! Serves me right really, doesn't it?

I've had some crazy haircuts too.

I looked like a hedgehog at one point. Then I swear I did a Justin Bieber before Bieber himself. It was pushed up at the front with spikes round the edges and was hollow in the middle. It was weird.

Dad says he can remember me asking the hairdresser for 'leopard hair', which basically sounds like I wanted highlights. There's a picture of me with one of those funny caps on that has the hair pulled through. After the photo was taken the hairdresser left me sitting there while she went to the shop and I screamed because the bleach started burning my head. After that I dyed the whole lot blond. I thought I looked like Eminem.

Then of course I had the 'walnut whip' when I first started *TOWIE* and the 'Fusey' undercut when I opened my shop. I couldn't believe it when loads of schoolkids started copying me after that. I started getting blamed for people getting expelled! A headmistress wrote an article last year saying that she blames shows like *TOWIE* and *Made In Chelsea* for 'infecting too many classrooms with a culture of stupidity'. And she described me as 'mind-numbingly dull'.

That might be the case but I bet she has rubbish hair.

Mushroom   Lemon

Broccoli   Carrot

Here's my hair through the years (described as vegetables)

I've just looked at my hair in the mirror. It's getting quite long on top. I've started wearing it in a ponytail. A 'mun' it's called – a male bun. Mine looks more like a pineapple.

CHAPTER 10

'ARE YOU SURE YOU'RE NOT UNDERAGE?'

Growing up is weird innit?

I can't remember my voice breaking; I thought it was the same as it's always been until I saw that DVD of me at Christmas earlier, opening those presents and shrieking like a little girl.

Then there's the whole big deal about facial hair. There was one kid at school who walked around with bum fluff on his top lip when he was about 12. But for the rest of us the only thing we could shave was our eyebrows.

I still can't grow a beard now and I'm 23. My mate dared me to try the other day, so right at this second, as you're reading this, I'm sat here with a tiny moustache. It hasn't grown anywhere else yet even though I keep looking in the mirror trying to talk to it (well, aren't you meant to talk to plants to make them grow?). I have to pull a stretchy smile to make it look alright.

Otherwise it looks like a waterfall. A hairy waterfall. I think I'll have to tell my mate it's not working out.

Some of the other boys got away with acting like they were 21 when they were 16 but me and my group of friends grew up a lot slower than most. We were still building camps and acting like little kids when we were 17. I don't think we ever wanted to grow up.

The first time I ever got drunk was on holiday in Spain with my dad. We used to go to Marbella all the time when I was young – sometimes for 6 weeks at a time. It wasn't quite the Marbs we know now though. My dad's favourite bar was called Sampsons, all our family friends and their kids would hang about there every day and it would be so much fun. I loved it. We nearly moved to Spain once after Mum died. I think Dad wanted to escape everything and we always had such happy memories there. The only word I could say was *hola* but I always say *oooohlaa* and people laugh.

So I had my first sneaky taste of alcohol when I was about 12. I was with a friend of mine called Daisy who I sort of fancied. We got some people to buy us some WKDs in the shop and ran up to a bit of grass on this hill. We just laughed and rolled around a bit. Then my dad came and found us giggling at the stars and I was sick outside the pub.

I first bought my own booze from a corner shop in Essex. It was miles away from anywhere but everyone at school used to say 'I've heard they don't check your ID' so me and Diags went there to try our luck.

We only looked about 10 . . .

They served us straight away. They wouldn't have cared if you rocked up in a nappy, they would still serve you.

When I was 15 we discovered a place in Chingford that was known for letting you in if you were underage. I remember once going to the front door and this kid Rory was in front of me, who was the smallest guy in the school, and the bouncer looked at him and said 'Are you underage?' He squeaked back 'Nnnnno . . .' really nervously.

The guy just waved him in.

'Go on then, in you go.'

Then he looked me up and down and nodded, 'And you.'

It was a terrible club. There were pictures of dead people on the walls and witches painted in the loo. We'd all stand around this giant speaker trying to look cool.

Tom decided we needed to get some fake IDs so we could go to better places. There was a company online where you could order them. It said on the website that it was 'only to be used as a joke to fool your friends' and there was a disclaimer saying you weren't allowed to use it in pubs or clubs.

Which was a stupid thing to write if you ask me.

Me and Tom had such baby faces that there was no way we were going to convince anyone this ID was real. Tom said we needed to do something with our facial expressions to try and look older in the pictures. So we sat there squinting our eyes and raising our eyebrows so we had as many wrinkles as possible. My photo is jokes. I look like a surprised seal.

We ordered three different types of fake ID (we decided you'd need to have more than one thing in your wallet in case they asked for proof). So we picked a European Driving Licence, a National Identification Card and some other card I can't remember. We didn't even put that we were 18 – we tried to make out we were 21! Luckily the places we ended up going were so lax they would let you in even if you looked 8.

By the time we were old enough to be served we didn't have enough money to buy any drinks. We'd go to bars and get a bottle of pink wine between us because it was cheaper and got us more pissed than spirits. If we met a girl we liked, all we could offer her was a glug of our wine. Sweet for that . . .

But the best time we had was abroad, where no one gave a shit how old we were. Our first lads' holiday was in Zante when we were around 16. It was me, Tom Pearce, Adam Hughes, Reece Wood and Steve Lott (Pixie Lott's brother). When we arrived, I remember Steve was lying on a sun lounger outside the hotel; he'd arrived the night before. He was moaning and groaning and half his ear was hanging off. There was blood dripping down his face and he was muttering 'I've been raped!' He kept this story going for two days saying it had happened on a mountain. We later found out he'd just tried to climb a fence. He was a right nutter.

There were loads of turtles in Zante so we decided to get henna tattoos saying 'Turtle hunters'. That was the name of our group for the rest of the holiday. We thought we were well 'ard until we nearly got killed by the police.

Before we left, all of our parents had warned us, 'Whatever you do, don't get into any trouble with the Greek police. They're very dodgy. Keep yourselves clean and you'll be OK.'

It cost 15 euros to rent out a speedboat. Because of the turtles, you weren't allowed to have those doughnut rings that sit on the back of the boats dragging people along – they were illegal. So we stupidly tried to improvise and threw out a life ring instead. I was in the ring, being pulled and dragged round by the speedboat when all of a sudden this massive police boat – that looked like a pirate ship – pulled up behind us, sirens blaring.

They were screaming at us through loud speakers. All we could hear was, 'You PLAY?? YOU PLAY?' Which was a stupid question because of course we were playing.

We were having fun. Couldn't they see that?

It took a few minutes to realise they were after money.

'We'll pay money!' we shouted back.

This wasn't good.

We were shitting ourselves.

They started shouting at us, frantically beckoning the boat over to theirs. But we were only kids and couldn't drive the thing properly. Plus it was a shitty little 15-euro job so was hard to control and, try as we might, we couldn't get it anywhere near the big boat. Instead we just kept driving it round and round in circles. The police thought we were taking the piss.

'You play! You play?!' – we were even more confused now. Did they want money or what? They could've wanted a game of tennis for all I could tell.

Tom took the wheel and started trying to drive towards the police. All of a sudden we saw the back of the ship looming and the propeller getting bigger. We honestly thought we were going to die. I closed my eyes, thinking my life would flash before me. All I saw was teeth.

The teeth of one of the policemen.

BOOM!

We hit the ship's propeller and went flying into the back of the speedboat. Smoke was coming out of the engine – we must've done thousands of pounds' worth of damage. Then, this policeman took out this massive hook, lunged it towards our boat and pulled it towards him. My mate Steve put his hands up to his head and shouted 'We're sorry'. The guy just swung the pole at his head.

Another policeman jumped on to our boat and we all shrieked. He was still shouting 'You PLAY!' and demanded 1,000 euros. Which of course we didn't have. When we shook our heads he grabbed one of the lads by the throat and with no effort at all threw him to the floor – BANG! I was screaming my head off and ran to the back of the boat.

'Let's jump! Let's swim away!' I said to Tom who looked at me as if to say, 'Who do you think you are, Tom Daley?'

'Where are you going to jump to?!!' he shouted.

'I don't know! But we're gonna die!' I screamed.

I was trying to do a runner in the sea. I honestly thought they were going to kill us. Then we turned round to look at them, but we had to squint because the sun was in our eyes. The policemen clearly thought we were taking the piss.

'YOU LAUGH? YOU SMILE?!' they were going mad now.

We were goners.

In the end we were saved by a local fisherman who happened

to be passing. He started speaking to the police and at one point it was like he was negotiating on our behalf. He got into our boat and helped us drive back to shore while the police took some of our mates. I was being such an idiot though because as soon as the policemen's backs were turned I was making signs at them. If they'd seen me I'd *definitely* have been dead.

We got back to shore to be greeted by more policemen. They started demanding our passports and a thousand euros each. 'We can't afford that!' we yelled. In the end we gave them 100 euros each, which went straight in their pockets.

We never set foot in a speedboat again.

We spent the rest of that holiday trying to pull girls instead.

'What do I do if I want to have sex with a girl?' I asked the lads as we stood in a bar one night. I was taking the piss obviously. We'd always have banter like this.

'Just go up to a girl and ask her,' grinned Tom.

He was winding me up to see if I would do it. And of course I did it.

'Hi there. Can I have sex with you please?'

'No, fuck off.'

Oh, OK.

We were all creasing up. The girl probably wondered what the hell was going on.

I wonder if she'd say yes if I asked her today . . .

From what I remember I did pull a girl that night though. She was a redhead and I snogged her in the back of a pub.

Another boys' holiday was in Magaluf the year after. This time Diags came and spent all his money in a strip club on the first night. He blew £700! The next morning he woke up and started crying. But one of the strippers had told me to give her my email address so she could contact me. Me and Diags got all excited thinking we were going to date her. Then she emailed saying 'Come and see me', which was great until we realised it was going to cost us £100 quid.

The following night a prostitute tried to nick Diags's phone.

We were laggin* on that holiday. We went on a boat trip where you could drink as much as you wanted and were in fits because Diags skidded right over on his arse. When we got back to the hotel we took his trunks off and pushed him in the pool. The only way we would give him his shorts back was if he went to the ledge of the building and jumped in naked. The whole hotel came out to watch. When he finally plucked up the courage and jumped in we still wouldn't give him the trunks. I was in tears I was laughing so much.

I remember putting tomato sauce all over the blades of the fan in our room before anyone came in (pretending I was in *Home Alone* again). Whenever someone entered the room and switched it on red stuff flew everywhere. The maid must've thought we'd murdered someone.

Another time I went to a place called Benalmádena with Tom Pearce. He got so drunk that he fell in the pool and couldn't swim. I had to drag him upstairs to our hotel room and I threw him in the bath. Then our mates came upstairs and thought 'What the hell's going on here?' We were crawling around on the floor like that funny scene in *The Wolf of Wall Street* when Leonardo DiCaprio tries to get into his car.

One of the group was a guy called Alex Salmon and his face got so sunburnt he blistered. So we spent the whole time calling him 'A salmon'. We found it hilarious and kept saying things like, 'Why would anyone write a cheque to A Salmon? What could a fish do with that money?' We were creasing up.

He didn't tell us 'til the next day but he weed on our toothbrushes to get his revenge.

My life was full of madness and I was always smiling and laughing, which I think annoyed some people. I don't know why but it's as if me having lots of mates was a bit of a threat.

One of those people was a guy called Ricky Rayment who went to my school. We'd never really got on because I thought he was a bit of a melt* and a try-hard (a few scraps later, we eventually sorted out our differences when we were both on *The Only Way is Essex*). One evening I'd been in Nu Bar, which was one of the places we all hang out. I was on my own because I was about to get a cab and Ricky was standing outside with a big group of lads.

'Look at Joey Essex all by himself!'

A *pretty pathetic thing to say really*.

I started crossing the road, not making eye contact.

'You alright?' I said.

'Where's all your mates?' Ricky snarled. He thought he was being really cool.

That got my back up. I turned round to look at him.

'Who the fuck are you talking to?'

He laughed. I carried on . . .

'Is this just because you've got all your pals behind you, you think you're hard? Do you think I'm scared of you?'

'Shut up you pussy,' he shouted and giggled.

'Oh I am. Am I?'

I squared up to him. He had a carton of sausage and chips in his hand (not exactly what you carry around with you if you're a hard man!). I leant across and flipped the whole thing right over. Chips and sausages fell on to the road.

I told you, I'm not scared of anyone. No matter how much someone fronts up to me I won't back down or be pushed.

'What the fuck!?' He was screwing.

I started walking down the road then one of his mates charged at me. He was much bigger than me and all of a sudden he lunged and head-butted me in the face. I tried to dodge him, running around cars and ducking from the punches. My nose was bleeding; I was a mess. I had blood all down my shirt. But I kept teasing them: 'You're not going to catch me.'

Then the police came and arrested me.

ME! What?!

I was put in a cell overnight (and most of the next day) and seriously thought that was my life done. When they were questioning me I started panicking. I couldn't exactly say 'I slapped a sausage out of someone's hand and then got head-butted' so

I just kept quiet. Was I going to prison?! Being in a police cell is just like you see on the TV shows, all cold and grimy. Except there's no fit policewoman coming to talk to you through the bars. I was in there for about 18 hours in total. It was soooo long! I wouldn't recommend it to anyone and it made me realise I never wanted to do anything like that ever again. Joey Essex was made for bigger and better things . . .

CHAPTER 11
LOSING IT (MY VIRGINITY)

<u>MY PERFECT WOMAN WOULD BE MADE FROM:</u>
Eyes — Cheryl Cole
Hair — Jennifer Aniston (when it was long and straight)
Legs — Rosie Huntington-Whiteley
Arms, nose and lips — Kendall Jenner
Bum — I would say Kim Kardashian's bum but it's way
   too big for my liking. So I'll say Rita Ora
Boobs — Victoria Beckham

<u>MY PERFECT MAN WOULD BE MADE FROM:</u>
Eyes — Joey Essex
Hair — A mix of David Beckham and Joey Essex
Nose — This is hard. I don't like Justin Bieber's nose.
   So I'll say Leonardo DiCaprio
Pecs — Justin Bieber
Six-pack — Joey Essex
Arms — Zac Efron

Lips — I think I have good lips. I don't know who has nicer ones than me. But it would be odd if I'd been studying some other fella's lips wouldn't it? So yes, Joey Essex's lips.

Legs — I don't like footballers' legs, they're too chunky. Maybe I'll choose the legs of a male versace model. Or I might just not have legs. I can't think of any I like . . .

Apparently when you have sex it means the girl automatically really likes you. Have you heard that? Diags was creasin*' when I told him my theory. 'It's not like some automatic switch!' he said. He also said if it was really like that, then people wouldn't regret one-night stands. And he should know!

I used to think babies came out of your belly button. And I found out an amazing shocking fact about girls the other day.

Are you ready?

Girls wee through a different hole to their noony*!

Trust me – NO boys know that. I guarantee you. Girls have another hole! How?

I was 16 when I first had sex.

It was like a planned operation. She was a girl who I had met a few times, but no one really knew her. Tom (who'd already been having secret sex sessions with girls by now) took me to this club where we knew she'd be and we asked if she wanted to come back to my house. Tom had just bought a car (I was jealous of his car, but more on that later) and he dropped us both off at my dad's house. I took her up to my loft.

It was over pretty quickly from what I remember and my dad was downstairs the whole time. After the deed was done, I tried to sneak her out of the house without anyone noticing. But Dad saw us come downstairs and was sat smiling on the sofa. He then tried chatting to my new 'friend'.

'Why doesn't she stay for a drink?' he shouted.

'No it's fine Dad, she's going now.'

I couldn't get her out the door quick enough.

The next day Tom was on the phone.

'Alright Joe?'

'Alright Tom?'

'You know that girl you roogsted* last night?'

'Yeah?'

'You don't mind if I go out with her do you?'

'Of course, you can do what you want!'

For the next few weeks, every time I went to call on him he was with her. I think he moved on to her sister after that. Dirty dog.

It was always pretty embarrassing having girls over to my house, a house I shared with my dad and Frankie.

Once, I was with a girl in my room and Frankie walked in wearing her dressing gown . . .

'Joey I'm just going to use the laptop quickly.'

Was she having a laugh?

'Frankie! Get out! What are you doing?'

'I need to go on the laptop!'

'Don't ever come in my room again!'

I felt like a right doughnut.

Another time, there was a girl in my room and Dad walked past the door shouting after the dog really loudly, 'Ralfie! Ralfie!' He was always whistling and banging everywhere.

Proper embarrassing. Thank God I could eventually afford my own flat.

But apart from my night as 'the inverter' and having my girl-friends to stay over, I'm not someone who sleeps around. Don't get me wrong, I do like the ladies (as you'll see throughout this book), I just don't believe in one-night stands. I don't like to do anything with anyone until I know I can fully trust them.

But once I fall for a girl? Then that's a whole other load of problems . . .

CHAPTER 12

SMITTEN WITH SYDNEY

My first love was called Sydney Beales. She had long brown hair, brown twinkly eyes, a really cute pretty face, wore designer clothes AND had a car with her own personalised number plate 'SYD' (her dad bought her a cream MINI convertible before she was even old enough to drive). She was the centre of attention everywhere she went and all the boys fancied her. She was your typical Essex girl and my ideal woman.

I'd been flirting with her for a few weeks but I officially asked her to be my girlfriend on New Year's Eve 2006 (I deliberately did it on New Year so I'd never forget our anniversary). A whole load of us had tickets to a party in a place called Manor Hall in Abridge and I was sat with her at a table while everyone else was dancing. I was wearing a fitted dark-grey shirt and she had on this sparkly sequinned dress that showed off her sexy slim figure.

'I've been chatting to you for quite a while now . . .'

She grinned at me. Wow she was fit.

'So . . . do you want to be my girlfriend?'

'Yeah.'

I remember feeling so chuffed. Everyone else wanted to snog her and now she was my girlfriend. I was in love.

I had butterflies every time I was around her. Just thinking about it now brings all the feelings back. I don't think you ever forget your first proper love. I don't know if I even knew what love was back then . . . I just know that I cared about her more than anything. Even Furbies.

The girls I mucked about with at school were nothing compared to Sydney. Once we started dating I looked back on all my other relationships and realised how pointless they were.

Remember the one I only spoke to on MSN?

But it wasn't just Sydney I fell in love with. I fell for her mum Dawn too. Growing up without a mum meant that there was a gaping hole in my life, so when I met Sydney's mum I wanted her to mother me. I was desperate for her affection, I needed her to like me – I wanted nothing more than to feel part of the family.

Sometimes I think I tried to woo her mum more than her. I'd buy Dawn flowers, take her out to dinner, spend hours round her house drinking tea and chatting to her about anything and everything. I'm still the same when I meet a girl I like now. Mums are so important to me.

I'd got so used to having meals cooked by my dad or sister that to have someone else's mum cook me dinner made me feel so special. I was still living at my dad's at the time but I spent most days at Sydney's. I loved being with her family and got on really well with her sister Brogan and her dad Jimmy too. But I adored Dawn . . . she was like my replacement mum. We would all go out for big family meals and I loved every second of it.

Sydney was really outspoken and chatty and, although I knew she loved me, she still did her own thing. She was independent not clingy. And she was very confident. I thought we looked like the best couple in the world when we went out.

I was with Syd for three and a half years. We were infatuated with each other but we argued a lot. If you ask my mates about Sydney now they'd probably say she had me wrapped round her little finger.

Why is it always the little finger? What's wrong with any of the others? Surely the little finger is too small to have something wrapped round it . . .?

The main cause of our arguments was jealousy. She'd get jealous if I looked at another girl and I'd worry about what she looked like when she went out because I knew all the guys would be staring at her. It got to a point where we didn't trust each other at all. I'd go to a club and I'd be too scared to talk to anyone. A girl would come over and say quite innocently, 'Hi Joey, are you OK?' and I'd just turn the other way and start looking at the wall. I'm sure most girls hated me at that time because I was so rude! Occasionally one of them would understand, so if I mumbled 'Sorry, I can't speak to you', they'd smile and say 'I know, I know, Sydney won't like it'.

Realistically we didn't have anything to argue about but we were both frightened about how the other would react. It was a young, fiery relationship.

To avoid arguments, I'd often lie about really stupid pointless things. I thought it was easier not to tell her the truth – that way she couldn't tell me off. That meant I'd get myself into even more of a tangle. I know what you're thinking – I thought you didn't like liars? Well these were white lies. Not proper lies. And they were carefully used to stop arguments! A white lie isn't actually that bad.

Here's an example of a stupid pointless lie:

I'm on the phone to Sydney.

Me: 'I'm going to bed soon, speak later.'

Her: 'OK bye.'

I leave my dad's house and go round to see Diags.

My phone rings. It's Sydney.

Her: 'Where are you?'

Me: 'I'm just in bed.'

Diags looks at me as if to say, 'Why the hell are you telling such a pointless lie?'

Her: 'OK, I'll ring your house phone.'

Me: 'OK.'

FUUUCKKK!

I phone my dad and say, 'Don't answer the phone! Tell Frankie not to answer her phone either!'

I rush back home in a mad sweat and wait by the phone until she calls again.

Here's an example of another stupid pointless lie:

I'm in Tesco with Diags (doing a 'Tesco Trip') and Sydney phones my mobile.

Her: 'Where are you?'

Me: 'I'm just eating a kebab in Loughton.'

Diags looks at me as if to say, 'Why the hell are you telling such a pointless lie?'

Her: 'OK I might come to Loughton soon so I can pick you up?'

Me: 'OK bye.'

FUUUUCCCKK!

Diags: 'Why didn't you tell her where you were?'

Me: 'If she knew I was in Tesco with you it would be embarrassing.'

Diags says I always make situations a lot harder for myself even now. I don't know why I do it.

Sometimes when Sydney would ring and my mates were with me I would put her on loudspeaker so everyone could hear. When they heard her shouting they were always shocked.

'Why do you let her talk to you like that?' they'll say. I think I must be attracted to girls who shout a lot!

I wasn't completely innocent though.

Me and Syd went on holiday together to Turkey. It was our first proper romantic trip on our own as a couple. We were getting ready to go out for the evening and she looked beautiful. She was wearing a lovely figure-hugging dress that showed off her figure. But instead of telling her how amazing she looked, all I noticed was her bra poking out the top of the dress. And it made me really angry.

'Why are you showing your bra? Do you want people to see it?'

'Well I can't just *not* wear a bra can I?'

'All the boys will fancy you!'

'Well I'll take it off then!'

'You can't take it off!'

But she did. She took it off just to prove a point. And that was it. We had murders*. I was shouting at her to put it back on. She was screaming back at me, 'No! Why should I?!' And all the while her boobs were more on display than they had been in the first place. That's how ridiculous our relationship was – we were arguing 24/7.

She scratched my eye by accident in an argument once and I was convinced it was bleeding. Really it was just grazed (it still hurt though!). We were at her house so I immediately went downstairs and started sobbing to her mum Dawn. Dawn looked at me sadly, 'It's just not working Joey. You're driving each other mad. You need to get away from each other.'

I sat there trying to use reverse psychology . . .

Believe it or not I do know what that is.

. . . and when Sydney came downstairs I said, 'OK then, let's split up, I don't mind.' Sydney broke down crying, 'No! But I don't want to!'

That's how it usually went. Until one day she walked away for good.

CHAPTER 13

'I'LL PAY YOU BACK DAD . . . I PROMISE'

Having a girlfriend was one thing. But the ultimate status symbol growing up in Essex was a set of wheels.

Not only did Tom lose his virginity before I did, he was also the first to learn to drive. What's more, he had a black Ford Zetec which was the *only car* to have if you wanted to look good.

I might not have been able to tell the time but I was determined to learn to drive. Even if it exploded my brain.

You see, I could see the value in learning to drive. I knew it would make my life better (e.g. I would look cooler). Unlike having to try and get my head round algebra that wouldn't be of any use to me on a daily basis, I could see the point of studying for this test. The driving part of it didn't worry me, it was the theory part of the exam that gave me the fear. I studied harder than I've ever studied before.

I failed my theory four times.

But every time, I'd pick myself up and go back to the books. Studying became my middle name. Joey 'Studying' Essex.

What are YOU sayin'?

When I finally did pass I was over the moon. I was so happy! Getting through the theory test felt like my biggest achievement ever. I was lucky too – you had to get 32 out of 50 in the first section and 44 out of 70 in the second and I got 32 and 44.

Sweet.

My first car was a silver Ford Fiesta. I got it for free from one of my dad's mates – I think he palmed it off on me because it was worth about a tenner. It had five doors and was the worst-looking car I've ever seen in my life. It was ugly and it didn't go with my look. It wasn't a black Zetec that's for sure.

Still, I was just grateful I had something to drive.

Dad didn't like getting in the car with me one bit. He thought I was the crappest driver on earth. This new car was an automatic and I'd only learnt with gears.

'Alright Joe . . .', he warned, 'remember you only use one foot with automatics.'

I was bunny-hopping all down our road. Dad went mad.

'What are you doing?' he shouted, 'I got you a car and you can't even drive it!'

It was all the car's fault. I bet I'd have been able to drive if I had a Zetec. Thankfully my crappy silver thing only lasted for two weeks before it blew up.

Me, Mum, Dad and Frankie on the doorstep of our house in Bermondsey. I'm around 2-years-old here.

I'm surprised I've not got my face painted too! Mc and Frankie with Mummy.

Ready to do my homework, obviously it wasn't learning to tell the time.

Every little boy my age wanted to be a Power Ranger.

Dressed up for my Uncle's wedding. The only reason I wore this outfit was because I was told I could wear a sword under the belt.

Always rocking the short shorts #Fashion.

Me, Mum and Dad in Tenerife. Dressing like my Dad!

I was a proper mummy's boy and would always cuddle up to her, we were all so close.

Definitely getting too old for the pram, but I thought it was cool being pushed around in it.

Me and Nanny Linda. I don't know why I look so grumpy, probably tired.

Blonde highlights were the fashion when I started secondary school, or did I start that trend too?

Being cool (with the highlights) in Marbella.

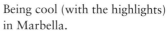

My first professional photo shoot. I've still got this jumper, but I've had the arms cut off. #wheresWally #wheresJoey.

At Frankie's 21st birthday party. We've been through so much together, love you Frankie!

Puppy love at Sydney's 18th.

The 'mystery man'. Mine and Sam's first photo together, I'll never forget this picture.

Our famous first date to the dump. It stunk but it worked.

One of my most
memorable scenes
in *TOWIE*. Blow-
drying my hair,
or should that be
hairdrying?

Everyone loved me and Sam together. We were like
the Essex version of Posh and Becks.

I was always told I was going to be a star. Turns out they were right...

I was on my way to Diags's house and . . . 'BANG! BOOF!' Suddenly all this smoke started coming out of it and I thought 'What the hell??' and left it on the road. The next day it got picked up by the garage and I was told the sprocket had gone.

Weird name: sprocket.

The garage said I could either pay £800 to get it repaired or they'd pay me £60 for it. I took the cash. I thought, 'What a good excuse to get rid of the old banger and get a proper Joey Essex mobile! You know what I'm sayin'?!'

It was time to plead with the old man.

'Dad, Dad, Dad pleeeeease . . . If you put the deposit down on a new car I'll pay you back . . .'

I managed to persuade him I needed a black Zetec.

They were the fashion.

And Joey Essex IS fashion.

As we sat in the garage, the fella started asking if I wanted 'gap insurance'.

What the hell's gap insurance?

I thought Gap was a clothes shop. What did they want with cars?

They told me 'gap insurance' was there to protect against your car getting stolen. And it would cost me extra money.

Nah. I didn't need that.

About four months into our relationship (me and the black

Zetec that is, not Sydney) I pulled up outside Dad's house. I'd just bought everyone a Chinese takeaway.

I was with Sydney and we parked the car then quickly nipped inside to give Dad the food we'd picked up for him. We were in the house for literally five minutes . . .

'Daaaaad!'

'What, Joey?'

'Where's my car gone?'

'What do you mean where's your car?'

'Dad, stop mucking about, this isn't funny now. Ha ha. Good joke.'

'What are you talking about?'

'Dad, you've nicked my car. Seriously stop doing this to me.'

My beautiful black Zetec had been stolen.

As it turned out someone had been nicking all the Zetecs in Essex. I found out afterwards that *everyone's* got taken. A group of people had been going round smashing people's car windows, reaching in, starting them up and driving off.

I was fuming. That was it. I was going to get them. Joey Essex was going to track down those cheeky thieves. So I did what most superhero car chasers would do. I got on my Go-Ped and sped off down the road.

'*Wweeeeemmm . . . weeeeeem.*'

Off I went into the darkness, chasing round Essex for the evil bastards who'd stolen my prize possession.

Within about 30 minutes I was back home empty-handed and pissed right off.

For a long while, the Go-Ped was all I had. Go-Peds are like skateboards with a handle and they run on petrol. So I had to scoot about on a mixture of a skateboard and a lawn mower. I felt so stupid.

It didn't help that Go-Peds were also illegal to use on the road.

On a Go-Ped it took 15 minutes to get from my house in Chigwell to Diags's place in Woodford.

'W*weeeeemmm . . . weeeeeem.*'

We were on our way to his one night when suddenly we heard the police coming up behind us.

'*Wooo! Wooo! Woo!*'

'Hello young man. Whose Go-Ped is this please? You do realise they're illegal to drive on the road.'

I gave him my best 'feel sorry for me' face.

'It's mine officer. My car got stolen so I'm having to drive around on this.'

I carried on . . .

'It's not like I want to be driving around on a Go-Ped at my age is it? It's a bit embarrassing and I know it's illegal, I'm sorry, I wasn't thinking.'

I think the policeman knew I was being honest and probably thought I was an innocent kid.

'We'll let you off this time young man.'

I reckon he also couldn't be arsed to carry a petrol-filled Go-Ped in his boot because it would stink the car out.

The Go-Ped might have been a lifesaver but it nearly killed me a few weeks later. Me and Diags were outside the shop round the corner and a scary-looking fella came out and brushed between us. We didn't even have time to complain before he'd got out a flick knife and held it to my throat.

'This is mine!' he said, pointing at the Go-Ped.

'No it's not. It's mine, mate,' I said. I was pretty brave.

Although Diags would probably say 'stupid' . . .

Diags was shitting himself. 'GIVE IT TO HIM!' he shouted.

I refused. I wouldn't let anyone get the better of me. My dad had always taught me to stand up to bullies.

'Give it to me now!' the guy growled.

'Fuck off mate,' I said and pushed him away.

I started up the Go-Ped and sped down the road. Diags was left running behind me screaming, 'Come back!'

The next car I got was a Golf. After that I fell in love with the Smart car. Everyone else thought they were girlie little two-seaters that would never catch on. I thought they were well cool. To me they were trendy and different.

My Smart car cost around £8,000. And somehow I had to get Dad to lend me the money.

I can recall the exact words I said to him.

'Whether it takes 25 years or 40 years . . . I promise I will pay you back Dad.'

What neither of us knew was that I'd soon be a TV star and be able to pay the whole lot back in one go.

JOEY'S FASCINATING FACTS:

#5 As it grows, sweetcorn makes a squeaking noise like two balloons rubbing against each other.

CHAPTER 14

'WHAT DO YOU MEAN I'M SACKED?'

Reasons I've been sacked from jobs:

- Falling asleep
- Having swollen lips and refusing to go in the freezer
- Falsely accused of being a cookie criminal
- Answering the phone to my girlfriend
- Running away
- Getting orders for coffee and tea mixed up
- Not having a clue what I'm meant to be doing . . .

Being Joey Essex (which to me meant having a nice car, suave clothes and a fit girlfriend) was flipping expensive. And having left school with worse grades than I'd got the first time around, my money-making opportunities weren't looking great. The rest of the beautiful blue-eyed gang – Tom and Diags – had very large brains which meant they were clever enough to go to sixth form and university, but me? I had no chance.

I might've been rubbish at school but I wasn't lazy. I offered to do jobs for anyone who'd have me, whether it was clearing people's rubbish or labouring. Sometimes I'd work all day for £30. Every penny I earned went on treating Sydney.

Luckily my dad was on hand to help. Somehow he'd managed to persuade someone on a stall at Billingsgate Fish Market to give me a job. It's really hard to get a job in the fish market – loads of people want to work there. I found out afterwards Dad had put me down on the list to work there when I was about two! He wanted to make sure I had something ready for me when I left school.

I lasted seven months.

I hated it there. Not only did I have to get up at 2am – because I lived with my dad there was no way I could be late – but I spent every day freezing my arse off and stinking of fish. I'd come home every day after work and spend hours scrubbing myself down in the shower. Sometimes I'd shower five times a day. There was no way I was going to be a smelly boyfriend.

When my dad used to take me there as a kid I loved it because there were so many characters down there and I was always made a fuss of. It's like one big playground, everyone shouting and laughing.

All my family loved working in the fish market but I knew it wasn't really for me. Dad was a porter, which is someone who trolleys the fish around the market for different firms and makes sure they have their orders in their van. You need a licence to be a porter.

I was a shop boy which meant I had to go and collect fish for the stall and basically run about and do what anyone asked. A typical day would usually consist of me trying to find a box to fall asleep behind. People even took pictures of me asleep and put them up on the wall! I worked for a company called Seahawk, which has become one of the biggest fish firms in there. Although I don't think that had anything to do with me! My worst job was having to go to the big freezer at the back where all the fish from the market were kept. It was literally like being in Lapland it was so cold. And if I spent too much time in there my lips would start to swell up. I was convinced it was because of the cold and would moan that it shouldn't be allowed. But really I think it was because I went on so many sunbeds and my lips were having a dodgy reaction. Then everyone would laugh and start calling me 'Mick Jagger' and 'Fishy Lips'.

There was one guy who knew how much I hated it and would send me deliberately just to wind me up. He also put chilli sauce in one of my gloves thinking it was funny. It wasn't.

I did have one friend down there though. His name was Tony Discipline and when I met him I thought he was really cool. He didn't have family down there so he'd got himself a job off his own back just by going round giving out his CV. Me and Tony used to sit outside behind the freezers, staring out at the docks where the HSBC building was being built.

I'd point towards the City.

'I'm going to be a stockbroker one day,' I said. 'That's where the money is.'

Tony had other ideas. He told me he was going to acting lessons and within five months he'd joined an agency and been offered a job on a show. I didn't realise which one it was until one day I turned on the TV and saw him playing Alfie Moon's nephew Tyler Moon in *EastEnders*! So I'd spend most of my days falling asleep or refusing to go into the freezer because of my lip-swelling. My heart wasn't in it and it was obvious. But because my dad had got me the job no one wanted to sack me without speaking to him first. 'Look, Joey isn't doing anything, he keeps falling asleep and he won't go into the cold room. You can tell he doesn't want to work here.' Dad gave them permission to get rid of me.

To this day my dad still thanks them for sacking me. If I'd been a master of fish maybe I wouldn't have found TOWIE . . .

I put a brave face on it when they broke the news but at home that night I was in floods of tears. I knew it was my fault but I was panicked. Who in their right mind was going to employ me now? Somehow or other I managed to get myself a job as an apprentice in a land-broking firm in the City. I was always smartly dressed so perhaps that's what swung it in the interview. I fooled them with my good looks! I'd have to dress up in a smart suit and get the tube to Liverpool Street. I'd always struggle trying to swerve McDonald's on the way to the office. I loved their breakfasts! When I got in at about 9am I'd have to start on the phones straight away. I was given a script to read (a little bit like that bit in *The Wolf Of Wall Street*!) and my job would be to try and get someone interested.

'Hello, it's Joey Essex here. Are you interested in buying any land?'

Something like that anyway. If they were interested then I'd pass them to someone who was higher than me who'd try and secure the deal. I didn't earn much when I was there but I was on commission, which meant you could make more money if you sold stuff . . . You weren't allowed to use phones when you were in the office. And having a girlfriend like Sydney who was always calling meant this was a problem for me. One day I was in a meeting and my phone was vibrating in my pocket '*zzz zzz*' so I quickly rushed to the toilet. She was calling to have a go at me about something. One of the other guys had seen and followed me to the loo. He was waiting outside when I came out of the cubicle.

'You were on the phone!' he started pointing at me and getting really agg.

That wound me right up.

'I've been working with you for three months without a penny, give me a break!' I shouted.

'Well, if you don't like it leave!'

'OK. I will.'

I was always being told I had a pretty face and of course I loved my clothes so I thought I'd see if I could use the Joey Essex looks to earn my fortune instead. I went to London and touted myself round a few model agencies giving them all my best grin and running my hands through my walnut whip hair. I joined a modelling agency called Cosmic. I liked the name Cosmic – it sounded fancy. I was sent away to get some photos done for my portfolio.

I styled myself. In one of the pictures I look like Danny Zuko from *Grease* in a black leather jacket and white T-shirt and in another I've gone all *High School Musical* with a bright stripy cardigan and short shorts (see, I was wearing them way back then!). I look about eight years old and am really orange and although I liked the pictures I could see they didn't look modelling material.

I didn't get sent to any catwalks around the world. So it was on to the next thing . . .

I'd heard there were jobs going at Abercrombie & Fitch so I dragged my friend Mitch to London and we booked ourselves on a trial day. The job was called 'impact', which sounded impressive but once we were taken downstairs we realised it basically meant you had to stand there folding clothes. There were rows of people down in the basement all staring at the counter, folding T-shirts with this special device that makes it all neat. It was like we were in a cheese factory.

Not that you fold clothes in cheese factories. They would smell.

I was given a T-shirt and told to start folding. I was on a massive downer because I'd had a row with Sydney the night before. I pulled my phone out of my pocket to see if she'd called.

'Put your phone away, you're not allowed a phone here!' someone barked from across the room.

Oh here we go again.

I did about three folds of the T-shirt and turned to the person next to me.

'Excuse me I need to quickly get something.'

I blurted* out of the store as quick as I could. It was way too weird in there.

My next job was back in the City working for a guy called Jay Rutland, who's now married to Tamara Ecclestone. He was a real face around Essex – everyone knew who he was. He drove a Ferrari, was good looking and always wore sharp suits. I wanted his life. Everyone who worked for him dressed immaculately – because that's how he rewarded his staff. Whoever did the best deal each month got gifted with a Hermès tie. He'd seen me about and knew how desperate I was to be a stockbroker so he gave me a chance.

And I think he knew I'd look reem in a Hermès tie.

I loved going to work in the City. Forget modelling, this was one big fashion show as far as I was concerned. I didn't know what I was meant to be doing but I looked the part and that was the most important thing surely? I'd get off at Bank station in the City. I loved seeing everyone walking past in their smart suits. I worked about 8.30am until 4pm. I was never late. There were two massive long tables and I was sat near the bottom end of one of them. You'd work in pairs, there would be someone called an 'opener' and a 'closer'. I was an opener, which basically meant I had to cold-call people and try and get them to not put the phone down on me.

'Hi, I'm Joey Essex . . . how are you?'

Most of the time you'd be hung up on.

With a surname like mine they probably thought I was taking the piss.

DURRRRR . . . there goes the dead dial tone.

I was pretty used to having the phone hung up on me by girl-friends so it didn't bother me.

If you managed to get someone talking then you'd pass the call on to your closer to do the deal. My closer was sat near me and was one of the top guys in Jay's firm. He was also really moody. He'd always be having a go at me, 'What are you doing you idiot? What are you saying to these people?'

I thought I was having some pretty good conversations to be honest.

One day he was in a typical bad mood and marched over when I was on a call. He slammed his hand on the desk and cut off the phone.

'You're a dickhead mate!' I shouted. No one would ever stand up to him. They were all scared of what he'd do. I wasn't. Which was probably my downfall.

About three days later the guy next to me put his hand in his jacket pocket and found some crumbs in there. One of the other guys had put a cookie in his pocket for a laugh and crunched it everywhere. He poured it out over the keypad and was shouting 'Who the fuck put it in my pocket?' The whole room was in stitches but because I was the one sat next to him suddenly all eyes were on me. I got the blame. My closer started effing and blinding trying to make me look an idiot. I wasn't going to be shouted at again so I said 'Fuck this' and left.

JOEY ESSEX

I went to Jay's office and shook his hand goodbye. I knew if I was getting the blame for stuff things would never change. So I got out before it got worse.

I'd been there 6 weeks.

Every time I lost a job I'd be shitting myself trying to work out what to say to Sydney. All I wanted to do was to look after her and show her I was a worthy boyfriend. I thought if I didn't have any money to buy her presents her family might judge me. I got to her house and burst into tears. Her mum Dawn took me inside and gave me a cup of tea. 'Don't cry Joey. You'll be fine.' But I was always worried Sydney would tell me off.

Arggh! What was I going to do now? Whether I'd been the one to leave or I'd been given the elbow, every time a job ended I really took it to heart. I'd cry for hours and sit worrying about how I was ever going to get anywhere and whether Sydney would dump me because I was skint.

'Can I come for an interview?'

There I was, back at Abercrombie & Fitch in London.

I'd decided they might not remember I walked out a few months earlier.

'So tell us Joey, why do you want to work here?'

I started banging on about how much I loved the clothes there and I was a hard worker and was good at time-keeping (I didn't mention that I sometimes fall asleep on the job).

They asked me if I'd already done the trial day and I nodded so they told me to come back the following Thursday. Brilliant! I was in!

Next Thursday I was waiting outside the Abercrombie & Fitch headquarters at 8am. I pressed the buzzer.

'Hello, I came for an interview three days ago. My name's Joey Essex. I was told I could start today.'

'OK one second.'

I waited.

I looked around.

Looked at my watch.

I couldn't read what time it was so I looked at my phone.

At least a minute had gone past.

I buzzed again, 'I'm here for a job.'

'Sorry. I think something's gone wrong. I'm afraid you can't work here.'

'What do you mean? I've come all the way from Chigwell. I got up really early to be here!'

'You're suspended from working at Abercrombie & Fitch – we've discovered you ran away from the first day's training . . .'

They might not have said it in those exact words but that was the gist of it.

I was screwing. I rang my dad up in tears.

'Dad I'm never going to get a job!'

'Don't worry Joey, we'll sort something out. You'll be OK.'

My poor dad.

So my dad used his contacts again (thanks Dad!) and got me a job in a big City firm. The place was called Schneider Trading Associates and it was a huge great company in Bishopsgate in London. They took me on as a runner.

It was serious business. It wasn't all smart designer suits and

Hermès ties. Being a runner was the bottom of the ladder, the idea being that while you were going about getting people's teas, coffees and lunches, you'd study in your spare time for your stockbroking exams. There were about two hundred people taking the exams and out of them only ten would pass. Of those ten only two would make it to the trading floor.

In my first day at Schneider the boss said to me, 'Don't take shit off anyone.' After I'd been there a couple of days I had an email from this guy sitting a few desks away which said, 'Send my stuff back to ASOS please.' The thing is, I knew I wasn't there to do people's odd jobs. I also knew I didn't have to take any shit. So I wrote back to him, 'I've never sent anything back to ASOS. I ordered some stuff from there once and it's still at home because I don't know how to send it. Sorry.'

He replied, 'You've got to do your job mate.'

I wrote back, 'I'm not going to send it because that's not the job I'm meant to be doing.'

The guy was fuming. He immediately walked over to my desk and slammed a box of shoes down in front of me. 'Do your job!' But I wasn't backing down. I stuck up for myself. 'If you want a coffee I'll get one but I'm not your slave.' So I didn't do it. My boss called me in the next day to ask what had happened and after that he held a meeting and reminded people that if they had odd jobs that needed doing people needed to get their wives to do it! Very sexist, but I liked my boss for standing up for me in his own way.

A normal day for me would be getting food and coffees for people. In my office they always wanted espresso shots – they were always tired (I tasted one once and it was rank). If you had a spare hour runners were meant to learn about the company. I remember people would try and teach me about the foreign stock exchange, but whenever anyone tried I'd just stare at the computer screen blankly and nothing would go in. It's like my head just thinks, 'I don't know how to do that' and switches off. Whenever I look at something and I know I'm not going to understand it, it makes me feel ill.

It was a losing battle from the start.

'Joey, I asked for black coffee and you've just given me tea with two sugars!'

'Joey – didn't I say I wanted red pepper couscous? Why have you given me a jacket potato?'

I couldn't even get the lunch orders right let alone understand what the foreign exchange was all about.

It wasn't long before I was taken to one side.

'Sorry Joey. I don't think it's working out.'

JOEY'S FASCINATING FACTS:

#6 All polar bears are Irish. They are descended from brown bears that lived in Ireland over 10,000 years ago. (Wonder if that means they really love listening to Westlife?)

CHAPTER 15

HELLO *TOWIE* . . . BYE BYE SYDNEY

A few weeks before I was sacked from the City for the third time I got a mysterious phone call. It was from a TV company called Lime Pictures. They said they were making a new reality show about Essex and had heard my name mentioned. Did I want to come in for a chat?

Rumours had been buzzing around already. This TV programme was apparently going to be like an Essex version of *The Hills*. It didn't sound that great to me. Plus there was no way Sydney would let me have anything to do with it. I knew that without even needing to talk to her. She'd go mental.

I told the producers I was fine, thank you very much and already had a job.

A few days later I got another call.

The production company told me their offices were based near my work in the City so I agreed to go and meet them one evening after work. That way I didn't need to tell an outright lie to Sydney about where I was. I was too scared to go to the interview on my own so I brought my friend Mitch with me.

The show was called *The Only Way Is Essex* and when it started out I think the producers wanted everyone to be really cool and suave. I told Mitch to wear his Prada coat. When we were in the meeting I kept clocking him out of the corner of my eye deliberately holding his arm up in an awkward position just so the producers could see the label. I still take the piss out of him about it now.

I was told to sit in front of a camera and they started asking me loads of questions about where I went out and what I did in the evening. They quizzed me for ages about whether Essex was really my surname. Then came the killer question . . .

'Do you have a girlfriend?'

I gulped nervously.

It just came out.

'It's complicated, but not really.'

I don't know why I said it. I think I knew in my head that they would prefer it if I was single. They kept me chatting for about an hour and a half. I could tell they liked me because they kept laughing at stuff I said.

I walked out and panicked. What would Sydney say if she found out?

I started seeing adverts for the show appearing all over the place after that. And I was getting more and more para* by the day. I didn't have a clue about the industry back then so I didn't know you needed to give your permission for footage of you to be used anywhere. Because they'd filmed my interview I kept thinking I'd suddenly see a clip of me popping up on TV saying:

'NO I DON'T HAVE A GIRLFRIEND!'

I was having nightmares about it.

Sydney would go mad and dump me if she ever found out and I loved her to pieces.

This couldn't be happening.

I rang my dad.

'Dad, I've been to a meeting for a reality show called *The Only Way Is Essex*. But I can't go on it. Sydney will kill me and I love her.'

I'd worked myself up into a right panic. I was so in love with Sydney that all I could think about was her. I didn't care that I'd lost about my 80th job by now and had zero money. I couldn't think about anything except making her happy.

I gave my dad the producer's number and begged him to tell them I didn't want anything to do with their TV programme. Dad got on the phone, 'My son recently came to see you. He's called Joey Essex. He told me he doesn't want to be on the show.' Thankfully the producers reassured him that the footage wouldn't be used.

Phew.

I remember sitting down to watch the first episode of *TOWIE* on TV. I was with Sydney and her family in their front room. It was sponsored by some cold-sore cream! I kept thinking, 'Imagine if Sydney found out I'd been asked to be on it.' That night everyone in Essex was calling each other to discuss it. Everyone was mugging* it off. But to me it seemed pretty cool.

One good thing that did come out of the show when it launched was the number of club nights that spun off the back of it. People were desperate to go out and taste a bit of the Essex lifestyle. I started chatting to my mate Steve about it one night and we suddenly had a brainwave – my second name was Essex, I was linked to nearly everyone in my area . . . we saw an opportunity, we were going to be promoters!

Our first night was in a club in London. We came up with the name 'Essex Nights' (see what I did there) and got a load of fliers done up for it. It took us about a month to get everything together but we were really excited. We had special logos made up and everything. For the first time ever I felt like I had a job that I might actually be good at. I knew in my heart it was going to be a success. All we needed to do was invite a load of people we knew (and we knew *a lot*! It was the Essex way!) and then we'd get money for each person who came into the club. Easy.

Everything was going so well. Too well.

Exactly a week before my first big club night – Sydney dumped me.

We were in her car having another row about something stupid. It was going the usual way and I was trying my reverse-psychology trick again:

'Just finish it with me then!' I shouted. 'If you want it to be over, you have to end it!'

I would never have dumped her. I loved her too much. If it was going to happen it would have to come from her.

'OK, it's finished.'

She'd said it. The words I'd dreaded for the last three and a half years had come out of her mouth. I felt sick. This wasn't meant to happen!

I backtracked:

'You can't dump me. It's my big promotion night this week. Don't you care?'

She just sat there stubbornly. I tried another tactic.

'If you do this I'm never going to see you again!'

But deep down I could tell that was it.

I knew she meant it this time. I remember seeing her number plate – 'SYD' – disappear down the road as she drove off and I shouted 'Nooooo' and burst into tears. I ran up the alley and over to Chigwell park and phoned Diags. It was 1am and he was at university in Bournemouth but that didn't matter. He was used to my late-night panicky phone calls by now and I needed a friend.

'She's finished it! Its over!' I could hardly get the words out.

He sighed.

'Joey, you say this all the time mate.'

'This time she's serious. I love her. I need to get her back!'

'Chill out Joey and go to sleep, it'll be fine. Trust me, I've heard this before. It's not over.'

But it was and I knew it. I cried myself to sleep. I was heart-broken. I cried the next day and the day after that.

When Justin Timberlake sung about crying a river he had nothing on this. I cried a whole sea.

My mates came over to try and cheer me up but there was nothing they could do. I knew in my heart there was no way back.

My big club night was coming up. Without Sydney, how the hell was I going to be able to hold it together?

CHAPTER 16

THE NAME'S ESSEX . . . JOEY ESSEX

'I've got the number. You have to call the producers back.'

My mate Steve Cass was right. With Sydney gone there was nothing stopping me speaking to *The Only Way Is Essex* people again. After the first couple of episodes it had got really popular and was the show everyone was talking about. I'd be stupid not to give it a go. But I was nervous.

'No man. I can't do it.'

'Come on. Here's the number. Ring it!'

He handed me a piece of paper.

'But what if Sydney wants to get back with me? If I do this there's no chance.'

To Steve, that was even more of a reason for me to do the show. My mates were fed up of hearing about my arguments and probably even more fed up of me calling them in tears in the middle of the night.

He looked me in the eye. 'It's done now. It's over with Sydney. Now you can finally start to do something proper with your life.'

He carried on, 'You're such a funny person to be around AND your second name is Essex. This show is made for you!'

I knew he was right.

I took a deep breath and called the producer, 'OK I'm in. I want to do the show.'

It was the day of our big club night 'Essex Nights'. We'd invited everyone we knew in Essex and some of the stars of *TOWIE*. We could tell it was going to be a good night and we were buzzing.

Sydney texted me saying she wanted to come to show her support. I think it was only because she'd suddenly realised there'd be loads of girls coming. Anyway, I was on too much of a high to let her or anyone else bother me. Essex Nights was about to happen!

Hundreds of people turned up. I'm not even joking. The whole of Essex was in my club. I was so chuffed. I felt on top of the world.

Joey Essex was Captain Invincible!

I didn't even notice when Sydney arrived.

Because I'd just met Sam Faiers . . .

I'd seen Sam out and about a few times before and we'd always got on. She was on the show but I wasn't thinking about that.

In the flesh she was stunning. I loved her voice, her long blonde hair and green cat-like eyes. It was like love at first sight.

Apparently 'feline' is the proper word for cat-like but when I was asked what it meant in a quiz once I thought it was a deer.

We chatted for a bit (in fact she was all over me that night!) then she leant in and whispered in my ear, 'Mystery man.'

What was she talking about? I must've looked confused because she said it again.

'You're my mystery man tonight.'

I didn't realise what she meant until I saw the Mail Online the next day. She'd tipped off a photographer and he'd papped us as we left the club. She'd planned it all along. She was the one on the telly but she wanted to get papped with me Joey Essex! Not that I cared. I fancied her. A LOT. We got a cab together and before we'd even closed the door I was snogging her face off in the back seat.

BAM! That was it. I was head over heels.

A few of us all stayed at my cousin Charlie's house that night. I woke up on his sofa spooning Sam with my hand on her knickers. 'Sorry about that,' I grinned and she laughed.

I didn't think about the consequences of us getting papped together until a few hours later when I'd gone home.

BEEP. It was a text from Sydney.

'WHO WAS THAT YOU WERE WITH? I'm coming to your house now!'

She came round and started quizzing me about *TOWIE*. She'd got wind of the fact I'd been to meetings and was thinking of going on the show. Then she said the words I'd been longing to hear:

'Shall we make another go of it?'

I was torn. I still loved her with all my heart but something had changed. I fancied Sam now.

She held my hands.

'I'll get back with you if you don't go on to *TOWIE*.'

I told her I needed time to think.

I avoided all contact with her until the next series of *TOWIE* aired.

About an hour before the show started I got a text from her.

'If you're on this show tonight I am going to go mad! I'm going to come round your house!'

I felt like a naughty kid. I was really scared but I was laughing nervously. My heart was in my stomach. I'd already filmed my first few scenes for *TOWIE* and tonight I was going to be on TV and there was nothing she could do about it.

I was at my dad's house watching the show with my mates, including Steve Cass. As soon as I popped up on TV the texts started coming. Sydney was NOT happy.

'That's it! I'm coming over!'

I couldn't handle another argument.

'I'm coming to yours and I'm going to beat you up!'

I told you she had a temper!

'No one let her in!' I shrieked. 'Dad! Frankie! Sydney's coming! Hide!'

My mates were nearly as scared of her as me so after the show finished we drove round the block in my car.

Eventually I answered the phone to her.

'Why did you do this?' she cried. She was sobbing, which made me start.

'What else was I going to do?' I cried. 'You didn't want me back, I didn't have a job. It's a good thing for me.'

A few series later the producers of *TOWIE* found out about Sydney. They wanted to get her on the show. But until this day I've never spoken about her.

They sat me down just before series three.

'Joey we need to ask if you've ever had a serious girlfriend. Have you had a previous relationship?'

My heart was racing.

'I don't know what you're talking about,' I said.

They kept pushing.

'Do you know a girl called Sydney Beales?'

All I could think to say was, 'Er, did you say Sydney or Widney?'

They gave me a funny look.

What kind of name was Widney?

I carried on bluffing, 'Hmm, let me think, Sydney Beales . . . no I've never heard of her.'

Sydney never wanted to be in the show. I knew I had to keep

her out of it so I never once mentioned her. And she's never spoken about me either – even when she was offered loads of money by the *News of the World*. They camped outside her house for ages trying to get her to talk about me. But she remained loyal to me and I'll always love her for that.

Sydney's got a kid now. One of my mates saw her in the street the other day pushing a buggy. It made me feel a bit funny inside when I heard. I know it sounds stupid as we split ages ago now but I suppose it just felt weird knowing I was with her for so long and now that's all gone. You can't get more final than someone you were once with having a kid that's not yours. But she was my first love and she is happy now.

Her mum still sends me Christmas cards too; they're the nicest family and are so proud of me. They sent me a 'Joey of the Jungle' card this year. I miss them sometimes.

JOEY'S FASCINATING FACTS:

#7 A female ferret will die if she doesn't have sex for a year (sounds like some of the girls around Essex . . .).

CHAPTER 17

ME AND MY SAM

When I saw myself on telly I thought I looked bare jokes*.

It was really weird. My first scene was in a bar called King William IV in Chigwell with my cousin Chloe who'd joined the show just before me. In the scene, I'm telling her that I'd got an annoying text asking if I'd 'rumped Sam' after the club night. *TOWIE* loved me and Sam together because it gave them a storyline. The producers needed Chloe to have a link to the show too so they wanted her to say something about a naked photo she'd been sent once. She wasn't sure about saying it, not that it was a lie, I just don't think she particularly wanted to be associated with all that when she had just started.

Even at this point I was getting butterflies about Sam and I had my sights set on her.

But first, I was about to try my luck with another of the girls on the show, Lucy Mecklenburgh.

There's a scene in Sugar Hut nightclub where I go over to Lucy and start trying (and failing) to chat her up. After that episode aired my Twitter followers almost doubled! I think people thought I was funny. Or mad. My opening line to Lucy is something about liking her eyes and then she starts asking me questions.

'What are you into Joey? What interests have you got?'

I didn't know what to say. I couldn't exactly say 'being a promoter' or 'clothes' because that was boring. So I said the first thing that came into my head.

'I'm into politics.'

She laughed. So did the camera crew.

She asked me who the prime minister was and at first I said 'What? Of Essex?', which made her laugh again. Then I said I thought it was 'Gordon Ramsay' who she said was a chef. She told me I meant Gordon Brown.

If you asked me today 'what is politics?' then I could describe what politics looks like, I just can't remember who anyone is. Politics to me is when you see a load of angry people waving bits of paper in the air. Politicians are just weirdos who care about parties and stuff like that. Someone asked me if I knew what a 'manifesto' was the other day. I said it sounded like loads of men having a party.

But the scene everyone always seems to remember when they talk about me on *TOWIE* is the bedroom scene with Chloe. It was the opener to episode three and there's a close-up of me drying my hair.

'My hair is looking reem,' I say.

Reem was a word me and my mates were using at the time. We thought it sounded cool. Reem means 'excellent, cool, wicked, lovely, nice, sick'. And 'sick' also means 'reem'. And 'creepy sick' means 'extra reem'.

Does that make sense to you? It does to me.

So I thought I'd say it on the show for a laugh. I didn't have a clue it would turn into such a massive deal.

Chloe was asking me if I knew what 'blow-dry' meant, which of course I didn't. I didn't realise 'blow-dry' was the same as 'hair-dry'. But I do now.

The word 'reem' was suddenly everywhere. Everyone was saying it (even the Queen, I reckon). One morning I saw on Facebook that a couple of geezers were promoting an event called 'Reem Nights'.

'That's my word!' I thought, so that day I went to see Kirk and his dad Mick Norcross who owns Sugar Hut in Brentwood and said I wanted to put on a night of my own. We called it 'Reem Parties' (and told the other fellas to change their name because Joey Essex had taken it back!).

By the time I started chatting to Sam on camera, in real life I'd already been seeing her for a few weeks. The producers of *TOWIE* expect you to tell them everything that goes on in your life so they can work out their storylines, but the truth is you can hold stuff back for yourself if you need to. They're going to find out *eventually* but sometimes you want things to happen off camera before it happens in front of the whole country! I knew it was serious straight away. I was getting butterflies all over again and whenever I saw her I had this really nervous feeling. I thought she was the best-looking girl in the universe. I'd say to my mates, 'Is it me or is Sam the most beautiful girl ever?' And they'd laugh and say, 'Joey, she's really pretty but there are millions of girls out there who are as good looking.' Not to me there weren't. I seriously thought Sam was the prettiest, best-looking girl I'd ever seen. And I couldn't look at anyone else.

Sam said in an interview once she made me wait five weeks for sex, as I remember it she did definitely make me wait but I don't think it was quite that long. Not that I was counting! The first time me and Sam spent the night together was after a night out with her and Jess Wright in London. We were all pretty pissed. We got a cab home together and dropped Jess off at her house before going back to my dad's. She'll probably kill me for saying this but that night it just sort of happened . . . but it wasn't proper! The next day she was late for *TOWIE* and she'd left her MINI somewhere, so I drove her to her scene in my Smart car. The producers didn't have a clue what was going on as we'd barely said 'hello' in the show.

The night Sam and I got together on camera was at Harry Derbidge's 17th birthday party. It was a fancy-dress theme and I went as Beach Ken. Everyone at school used to say I looked like the Ken doll so I thought I might as well embrace it. Anyway I had an excuse to bag myself a Barbie!

Sam was wearing a white bikini. She'd gone as a Bond girl. She looked stunning and I couldn't take my eyes off her. At the end of the episode we were sitting outside with our feet dangling in the swimming pool.

Sam was giggling, 'Why did you bring me out here? Do you fancy me?'

I grinned back at her, 'Do *you* fancy *me*?'

She laughed, 'I asked you, you idiot!'

I started stroking her legs then we jumped in the pool and I took my top off.

Say say! What what!* What are YOU sayin'?

I asked if she'd give me a kiss and the camera lingered on us for what seemed like ages. To this day I still think it's one of the best scenes I've ever done on *TOWIE*. I love watching it back. I didn't mind that we were kissing on national television – in fact, I was buzzing off it.

So Sam Faiers and Joey Essex were official.

After the kissing scene Mark confronted Sam and told her, 'That was a bit strong the other night wasn't it?'

I was the new guy on the show and I think he might have been starting to think that I was treading on his toes.

I knew Mark before I joined the show and a few days before I'd shot my first scene he'd called me up trying to do some digging . . .

'A little birdie tells me you're coming into *TOWIE*.'

At the time I was thinking, 'A birdie? How's a bird on the phone suddenly talking about TOWIE?' *I was well baffed*.*

He'd clearly been worried from the start about what effect I was going to have on the show. And now a few weeks later he was even more worried because me and Sam were the new couple in Essex!

I wanted to make our first TV date special. So I decided to take Sam on a little 'Joey adventure'.

I took her to the dump.

She was a bit baffed at first – she'd hoped I'd be whisking her up to London in a chauffeur-driven car. But to me this was much more special; I was taking her on a trip to the places I used to play as a kid.

I even made her a packed lunch (it got a bit squashed in my rucksack though).

I turned up at her house clutching two peddle bikes and helmets. I was wearing a white T-shirt and very short tight blue shorts. She was wearing a floral dress that showed her boobs, a gold necklace and wedges.

The first thing she said was, 'I haven't ridden a bike in ages.'

'Trust me, you'll love it,' I replied.

She did love it (even though she kept moaning that the bike seat hurt her bum!).

I took her to the dump and told her about how I used to get bits of rubbish from there to build my treehouses and 'base camps' in the brook.

We had a picnic and she couldn't stop laughing. It obviously wasn't what she'd expected but it was definitely a date she'd never forget. Anyone could take her to a boring restaurant but only Joey Essex would take her to the tip!

I asked for another kiss.

'Am I a good kisser?' I grinned.

'Do you know what? I would actually say that you are,' she smiled and we kissed again. She told me that when Mark used to kiss her she could tell he didn't mean it but with me it felt 'nice'. I told her I knew exactly what she meant.

The next couple of months were brilliant. I was so happy. I fancied Sam so much and we spent nearly every night together.

It wasn't just me and Sam who became the talk of Essex. My outfits were starting to get a bit of attention too. I turned up in one episode wearing orange Ugg boots and super-skin-tight jeans. Sam was horrified.

'What have you got on your feet? They look stupid!' she laughed.

I didn't care. To me I looked cool. As I said before, clothes are fun – they're not meant to be serious.

'Your jeans are really tight, you can see your willy,' she carried on, 'it's like you're wearing leggings.'

She told me I looked like more of a girl than her, which I probably did at the time. I was also wearing my 'H' Hermès belt (this time it was a real one not a fake) and driving my Smart car.

Everyone started copying me after that so it can't have been that bad, can it?

In the same way as I'd bonded with Sydney's mum Dawn, I got really close to Sam and Billie's mum Sue. She's an amazing lady and I have a huge place for her in my heart. I adore her, we used to have such good chats (much to Sam's annoyance a lot of the time because she'd often take my side in an argument!). Sue is always really supportive to me and would treat me like a son. I loved going to visit her and I'd always bring her flowers. I turned up one day with a huge bunch and I think Sam was disappointed they weren't for her! Sue if you're reading this I just want to say thank you for always being so nice to me. I know I wasn't easy.

Off-screen everyone seemed to want a piece of us. We were doing TV shows and magazine interviews every week. And when we got nominated for a BAFTA I was asked to go on ITV's *Daybreak* to talk about it.

BAFTA – I still don't even know what that stands for . . .
British
Awards
Finally
After
The
Amazing show
?

Christine Bleakley told me *TOWIE* was up against something called *Downton Abbey* and asked me what I thought of it. 'What's *Downton Abbey*?' I asked and everyone laughed for some reason.

I still don't know what it is. Is it like EastEnders?

They had me trying to read the weather but I got everything muddled – they told me I was pointing to Wales when I was trying to say what the temperature was in London. They told me it was going to be raining in Manchester, which I said was 'not reem' and they all creased up again. We ended up winning a BAFTA in the end. At the time I didn't realise what a massive deal it was. We collected our award off *The Inbetweeners* actors. The other people in our category were apparently really pissed off. We were also up against something called *Sherlock*.

Never heard of it.

I didn't recognise any celebrities at the party apart from the guy who shouts the names of the balls in the National Lottery. I went over to him really excitedly and said 'Number 21!' I'm sure there were loads of famous people in there but I didn't know who anyone was.

It was all going so well. At least I thought it was.

I didn't know it but Sam was starting to have second thoughts. She thought I was getting too keen and started telling her sister Billie that she thought it was 'moving a bit too fast'.

TOWIE broke up for the summer and everyone went to Marbella on holiday. 'No carbs before Marbs' had become another big saying from the show and whenever we saw anyone out there that's what they'd shout.

I don't eat a lot of carbs anyway. Someone told me bread sits in your stomach and doesn't move. Do you think that's true?

Sam went to Marbella with her mates and I went out with a group of lads I knew. It was a strange feeling, going on holiday with everyone knowing your name. Being drunk and acting like a bean with your mates was one thing, but this time there were paps following us about watching us every second!

I should've been able to tell things were starting to go wrong with Sam but I was so into her I'd never have allowed myself to believe it.

We saw each other while we were out there but she kept wanting to go off with her mates and whenever we were out it felt like she didn't really want to spend that much time with me.

Then everything started to go wrong.

I'd been staying in a villa with my mate Steve Cass and another group of lads we knew. We'd stayed out one night with Sam and her mates and as I got back to the villa I got a phone call.

It was one of the *TOWIE* producers.

'The papers know about your mum.'

My heart went into my mouth. I thought I was going to be sick. I knew it was only a matter of time before the press found out about my mum's suicide but it didn't make hearing about it any better. I was more worried about my family.

'Joey's hell at suicide mother' said the paper.

I spoke to my dad and Frankie on the phone and we were all in tears. It hurt so much. It was almost like it had happened all over again. Just having it out there in the public and knowing people would be talking about it. It's such a private thing. Just because I was on TV didn't mean people had the right to know about something so personal.

I just sat there sobbing my eyes out.

I just wanted to get away for a bit but as I went up the steps to our villa I suddenly got a weird feeling in my stomach. Something wasn't right. I saw my passport sitting on the table outside my room. My room had been locked because I'd been out for the night with Sam. My passport was in my room when I'd locked it.

I'd been robbed.

I quickly opened my door and saw the window to my room had been smashed.

Everything had gone – I'd had a brand-new Louis Vuitton suitcase full of designer clothes that I'd bought especially for the trip. There was a man-bag with £4,000 in it. All gone.

Could it get any worse?!

The other lads were all stood there, looking on in shock. But there was something about the way they were acting that made me suspicious. The only one who had genuine concern was my mate Steve and he'd been with me the whole time.

My head was whirring. I looked from my room to the table outside.

How had my passport been moved back inside the house? If someone had broken through the window and stolen my stuff, why would they then put my passport back? It didn't make sense.

Only it did. The lads had done it themselves. They'd taken all my stuff, hidden it somewhere and then panicked because they knew I'd need my passport to get back home. So they'd quickly put it on the table hoping I wouldn't remember where I'd left it. They weren't my usual group of mates. They were just some fellas I'd got to know the last year or so. And I knew deep down that they were behind it.

'You robbed me! You robbed me!' I yelled at them.

Of course they all stood there protesting and pretending they had nothing to do with it. But I knew. In my mind there was no doubt.

'Fuck you all!' I shouted. 'I don't like any of you anyway.'

I was too upset to even bother talking to the police. It wasn't worth it.

Me and Steve spent the rest of the holiday penniless without any clothes to wear. Sam was still there having a great time with her mates and although she was there for me and let us stay with her, I felt like she was looking down at me for some reason. And having to rely on her for money made me feel so small. It was probably all in my head, and to be fair I wasn't the best person to be around as I was on a big downer. Not only had my clothes got nicked but they had also taken my tickets to the champagne spray party at the Ocean Club. I had to stand outside watching as Sam enjoyed herself on the top deck inside the VIP area – she didn't seem to care that I couldn't get in. She was having a great time and I wasn't part of it. In the end Mick Norcross saw us and sorted us out with tickets.

Not that Sam noticed. Her feelings towards me had obviously changed.

CHAPTER 18
BRAND JOEY

As soon as I appeared on TV I had agents trying to meet up with me to represent me. One meeting I had was with a guy called Dave Read from Neon Management. Dave already looked after a few people from *TOWIE* and from what I could see he was doing a good job getting them seen all over town. He also seemed like a nice straightforward bloke, which to me was the most important thing.

Dave must've thought he had his work cut out with me. I couldn't tell the time or blow my nose. But he soon realised I wasn't as stupid as I seemed. I even managed to do a sly turner* by negotiating with him in our first meeting. *TOWIE* didn't pay much money – I think it's gone up now – but I knew it was about looking at the bigger picture.

'I can make you loads of money,' Dave told me matter of factly.

OK, I thought, let's see how serious he is.

'Can I have £8,000 up front?' I asked cheekily. I still owed my dad money for the Smart car (See! Not so stupid!). Dave hardly flinched.

'By the time I send you the cheque you'll already have earned well over that anyway.'

He was right. By the end of my first month signed to Neon Management I'd made £12,000. I gave my dad the money he'd leant me all in one go and he nearly fainted.

Dave booked me PAs all across the country. All I'd have to do was turn up to a nightclub, have my picture taken with a few people, smile a lot, say 'reem' a few times and I was done. I'll always remember getting my first pay cheque. I'd been to a nightclub for no more than two hours and I'd earned over a grand. That was more than I got paid in a month at the fish market.

Dave was good to me. We've been together about three years and he's become one of my best mates. But just like any relationship, there have been a few dramas on the way.

After I'd been with Dave a few months I started getting carried away with the whole fame thing. I'd gone to a party with Amy Childs; she'd left *TOWIE* after series two and was signed up with an agent called Claire Powell who also looked after Peter Andre. Sam's mum Sue was at the party too and she was telling me how she thought Claire would be good for me. It seemed like one minute I was chatting to Claire and the next I'd signed up to CAN Associates. I said goodbye to Dave. But a few weeks into being with CAN I knew I'd made a mistake. Although Claire had promised me the world, I felt like I hardly saw her. She'd said all this stuff would happen – calendars, hair products and endorsements – but as far as I could tell I was working less and earning less than when I was with Dave. In the end I started booking PAs for myself. They'd got me a few, don't get me wrong, but Dave had taught me what I could earn and I didn't feel like CAN were getting me what they should.

It all came to a head at New Year's Eve. I'd booked myself four different PAs at clubs across Liverpool, which would've bagged me a fair bit of money. I'd made all the arrangements with the nightclub owners, then CAN told me they'd booked for me to appear at GAY in London on the same night. I politely asked them to cancel it and said it wouldn't work as I'd already sorted my work for that night.

This was a few weeks ahead of the event and I thought I'd made myself clear. But on New Year's Eve itself I got a text from CAN.

'Don't forget your gig at GAY tonight.'

I was confused. I'd told them to cancel it hadn't I?

I don't know what happened with the message (I actually had a screensaver of the text I sent them telling them to cancel it but there was no point trying to get into a fight about it) but in the end they informed me that I was contracted to them so I had no choice but to do GAY and break my other arrangements. This meant I had to let down four clubs at the last minute. I felt so bad.

'OK, I'll do GAY,' I said over the phone, 'but after that I'm leaving CAN Associates.'

A few days later I was on the phone to Dave.

I sheepishly told him I'd made a mistake and asked if he'd have me back. He was great about it and he's told me since he's glad I left when I did. It's made our relationship stronger and there's more respect. I've realised the grass isn't always greener on the other side.

What does that mean anyway? Just that it gets watered a bit more and it's in a sunny patch?

So me and Dave picked up where we left off. And the next time we met up he pulled out some paperwork with details of a deal he'd been working on to get me my own hair-care range. He'd had it there all along but hadn't used it as bribery to make me stay with him when I'd said I was off to CAN. That's not his style. He'd just quietly been working on getting it sorted for me. In the end he was the best agent I could ever have – he's helped secure me all sorts of endorsements from hair products, to calendars, clothes and perfume, he's also negotiated some very lucrative deals for me to appear on brilliant TV shows. A few of my *TOWIE* friends have all taken big money to appear on *Big Brother* for Channel 5 but Dave has always told me to be patient and wait for the right offer to come and by that he didn't mean the highest bid. He explained that although we are all in business to make money it is very important to make the correct decisions for the long-term plan.

What's great about our relationship is that I really feel that he is there for me, working in my best interest. It's definitely helped me these last few years and kept my feet on the ground.

I've jumped ahead a bit here so we'd better catch up. Before any of this wicked news I'm about to get dumped by Sam first . . .

CHAPTER 19

'WE NEED TO TALK' (IN OTHER WORDS, YOU'RE DUMPED)

She was in Manchester by herself, she said. I was at Tom Pearce's house playing ping pong.

'We need to talk.'

It was such a 'film' thing to write. Why would you ever say to anyone 'We need to talk'? It basically means you're dumped. Why do you then need to talk about it? I've never understood why people say that. Why not just be honest and say 'It's over'. I called her even though I knew what was coming, the conversation lasted about 40 seconds before I hung up the phone.

I was heartbroken.

I phoned Diags.

'She's dumped me.'

'Come to mine,' he said.

That night we both drove to his place in Bournemouth where

he was at university. We went out and got so laggin that when we got back to his house I started around turning all the lights on and off, then sprayed the fire extinguisher all over the kitchen, lounge, stairs . . . EVERYWHERE.

The next morning we called our mate Mitch in Ibiza.

'She's finished with me,' I cried.

'Come out here then,' he replied.

So we booked our flights that morning – me, Steve and Diags – and flew out that night. I've never done something so sudden before. I remember Steve saying, 'Are we *really* going to do this? Book a flight and go tonight?'

It was the best holiday I've ever had.

As soon as we landed we headed to the Ibiza Rocks Hotel. It was like being in another world. Mitch appeared looking ridiculously brown with a massive grin on his face and he took us to his apartment overlooking the sea. There were three people I knew from school – I couldn't believe it! – and about five *really* fit girls. The apartment was amazing. Mitch took us to a club called Space and we'd never seen anything like it. We were dressed up all smart like Essex boys in our £100 shorts and tight-fitting T-shirts. But everyone there was wearing battered vests, £2 Adidas shorts and flip-flops. Maybe I was about to discover a new look for Joey Essex!

We were only there for three days but it was brilliant. There were beautiful girls everywhere. We went to another night called the Zoo Project, which confused the hell out of me to start with.

What the fuck was it? A nightclub full of elephants?

It was a club night held in an abandoned zoo so we all had our faces painted like zebras and tigers. There was a girl who came round to the apartment to do the make-up for us. She was fit. Once inside everyone was dancing in the seal pit, which had steps all around like in a stadium. We were all jumping and waving our hands towards the DJ like he was God or something.

Just before we were due to go home I had a phone call from Giles, one of the producers on *TOWIE*.

'Are you in Ibiza? There are some pap pictures of you. Sam's really upset, why have you gone?'

'Hang on! She finished with me.'

'But she wants to sort it out.'

I was still upset.

'It's too late; the way she did it really hurt.'

I didn't want them telling me what to do.

Sam had been calling me, asking me to come back and talk to her. There it was again, 'the talk'. What was there to talk about? Anyway, I was trying to forget about it all and have some fun.

When we got back the whole *TOWIE* cast were invited as guests to Channel 4's T4 on the Beach – a big music concert in Weston-super-Mare. I had never seen so many screaming kids. And the crazy part was – everyone knew my name.

Mark and Arg were doing some presenting on stage and I poked my head round the corner to look at the crowd. Suddenly all I could hear was this chanting – 'Joey! Joey!' It was mental.

Sam was there too. When I saw her again it still gave me butterflies. She always has that effect on me no matter what's happened between us. Just looking at her face makes me feel all funny inside.

I was still upset with her but I was obsessed with knowing whether or not she was wearing this ring I'd bought her. I'd given her a promise ring a month or so earlier. She'd been wearing another ring of her own on her engagement finger and had flashed it to the cameras when we were in a restaurant once which made all the papers think we were engaged for a few days. So I'd gone out and bought her a special one to prove I'd always be a good boyfriend. It had a baguette diamond in the middle and was in the shape of a heart.

When I saw her at T4 on the Beach I kept looking at her finger. All I wanted to know was whether she still had it on. She'd told me once that when you have a ring with a heart on you have to wear it in a way that faces upwards when you show it to someone else. That way it means you're in love with the person who gave it to you. So there I was squinting my eyes to see whether a) she had it on and b) it was the right way up. It was facing the wrong way.

I felt sick. I knew she'd done it on purpose to make me feel bad.

She denied it at the time but has since admitted she did do it. She was really upset about it all too.

Then it was time for series three of *TOWIE*. Me and Sam had to meet up and talk on camera about what had happened. It was so hard.

'Why did you split up with me?' I asked her.

'I just felt like it wasn't the right time, we got together really quickly . . .' she said.

We were sat on a park bench. I would have done anything to have her back but I sat there pretending I was OK.

She carried on . . .

'It was a bit of a whirlwind. Don't get me wrong I was completely wrong, I should have just said "I think we need to have a break . . ."'

I told her it felt out of the blue and that's why it had been such a shock. Then she started saying, 'I did say, let's talk about it . . . but you didn't want to.'

'Why would I want to talk about it?' I said. 'It's like me saying, "You're dumped – but can I see you tomorrow?"'

Although I was single and still had feelings for Sam, in series three of *TOWIE* I felt like I was able to show a bit more of what I was really like at home. In other words, I wore some sick clothes (e.g. a beret and green jacket, some very short denims, a vintage shirt with horses on, vests and Speedos). My sister Frankie joined in this series, which was good because it meant I got to see her a bit more. Because she did a lot of scenes with Chloe, the producers started to get me doing more scenes with Kirk Norcross instead, which worked because we had a fun bromance.

'Cheers united' was a favourite saying of mine. I liked being stupid and I felt like I could open up and have a bit more fun now I was single and hanging around with the guys a bit more. I knew I genuinely didn't understand a lot of stuff but I would also say some things deliberately just to make people laugh. Like when Kirk bought a new car and told me it had 485 brake horsepower.

'What do you mean horse power?' I asked, 'have they got little horses in the back that power it?'

I didn't seriously think there were horses in Kirk's car. Although that would've been jokes.

I heard that Sam had started seeing some guy who wasn't in the show. Weirdly it didn't matter to me who it was, to me he was just some random little bean! I only cared about her.

I, on the other hand, was sent by *TOWIE* to a speed-dating party. Here are some of my best Joey Essex chat-up lines . . .

'What's your favourite animal? I like elephants. I would say a dinosaur but they don't exist anymore.'

'Have you got a favourite fruit? Mine's a tomato.'

'What's your biggest secret? Mine is that I can't wear my socks the right way round. It's a good secret isn't it?'

One girl asked me if I was alright because I kept touching myself. I told her it was because my jeans were too small and I could hardly walk.

Billi Mucklow and Cara Kilbey joined *TOWIE* in series three. I knew them both from around Essex and thought Cara was a sort* at the time.

I threw a pool party for my 21st birthday and made everyone wear face paint like in Ibiza. I went as a zebra, Gemma Collins was a rabbit and Frankie was a snake. Lauren Goodger was at the party too. She told me that Sam and Mark had gone on a date.

I was confused. Why would he do that to me when he knew me and Sam had only just broken up? And what was Sam playing at? I thought she had a boyfriend at home. Why was she dating Mark now? Did she just want a storyline on camera.

After we'd finished filming, me and Cara got a cab into London and went to Fabric nightclub. Her dad owns it, which meant we could just walk in and sit at the best table. We were really pissed as we'd been drinking all day and both still had our face paint on. I was even still wearing my swimming trunks! I don't remember much that night apart from partying with Cara and my mates. Me, the two Tom's and Cara went back to his flat as it was nearby.

The next day I was sat with everyone having breakfast and I saw a picture on my phone.

'Look!' I said. 'There's a picture of Katy Perry leaving Fabric last night!'

Cara laughed.

'She was sat with us in our booth, Joey!'

Apparently we'd been hanging out with her in the VIP area all night. Only I was so bladdered I didn't even realise.

'She was sitting on your lap at one point,' Cara told me.

Sam and Billie were attacked by some girls outside a nightclub and ended up with bashed faces and black eyes. I don't know what the full story was but something must have happened to start the argument. I was filming in B&Q when I found out and I couldn't think straight after that. I got a phone call from one of the boys saying that Sam was in hospital and my heart dropped. I was in such a mess that they cut the scene in the end – the producers said they couldn't use the footage. The 'incident' was brushed over on TOWIE but for some reason Sam decided to still be on camera.

JOEY ESSEX

I really wanted to go and see her to check she was OK. But when I got round there I saw that Mark had been to the house already delivering giant teddy bears and flowers. I felt so sick seeing her face. I properly cared about her. And for me it wasn't just a storyline.

When he eventually spoke to me about him and Sam it was on camera at a *TOWIE* Halloween party. I told him he could do what he wanted because me and Sam were over. But it wasn't me he should've worried about because a few minutes later he started snogging Sam – and his ex Lauren was watching them and sobbing behind the bushes.

And remember, although I think she'd cooled things with this other fella, it wouldn't have looked great at the time. Apparently he only found out when he was at home watching it on TV. One of my mates told me afterwards he had been eating a pizza and was so shocked when he saw them that he spat it out at the TV. Poor bloke.

Mark left the show at the end of series three. He'd been signed up to do *I'm a Celebrity . . . Get Me out of Here!*. As he left he asked Sam if she'd give him a proper go as her boyfriend. She said she couldn't trust him and that what she was looking for was someone who pays her attention, respects her and looks after her.

Basically she was describing me . . .

CHAPTER 20

NEW MATES AND A NEW MOUTH

It was off to Lapland to film the *TOWIE* Christmas special. I'd just had veneers put on my teeth and one of them nearly fell off on Santa's lap. I also had to drink everything through a straw because I was so paranoid about them getting stained.

People always said I had nice teeth before so I don't know why I got them done really. But ever since losing one of my front teeth in my bike accident when I was a kid I had one tooth that looked a different colour to the rest. My mum had done everything possible to try and get me a perfect new tooth but no matter what we did it still looked odd compared to the others. I was convinced it kept shrinking too. So I was known as 'Joey Shrink-tooth' for a while. Long*.

Ever since school, I'd always dreamed of having perfect pearly white teeth. I wanted to be able to walk down the road with a deep tan and a mouth that glowed in the dark. You might not believe it to look at me, but when it came to getting a new set

I decided to go for some that looked a bit more natural. And when he showed me the 'white scale' I went for the third one down. So when people say 'I'm blinded by your teeth' they should have seen the top colour!

Sometimes I look in the mirror and wish I had my normal teeth back but I couldn't because then I'd be stuck with the deformed one again.

I met Rylan Clark, who was on the X *Factor* and now presents the spin-off show for Channel 5's *Big Brother*, at the filming of *Celebrity Juice* the other day and he said he'd been to the same dentist as me when he got his veneers done. Now they are some TEETH! He chose the whitest ones on the scale. He told me he likes them big and fake looking – so that's all that matters!

Lapland was fun. We had to write letters to Santa, so I asked him for some new short shorts and a poisonous frog.

When we returned, Arg threw a medieval birthday party dressed as Henry VIII. He was wearing tights and stuffed his pants with socks to make him look like he had a bigger willy. All the girls were wearing these corset things which made their boobs look huge. Being in the royal family back then must have been pretty good!

I was trying to remember who's in our royal family the other day. I know there's Prince William and Prince Charles, then I thought there was someone called Charles Dickens. But someone told me afterwards he writes books. I also thought the prime minister was in the royal family. I thought he was their dad. I know Prince William has got a baby with that girl he met at university. I couldn't remember the name of their kid though . . . I think it's Blue.

I also think that secretly the Queen isn't all that posh. I reckon she just eats cereal all day. Or sometimes a sausage sandwich. I bet she says to her butler, 'Giz a cuppa tea with two sugars – and for dinner I'll have a Big Mac. Fuck it, I'm on a lively one today.'

With Mark gone from the show, I started hanging out with Arg a lot more. He's a really lovely bloke. He's also slow, forgetful, always on a diet (or talking about being on one) and LOVES a gossip. If you tell him a secret you have to beg him not to say it to anyone else. And most of the time he still can't resist it. His laziness is the worst though. It annoys people sometimes.

Here's an example of him being slow (this happened when I went to his house to drop off his gym kit the other day):

It was freezing and raining outside so I phoned him when I was about 30 seconds away because I know how long it takes him to get downstairs.

'Arg, I'm outside.'

'OK I'm coming down.'

I sat in my car on his drive.

I waited.

And waited.

At least a minute went by (I know because I'm very good at counting in my head).

I opened the car door and accidentally ran into a thorn bush.

I knocked on the front door.

Another 20 seconds went by.

Finally he let me in.

As soon as I got inside I said to him, 'Why didn't you answer the door?'

'I was just doing something.'

I told him this was where he always goes wrong.

'You can't be bothered and it annoys people.'

I'm honest with Arg – I tell him straight and he respects that. But then he'll do it again.

'Can I use your Wi-Fi password?' I asked him.

'I don't know it.'

'Yes you do Arg, you've got a computer.'

'It's in my dad's room and it's locked.'

'No it isn't. You're lying.'

He just couldn't be bothered to get it. He paused for a few seconds then said, 'Hang on, let me remember, I think I know it off by heart' and told me the whole thing off perfectly.

See! Lazy!

I've said to him before, 'Arg, you have to stop doing things like this. You're being selfish and not thinking about other people.'

It's only the past two years that he's become so lazy. I personally think it's because he's still in love with his ex-girlfriend Lydia, and I think he knows that's the reason too. I'd love to sit her down and ask her to give him one more chance. They were a good couple. I reckon he realises he didn't treat her so well towards the end, which pushed her away.

By series four of *TOWIE* I'd also managed to persuade the producers to let Diags join the show. Me, Arg and Diags were like 'the three musketeers' or as Arg called us, 'the thick, the fat and the ugly'. In Diags's first scene he asked me why I didn't think he had much luck with the ladies. I told him it was because his teeth looked like balloons.

I was single and ready to mingle. At the end of series three I'd had a bit of a thing with Mark Wright's sister Jess. I snogged her at the end of series three. I found her attractive at first but then she got a bit boring. Anyway, her future fiancé joined the show in series four so it's probably a good thing we didn't work out.

When Ricky Rayment joined the cast, I didn't tell the producers about our history but it was only a matter of time before he did something to wind me up. We had a massive fight at the opening of Lauren Goodger's beauty salon.

What a manly place to have a scrap.

I'd heard he'd been taking the piss out of me behind my back.

When he arrived at the party I squared up to him, 'What are you doing going behind my back telling girls I'm a little boy?'

'I didn't even know I said it,' he said. I didn't believe him.

'If you've got something to say why don't you say it to my face?'

I couldn't let it go.

'I'm not denying it, but I don't remember saying it or doing it. I don't even remember being at that place. I was that out of my nut. Then as soon as I found out I did I tried to get your number, I tried to talk to you . . .'

He was just making crap excuses.

'WHY are you talking behind my back??' I shouted.

'Well, get pissed and go and talk about me behind my back then! I couldn't care less!' He was getting all sarcastic now.

'That's the point, I wouldn't do that,' I said.

'If you want to fucking whack me up, whack me up right now!' he shouted, before adding, 'If I was a little boy like you I'd slap me up but I'm not.'

I tried to walk away. I'd had enough and he was winding me up. Then Frankie told him he was being embarrassing and he started swearing at her saying 'No one cares about you'. That was it, I was screwing. He walked out of the shop and as he did I went after him.

The girls were screaming and trying to hold me back but I couldn't help myself. I ran after him and tried to punch him in the head. I wasn't going to let anyone mug* me or my sister off on TV.

Definitely not Ricky Rayment.

That summer, Arg was on another diet mission. He went to Marbella to do a boot camp with Gemma Collins and invited me to join them.

I saved Gemma from drowning on that trip. She was in the sea one day waving about and screaming. Me and Arg thought it was funny to start with. Then I thought, 'Crap, is she actually drowning?' So I swam out to save her. I've never done a life-saving course so I just had to wrap as much of my body around her as possible and swim with all my strength. Afterwards she was looking at me all dreamily saying 'You're my hero'. I thought I was in *Baywatch*.

Me and Arg went to a strip club while we were out there – I remember us both getting lap dances and giving each other high fives. Not sure that was part of the 'boot camp experience' though.

The boot camp was when something first happened between Gemma and Arg. He didn't tell me until a couple of weeks afterwards. But he did say she had 'very good techers*'. Gemma is a brilliant girl and I've got a lot of time for her. But she's properly in love with Arg and I find that weird. Especially when he says stuff like, 'If you were four stone lighter you could be my girlfriend.'

Arg ended up losing two stone. And he ran the marathon. I really admired him for doing that – we all went to cheer him on and he was in such pain he was crying towards the end.

CHAPTER 21

I WANT YOU BACK

The Joey Essex house rules:

1. Be tidy
2. Don't snore
3. Clean up
4. Do your bed in the morning
5. Don't nick my food
6. Take your shoes off
7. Don't wee on the toilet seat and flush the chain

I bought a flat! Me, Joey Essex, had earned enough money to get myself a proper place of my own. I was 21.

I think Dad and Frankie were sad when I left. Although I don't know how they put up with me for so long. I was always causing murders of some kind. I nearly pulled the house down after my 21st birthday party (this was my proper 21st, not the one I had on camera for *TOWIE*). I'd told Dad I wanted to get a big marquee in the garden, so me, Tom and Diags put it up.

We tried to anyway. We didn't realise it had to be secured to the ground so instead we just tied it to anything we could see – the pipes, the water tap, the patio chairs. It was held on by about a million things. Dad had told me to 'weigh it down' but I didn't know what he meant. Three weeks later it was flapping all over the place and had nearly ripped the drain pipes off the wall.

I couldn't believe I had my own place. I was buzzing. It's such a sick flat. My bedroom's got a walk-in wardrobe that lights up as soon as you go in and the building has a gym and an underground swimming pool with stars on the ceiling and a sauna! I had to put in every single bit of money I'd earned to buy it. But it was worth it. The boys loved it too – we had pool parties nearly every night for about four months!

The Joey Essex gym routine
  (in case you want to look like me)

- 30 press-ups
- 30 crunches
- 30 sit-ups

Repeat that five times and do it once or twice a day for a month.

The next house I buy needs to have a nightclub inside. I'll never have to leave! People will be queuing up to come to the best club in the land – Essex Land! It wouldn't be an actual club though. It would just be a room with some speakers in. I want to have a massive slide in it that comes down from my bedroom and

goes outside and then in again. People will be walking down the
road and see me flying past going 'Owhhhaaey!'

When I first bought the flat it was a showroom so it was all
cream and I didn't like the furniture. The beds were for midgets
– I think they had them like that to make it look bigger when
they were showing people around.

Billi Mucklow's mum Paula is an interior designer and she
decorated it for me. I told her, 'I don't know how much it's
going to cost but I want snakeskin wallpaper and snakeskin
everything.' She found this grey stuff for my walls that looks
like pale leather snakeskin shoes, you can stroke it and everything. My couch looks like a big grey crocodile made of the
same stuff. And I've got a bed that looks like a crown with 'J
E' carved in it.

I don't know many of the other people in my building but
there's one guy who lives in the penthouse upstairs who I'm really
close to. He's called Mozza. That's not his real name but that's
what I call him. He's older than me and he's really sound. We
go to the gym downstairs together sometimes. He's one of the
only people I trust to look after the flat when I'm not there. And
I don't trust very many people.

Arg keeps texting me because he wants to go out. I've just told
him his new nickname is Pesto Pasta*. Because he's being a pest.

Tom Pearce moved in with me for a few weeks but, as I told you,
he's clumsy and breaks stuff so I didn't give him his own key. It
was series five of *TOWIE* by now and he was now on the show

as well. So I felt like I had my proper mates with me. All we ever did was muck about and laugh. Usually in our boxers.

But it wasn't a lad's pad for long because I'd started to see Sam again.

Sam had split with the guy she was seeing by this point and one thing led to another one night at Sugar Hut.

The boys were worried I was going to get hurt again. I tell them everything so they knew how much I'd cried over her the first time around. And I don't think Frankie trusted what she was after – she told Chloe she thought Sam was only back with me because I had a swimming pool! Which is hilarious.

I wasn't sure how Sam felt to start with – she hardly ever says how she feels while I wear my heart on my sleeve.

That's a weird saying isn't it? Would be a bit mad if your heart was on your sleeve, it wouldn't be in your body then would it? And you'd probably die.

She saw a picture of me leaving a club one night with another girl and although nothing happened I think it made her realise what she wanted. It was a stupid thing for me to have done and I thought I'd messed it up for a minute but in the end it brought us closer together. She told me she loved me and that the thought of me with another girl made her feel sick.

I realised that Sam was the girl I wanted to marry. I was so in love with her.

So I pulled out all the stops to impress her. I paid for a helicopter ride and hired out a restaurant just for us. Sam couldn't stop smiling; she was so chuffed (probably because it wasn't the dump this time). She wore a tight red dress and looked stunning. The butterflies were back!

Our sex life was really good too and made me think that we were really on to something good. Sam wrote in her book that we had a rubbish sex life when we first went out, which pissed me off a bit. But we've chatted about it since and she said she regrets writing about it in that way. What she meant was that when she lived at home we were stuck in her box room directly above her mum and dad's room. I was always worried about making noise or that her dad would walk in on us – it was pretty cringey so I get what she was saying. But when we both had our own flats that soon changed. We couldn't keep our hands off each other. I definitely didn't hear her complaining!

Sam was the girl for me. And for a while all we ever did was laugh and have fun together.

It was also nice to be in the show and not be the one having all the arguments. There were more than a few dramas between others though. One massive row kicked off between Jess Wright, Billi and Cara after Arg told Jess he'd overheard them call Jess's mum Carol 'mutton dressed as lamb'.

I don't know what that means. I thought they were saying Carol was wearing something furry and looked like a lamb.

Lucy Mecklenburgh got engaged to Mario Falcone in Marbella but there were loads of blazing rows when she found out he'd cheated on her. At one point he tried to blame me and Sam for spreading the rumours so I called him a 'Capri Sun*'. I think I also called him a 'Slush Puppy*'. He tried to fight back by saying I was a 'protein shake', which was quite a good reply to be fair but only if the person he was saying it to had big muscles and looked like him.

I don't like using normal swear words if I can help it. I like them to be Joey Essex words. Another good one (which I used on a guy called Jamie Reid who was disrespecting Frankie by saying he slept with her) is a 'lunchbox*'. Your lunchbox is something you're embarrassed about so that's a good diss.

Tom Kilbey started seeing Arg's ex Lydia, which made Arg go a bit mad. Arg then dated Gemma on and off but she was always crying. He'd say he loved her one minute and then insult her the next. She broke down in tears at dinner once because he said she looked like some woman called Vanessa Feltz.

I didn't know who she was – is she the woman who does the voice over for TOWIE?

But life couldn't be better for me and Sam. I wrote her a love letter to tell her how I felt.

I told her she meant so much to me and that I knew our love was a 'sure fing'. And I reminded her of the first night we met, 'When we woke upon Charlie's sticky leather sofa! I know I always say this but you are the love of my life and that will never change. I love you.'

We even talked about marriage. We felt so comfortable around each other – I'd walk about naked and make her laugh and she'd cook for me! I could properly be myself around her.

Here's how I'd describe myself naked in five words:
- Slim
- Brown
- Skeen*
- Lean
- Sweet

Here's how I'd describe Sam naked in five words:
- Beautiful
- Silky
- Cute
- Love heart

I know that sounds weird but when I try to picture what she looks like that's the shape that comes into my head

- Tender

Actually, what does tender mean? I want to say 'pillowy like a cushion'.

I'd always compliment Sam on the way she looked and text her nice things when we weren't together. She was insecure about her body sometimes – like most girls are. And she had this thing that meant she pulled out her eyelashes all the time. It was a condition she'd suffered with from when she was a kid. I'd try to stop her doing it but sometimes it happened in her sleep. She'd wake up with swollen eyes and bruised eyelids and hated the way she looked. But she always looked beautiful to me.

We talked about moving in together but I think Chloe and my mates thought it was a bad idea. We were starting to have a few arguments and afterwards I'd get really upset and go and tell Chloe about it. I was honest with her though, I didn't just give my side of the story. I knew I was stubborn and could get really jealous and possessive, so Chloe always knew what was really going on. But she told me 'love is a dangerous game' and I could see she thought I was in too deep.

At one point me and Sam went to see someone who was going to tell us whether moving in was a good idea or not. I thought it was a psychiatrist but Sam said, 'No, that's someone for crazy people', and that we were going to see someone called a 'prediction teller'. Or something like that anyway. Whoever he was he read our coffee cups. He was a bit strange. He told Sam she was a witch in a previous life and then told us that he could see there would be 'three of you living together', which Sam took to mean we were going to have kids.

And kids were one of the biggest things we argued about . . .

JOEY'S FASCINATING FACTS:

#8 Every human being starts out life as an arsehole, it's the first part of the body to form in the womb. (How jokes is THAT for a fact?)

CHAPTER 22

MUGGED OFF

Sam started to talk about wanting kids. She'd act like she was joking at first but I knew she was serious. She'd bring it up in magazine interviews all the time:

'We're going to have four babies aren't we Joey?'

I'd just sit there thinking, 'I'm too young. I don't want this.'

It got to the point where I was calling Tom or Diags in a constant state of panic.

'I'm worried she's going to get pregnant!'

I'd say to Sam, 'But what if you get pregnant?'

'Well I'll obviously keep it!'

One day I went to see her mum Sue. I was so stressed about the idea of being a dad. I could hardly look after myself let alone anyone else. 'I really think Sam wants a baby,' I told her with a worried look on my face.

'Don't be silly Joey, you're both too young for all that!' Sue would make me feel better about it all. Then Sam would find out we'd spoken about it and have a fit.

We began arguing over everything – whether I wanted eggs on toast or on the side, what colour a chair was, leaving towels in the sink. Everything. Sometimes we'd go for days without even speaking it got that bad.

We are obviously both as bad as each other, but our arguments would often get so out of control that it would scare me.

Not long into us dating the second time around she phoned me from Sugar Hut. I was panicking as I didn't want her to get into any trouble so I went over to check she was OK. As soon as she saw me she came over and shouted, 'Why are you wearing a raincoat? It's not raining inside, take it off!' When I said no she said, 'Take it off or I'll throw this drink in your face'.

'Go on then,' I said, and she did.

I guess I did ask for it. I ran into the toilets wiping drink and tears off my face. What upset me more about rows like that was that she would just disappear – it felt like she was never the one to say sorry. When I came out she was gone, she had gone back to her house and had a party. When she was like that I felt like she didn't give a shit.

Every time we had an argument I got scared that it was over. I was so worried about it ending. It gave me palpitations and I'd panic and worry for hours.

I'd sit crying to the boys, 'It's killing me. I love her. I don't want to split up.'

Tom would ask, 'Is it really making you happy mate?' while Diags would try and make me feel better, 'You don't know this is it. Just because you're rowing doesn't mean you'll split up.'

My sister Frankie thinks I've got issues about people leaving me because of my mum. She says that when I get upset about girl-friends dumping me it's like a rejection thing and it's because of my mum's death. She might be right. I absolutely hate the thought of someone leaving me. I get so upset. It's embarrassing though. I don't want to be someone who's a pussy around girls.

Then there was the jealousy. I trusted Sam but I'd always hear little things, stories, rumours and it would make me paranoid and start to doubt her. I know it was wrong and I should have trusted her but with my history I just found it really difficult.

She went on holiday to Las Vegas with some of her mates and there were pictures of her on the *Daily Mail* website with a group of lads. She was rubbing sun cream on one of their backs, smiling and laughing.

I'd been talking to her on the phone the night before and she was pissed in her hotel room. I thought I heard someone walk into the room and her phone went dead. I tried ringing her back four or five times but she didn't answer. It wasn't until the next day that she called me back, at breakfast. I was fuming. Why did she wait 'til she was at breakfast to call me? If she'd fallen asleep drunk, fair enough, she'd have seen the missed calls from me and would have known I'd be worrying. I was suspicious, but deep down I knew I had nothing to worry about.

To make matters worse, I got mugged the next day.

I was on my way to see my agent Dave in his offices in Hammersmith and it was a scorching sunny day. Before I drove into London I'd been to visit my dad. We sat talking about watches – he collected them and, as I was earning money, I saw them as an investment too. I was going to buy myself a £33,000 watch. It was an Audemars Skeleton and I'd been eyeing it up for ages. Dad looked at me all concerned, 'Joe, please don't wear that watch. You'll get mugged one day you know.'

That conversation was fate. As soon as he said it, I looked at my wrist. I was already wearing an expensive watch as it was – it had cost me £17,000 and was a Rolex Daytona. I thought to myself, 'Maybe I should leave this one here and wear one of my other watches into town.' So I swapped it for another one, but that had still cost me £5,000! I know it seems like a lot of money but it was my one indulgence – as I say, they were investments for the future and I really like watches even though I can't tell the time. Weird.

I left my dad's and drove to Hammersmith at around midday. I was in my Smart car and pulled up in a parking bay. As I reversed, there was a knock on my window. There were two lads wearing Ray-Bans and smiling at me.

'Joey can we have our picture taken with you?'

'OK,' I replied. 'Two minutes.'

They were lingering by the car and I started to get a weird feeling. I sat in the car pretending to look for change for the machine. I thought they might go away if I stayed there long enough. But they didn't so I had no choice but to get out.

'Come on then.'

I stood next to one of the lads for a picture. He put his arm around my neck and was gripping it quite tightly so I smiled for the photo then pulled away as quick as I could.

'See you later,' I said and turned to put money in the ticket machine.

As soon as my back was turned I felt a bang on the side of my head. I instantly hit the floor. My vision was blurry but I saw one of the lads bend down and look me in the eyes then grab something that had dropped on the floor. It was my watch. He started running off so I picked myself up – which wasn't easy – and legged it towards him. As I got nearer he pulled out a blade and started screaming, 'Come on then let's have a fucking fight!'

I started running back to the car.

The guy started to walk off. As his back was turned I found a stick on the floor and tried to hit him with it, running after him again. He was trying to get into his car. His mate had the door open but he couldn't get in – he probably thought if his back was turned I'd smash one of the windows. It must've gone on like this for about ten minutes.

Eventually they managed to shut the door and drive off. In the madness of it all, I'd forgotten to get their licence plate.

I shouted and swore after them.

The police came to my house afterwards and took away my man-bag telling me they were going to search it for DNA. But I knew they wouldn't find anything. It was pointless.

But thank God I'd listened to my dad's advice.

CHAPTER 23

HOW DID IT GET TO THIS?

Dad always loved Sam. If I had a row with her he'd just say, 'Oh come on Joey son, make it up will ya? She's a lovely gal.'

I couldn't really tell him about my feelings or cry in front of him. He doesn't like showing his emotions much and just brushes things away. If I'd told him Sam held an AK-47 up to my face he'd probably laugh and say, 'Oh son. She doesn't mean it!'

But I told my cousin Chloe *everything*. And sometimes that meant she knew a little more than she probably felt comfortable with. I'd tell her what happened between me and Sam behind closed doors then beg her not to say anything. Which sometimes put her in a very awkward position.

Especially after I told her Sam had slapped me.

We'd gone to Dubai for a mini-break. There were a few of us there including Chloe's ex-boyfriend who's a mate of mine and Sam's.

One evening we were in a club and we were getting drunk. We'd been rowing again over stupid stuff and on this particular night it really got nasty.

I went to the toilet while Sam stayed with our mate; they were meant to be waiting for me. But somehow they got lost and when they found me again she was screwing.

'Where have you been?' she shouted and pushed me really hard. I was shocked.

'Calm down!' I shouted back. 'What are you doing?'

It was like she didn't even think anything was wrong.

'Well you shouldn't have left me should you?!' she said and stormed off to a table.

Sam could be pretty short tempered, and when she pushed me like that it made me feel really small. It would get me down and I'd feel very sad. I tried not to get angry in return, which is probably the reason I kept getting so upset. After we split she actually told a magazine, 'What I didn't like about Joey is that no matter what I'd do to him he'd never get angry with me.' Sam's right in that I would never lay a finger on a girl but I did let my temper get to me sometimes. Once I got so mad with Sam I smashed her phone on the floor and broke her screen. I felt really bad afterwards.

In the end, Sam stormed back to the hotel. I followed behind with our mate and when we got back she was in bed pretending to be asleep. We had a big suite so our mate stayed in the lounge area while I crept into the bedroom and tried to wake Sam up to see if she was OK. I was pissed too so was probably being a bit annoying shouting, 'Wake up Sam!'

She lashed out at me. I was in shock. I was so upset.

When I woke up the next morning she wasn't in the bed with me.

Where had she gone?

I looked at myself in the mirror. My eye was bruised and I had a little cut on my lip. And Sam was nowhere to be seen.

She sent me a text that said, 'Come to the beach.'

After all that she'd got up at seven in the morning and left the hotel to go to the beach and sunbathe! Her text was all cheery, as if nothing had happened.

I texted her back, 'What have you done to me? Why have you left me? You should've stayed with me, you should've said sorry.'

'Well I'm at the beach now sunbathing.'

I felt really humiliated and upset. I got to the beach and she was laying there in her bikini. 'Come over here,' she said. But I refused.

'Say sorry then,' I told her.

I sat on the beach crying in front of her. I couldn't believe what had happened.

'What are you talking about?' she said.

I took my shades off and showed her the bruise. 'You've done this to me. I can't go on like this.'

I kept on crying. She started cuddling me and told me it would be OK.

For the rest of the holiday she'd cover the bruise in make-up when we went out. One day soon after we got home we bumped into someone from *Now* magazine and she looked at me strangely.

'Have you got a black eye?' she asked.

I hadn't prepared an excuse. I was embarrassed. I felt like I was in a scene on TV when a wife is pretending her husband hasn't bashed her.

'Oh no, I walked into a door,' I mumbled, or something like that.

Afterwards I was so angry. I said to Sam, 'You've humiliated me. I feel like a weak little weirdo.'

I'm not trying to ask for sympathy. I know I caused as many arguments as Sam did. I could be overprotective, oversensitive and would get wound up about stupid things sometimes. And maybe I should have let her be herself a bit more when we were out.

Sam texted Chloe while we were out there and told her that we'd had a fight, but Chloe didn't know how bad it was until I turned up at her house and she saw my face. She was shocked and angry but I begged her not to say anything to anyone else. I didn't want it to get out. I didn't want it to be talked about on TV. No matter what Sam had done, I wanted to protect her. I knew how it would come across and I didn't want people to judge her.

When Sam did admit it on TV in series nine the press went nuts. Domestic-abuse charities were talking about it and there were all these internet forums calling her a 'thug' and a 'vile human being'. I hated it. She's not a thug or a vile human being at all . . . I still wanted to look after her. I wished she'd never said anything.

Not long after Dubai we had to film a special episode of the TV show. This was *TOWIE Live* and was a total disaster if you ask me.

There were new producers working on it and they were just getting used to the demands of normal *TOWIE. TOWIE* is a tough show to work on because they're trying to follow the lives of real people and it's a really fast turn-around as they shoot, edit and put it on TV in a matter of days.

I phoned up my agent, Dave.

'*TOWIE* have just asked me if I want to propose to Sam on the live show,' I said. 'When I told them I didn't have a ring they said "Don't worry about the details, do you want to ask Sam to marry you?"' This was something I had been thinking about but it still felt too soon.

'Live on TV? Are you having a laugh? That's embarrassing!' he replied.

I refused to do it. I was in love with Sam but I wasn't ready to propose just yet. And definitely not live on TV – I would be too nervous.

At the time I was at a crossroads with Sam. I loved her and wanted to marry her but we'd been arguing a lot, I didn't know if I wanted to propose or break up with her. The producers wanted me to share this on camera and I felt the pressure of being the big story line of that episode. I started panicking.

Anyone who watched *TOWIE Live* will be able to see how nervous I was. I was shaking the whole way through, I was so stressed. I felt like the ending of the whole series was all down to me and what I did on camera. I knew the producers wanted me to make a decision on Sam; either propose or dump her but I didn't really know what I wanted to do so in the end I just left the scene. I said, 'I need to go outside, I can't do this anymore.' There, that was their ending.

There wasn't just tears though. Series seven of *TOWIE* had some jokes moments. My favourite was when I tried to walk on water.

I was with Arg, Diags and Tom and I'd decided to test out

some new water-repellent trainers I'd got. I was wearing a onesie (I wore a lot of them in this series) and none of the lads believed I could do it.

'It's about believing in yourself!' I said. But first, I needed a superhero name.

'Duck Face!' said Arg.

'Fish Lips!' said Tom.

'Goose Face!' said Diags.

They were all rubbish. I said I needed something that hovers on water – 'HOVER MAN!' That was it!

'Hover Man! Hover Man!' they chanted as I did a long run into the lake.

'Do you believe in me?' I shouted.

'We believe in you Hover Man!' they cried.

I sped up, my legs were flying everywhere. I splashed about a bit. Then fell in.

They were all rolling about on the grass pissing themselves with laughter. They made me have one more go at it and this time I swear I did it (look it up on YouTube if you don't believe me).

'You've beaten science!' Arg laughed, and they all started laughing again. The water was well dirty. I think I swallowed a weed.

Sam took me to New York that December. It was a present she'd got for my birthday in July and it was meant to be a pre-Christmas treat.

I got a bit confused about which day Christmas was – was it the 23rd or 22nd?

We were there for four days and had a brilliant time shopping, hanging out in nice bars and restaurants. Well, except for one big row. This time it was over Mark Wright.

I'd been asked to appear on a new ITV show called *Splash!* with the Olympic diver Tom Daley at the same time as I was filming the *TOWIE* Christmas special. What I didn't know was that while I was out of the way training for *Splash!* they sent Mark Wright back into it for one scene with Sam. Me and Sam were in New York when it aired so I was following what happened on Twitter. I got jealous and demanded to know what she'd said to him and whether she'd been happy to see him on camera. She told me she wasn't and it was no big deal. But I didn't believe her.

The Twitter comments started coming in as the show went out on TV in the UK. They were all talking about Sam and Mark. One of them said, '*When Mark goes to Sam's house, her eyes light up like a Christmas tree*'. I was fuming and started calling my mates back home asking them what they thought of it. It was all in my head but I felt like she was trying to make me look stupid on TV. If there was someone my family, friends or Sam didn't like for the right reasons I wouldn't talk to them, but that's the way I am. I don't know why I started such a pointless row, I was in the wrong, sometimes I get wound up too easily, especially when it comes to me and Sam.

Our first proper Christmas together should've been the happiest day of my life. But we had another huge argument which ended badly.

I'd bought Sam a designer watch as her present and wanted to give it to her on Christmas Day so I went over to hers in the evening. We ended up bickering about something, I started a row about something silly . . . this time it was tracksuit bottoms(!). We were properly shouting at each other. We were on the landing still arguing when before I knew it we were tumbling down the stairs. What exactly happened is still a blur but I know I sprained my wrist.

Afterwards I was gutted that we'd ruined what should have been a special day by having a row.

CHAPTER 24

NEW BEGINNINGS

The Joey Essex style rules:

Onesies – Not for going to the shops (that's very 2013). Good to wear when you visit your girlfriend or cotch at home with your mates.

T-shirts – Need to have long sleeves that you can roll up, but don't roll them up too high, that's chavvy.

Shades – Good to wear in nightclubs. They make you enjoy your evening more because you can't tell what's going on and can't get hassled.

Jeans – Not too tight. That's last year's look. Plus they can stop you having babies and cut off your circulation.

Chains – Must be long with an emblem.

Trainers – Should be hierarchy. They're reem. I wore them before everyone else.

Capes – I'll be wearing these a lot in 2014.

Socks – Must be worn inside out. Much more comfortable that way.

Shoes – Wear the right size. I used to get them two sizes too small so they didn't crease (I'm a nine but I wore a seven) but if they don't fit they make you walk like a doughnut.

Roll necks – Good but only wear one when it's cold or it's pointless.

Short shorts – Always and forever. The shorter the better.

Man-bags – I have loads. I love them. D&G, Prada, Gucci. They carry everything: money, chewing gum, diary, receipts, bank cards. I don't know how I lived without a man-bag. I wear one in the house cooking sometimes. If I go out without a man-bag it's like I'm missing something.

Uggs – OK to wear for a laugh round the house or for a drive but not walking down the street. That's been done.

The next year started with a splash – literally. I took part in the show *Splash!* where celebrities had to compete against each other in a diving contest. I wore extra tight, extra short trunks. They even had 'Essex' printed on the back.

There were a load of other celebs on there but, me being me, I didn't recognise any of them. Jennifer Metcalfe from *Hollyoaks* was supposed to do it but she'd just split up with her boyfriend so she pulled out because she was too upset. There was a comedian guy on it called Dom Joly who was a bit weird and I didn't think he was very funny. He didn't say much. Caprice the model was in it too. She was pretty hot at diving . . . and in her swimsuit.

I knew who Tom Daley was because I'd watched him in the Olympics. I reckon I could tell even then he was gay. He laughed at me a lot but we didn't speak much. My theory is that he didn't want people to know he was gay and that's why he didn't chat to me – not saying he would have fancied me, that would be a bit big headed, but maybe he was conscious of people knowing back then. He's a lovely guy though. When he told me the 20-metre board was his 'second home' I thought that meant he lived there.

Splash! was way harder than I thought it would be. In training I did a face flop and it hurt everywhere. I was dizzy as hell. It was like I could literally see stars flying round my head. I had torn muscles and everything. Sam was worried about me which gave us a good excuse to cuddle instead of arguing.

Most of the other contestants went off the 3-metre board but I decided to dive off the top of a 10-metre board at the last minute. Everyone said it was a daredevil thing to do but I did it with no belly flops so I was chuffed.

One of the judges, who was called Leon, said my technical ability wasn't up to scratch so I asked him if he could've done it better. Vernon Kay the presenter laughed and said, 'He's an Olympian, Joey!'

I didn't win *Splash!* but I did get a new haircut. I called it 'fusey', which was a word me and my mates had been using for ages. Fusey means suave and cool – unique. It means a bit better than reem.

The haircut was long on top and shaved all around the bottom. I'd wanted to do it for ages. After I'd done it I was buzzin'. I rang Dave – 'I've cut half my head off!'

He was probably worried. How would I cope walking around with no head?!

As I mentioned earlier, the craziest thing was that loads of other people started doing it. There were stories in the papers about schools banning the kids from doing a 'Joey Essex'.

It was around this time that Dave had completed the deal for me to have my hair-care range 'D'Reem' so the new haircut was perfect timing. It had taken nearly two years to finish – I'd helped pick all the smells and everything. I'd always loved playing about with my hair when I was a kid and I couldn't believe it when it came out. I kept staring at it on the shelves as if it was a ghost.

I lie in bed and think about ghosts sometimes. There's one who comes into my room. It's well annoying. Honestly I see it all the time, it walks round my house. I used to be scared of ghosts but because I see this one a lot I'm used to it. He's my mate. I go into the kitchen and say 'Alright ghost?' It's like a boy of about 18. I don't really see him properly though, I just see him whizz past me in time for me to say 'What's happenin'?' I never really thought about ghosts when I was younger because I didn't see them. But now I see dead people . . .Whooooaaaaah.

When Dave had started talking to people about me doing a range of hair products, not a lot of people trusted that I could do it. I think he went to Asda first but they didn't think it would sell – having seen the sales of my hair products I bet someone in their buying team is kicking themselves now! Tesco believed in me and put it in all their stores. I had a launch party and we'd got these little kids to be mini Joey's with me on the red carpet. Everyone came and I just felt so chuffed that I'd got this far. The products started flying off the shelves and within days Tesco said they wanted more!

Fusey was also the name I gave to my clothes shop in Essex. I opened it with my friend Jake's mum Tracy, who's like a second mum to me. I've grown up with her and she does everything for me (she does all my washing and comes to clean the house – thanks Tracy!). She didn't have much money and I wanted to help her in some way, to repay her for everything she'd done. So I suggested we open a clothes shop. We found a place in Brentwood and I decided I wanted to have a logo that was a duck. A duck called Fusey.

I'd grown out of frogs by this time and ducks had taken their place.

I like them both but ducks are funnier. I never understood why their feathers stay dry even when they dip themselves in water. They're a bit pointless but they're cool.

I've got loads of plastic ones dotted about the shop. I had a little married couple of ducks too that I said were like me and Sam.

Sam helped me so much with setting up the shop, she went to all the meetings with me, helped buy the clothes, and get everything in place. She's got a shop of her own – Minnies – so she knew what needed to be done.

The start of the next series of *TOWIE* was edited to make people think me and Sam were getting married. In the opening scene Diags said to Arg, 'Have you heard about Joey? It's a lot of responsibility for someone so young.'

And then you see Frankie saying, 'I didn't know anything about it.'

Then I carry Sam over the threshold.

Into my shop.

At the opening party for Fusey I had a little speech prepared for Sam. I wanted people to know that we loved each other and even though we rowed sometimes she was the one for me. I said:

> 'I met Sam four or five years ago now. It's so strange to think we were only friends and now we're so close. When I first kissed Sam I was like "yes". What a little sort! And now I kiss Sam and it's special. I'm so proud of you, I love you'

I gave her a box. It was diamond earrings. Tom said that he thought I was going to propose!

When we opened the shop to the public I couldn't believe the amount of people who turned up. These little kids had been camping outside in the wind and snow since 5am. I felt so guilty! They were all chanting my name banging on the door to come in. Never in a million years did I think this could happen to me. It was such a surreal moment.

I couldn't work out how to use the till, even though Sam did try to teach me.

'If someone gives you £20 how much change do you get?'

I was baffed.

'Who?'

'The customer.'

'What customer? I don't know what she looks like!' I said.

It was well confusing.

Instead I just walked around the shop with my hands clasped behind my back because I thought it made me look important. I think I'd seen a manager do that in Topman once.

We sold out on the opening day. It was madness. I looked at Sam and held her by the hands.

'Everything we earn from this shop is going towards our future – the house, the dogs, kids, marriage,' I told her with a big grin.

'Aaah,' she said, 'you're setting up our foundation for the future. I'm really proud of you.'

Things were going really well for us, everything seemed to be working out in my life.

I don't know what she meant by a 'foundation'. I think it's one of those things where you put your money into a bank account.

My mum would have been so proud of me too. I think about her all the time but whenever I've done something big I always think she's had something to do with it. Like she's made it happen. Like it's fate somehow.

My mum's birthday and Mother's Day fall around the same time of year. It's always so painful but they're some of the hardest times for me. I'd never talked about her on camera but *TOWIE* wanted me to do a scene with Sam about it. I didn't really want to at first, but I thought it might help others going through the same thing. I remember sitting on the sofa at Sam's house looking at photos together. I just sat there sobbing into her arms.

I miss her. It never gets any easier.

This Mother's Day I did a onesie walk for charity. I always wanted to find a charity that meant something to me. The charity is called Child Bereavement UK and is for children who've lost a parent and I feel really glad I can give something back and help others who're going through the same as I did.

On the show, I asked Sam to come with me to see my mum's grave at the cemetery. At the start of that episode there's a scene where me and Sam are in the shower together and I'm singing 'Unbreak My Heart' and Sam's washing my back.

That was a strange scene.

I had written my mum a 'Happy 50th' birthday card. As I laid it down on her grave I was sobbing and shaking. 'Your mum would be very proud of you,' said Sam and gave me a hug. But it was so hard. Every time I come to her grave it's always the same, it never changes. It never gets any easier. I stood there thinking of what she might look like if she'd lived to 50. She would have been so beautiful.

CHAPTER 25

POPPING THE QUESTION ('ER, WHAT KNEE IS IT AGAIN?')

I knew I wanted to propose to Sam. OK, we argued but didn't all couples have tiffs? She was my little mouse and I couldn't imagine life without her in it. When it was good between us it was amazing.

That didn't stop people worrying about me though. It didn't help that I was so emotional and cried in front of my mates every time we had a fight.

Diags spoke to Chloe about it.

'I'm concerned about Joey. The other night he burst into tears for 15 minutes straight and there's nothing any of the boys could say that would make a difference.'

'I think they're moving too quickly,' said Chloe.

But she knew I loved Sam and she wanted me to be happy.

When I'd told Chloe about the arguments we'd be having she'd promised not to say anything on TV. But she was angry and upset and felt she still needed to talk to Sam on camera to clear some of the tension. Chloe and Frankie had hardly said a word to Sam over the last few weeks and it was starting to get awkward when we had to do scenes together. So Chloe went to her house.

'I wanted to have a chat with you.' She said to Sam, 'Obviously you and I both know that Joey does flare up after arguments. And he'll turn up at my house. And you know what a state he gets into.'

Sam sat there and nodded. Chloe carried on:

'You're welcome in my family; if you both get a house and settle down we'll be in each other's lives. It's not like I want to interfere but at the same time it's really hard to see him upset and crying.'

Sam defended herself:

'There's always two sides to a story and I know I sometimes take it too far but I've heard him on the phone to other people before and I'm sat there thinking, "Why are you twisting it like that?"'

Chloe looked at her and told her, 'I think he's shown and told me more than you're aware of, he's shown me text messages and stuff. It's not just the small arguments either, it's the bigger rows and the aggression . . .'

Sam paused then said, 'I'm not an aggressive person at all but sometimes Joey pushes me so far to the limit. He pushes the wrong buttons and sometimes he can be a handful and I go off on one and go mad. He does push it to that point sometimes. I haven't done it for ages . . .'

They were both talking about the slap without saying what it was. It was a really pointless conversation to watch back and must have seemed odd for all the viewers who didn't know anything about all that.

Sam spoke to me about it afterwards and said we needed to speak to each other about our problems rather than everyone else. Then she kissed me and said, 'We're allowed to argue though!' before kissing me again. 'If we didn't argue it would be boring.' If I'm honest I know I can be hard work, I'm probably not the best boyfriend sometimes. I can be controlling, possessive, jealous, high maintenance, moody and I like things my own way. Other than that I'm perfect.

I'd planned my proposal. I'd bought the ring. I'd shown her sister Billie who nearly cried – 'It's perfect,' she smiled. I'd spoken to her mum Sue and I'd written a letter asking Sam's stepdad Dave, who was in prison, for permission . . .

I love Sam more than anything in the world and I wanted to ask you permission to marry your beautiful daughter. I've already asked Sue and Billie and I hope you feel the same way. Please call me, I will be waiting for you to come home.

Love Joey.

'The only way you'll get me to do it on TV is if you send us somewhere special,' I told the producers. I wasn't going to ask the woman I loved to marry me in the backyard of a pub or in some silly park in the middle of Essex, like they'd tried to get me to do in the live episode. I didn't want to do it while everyone else was around either. I said I wanted to take her to Dubai. And if they didn't send us then I'd just do it on my own without the cameras there.

'We're not sure Joey. It's not really in the budget.'

They said they'd think about it. A day later I heard back from them.

'OK, we're on.'

I was so nervous. I planned the whole thing with Billie.

'She's going to be so shocked!' said Billie.

'Will she be happy?' I asked.

'One hundred million per cent,' she grinned.

I got on well with Billie. We always had a laugh together and she knew how I felt about Sam and that I'd do anything for her. She also used to tell Sam she needed to open up about her feelings towards me sometimes and that she could tell I was just insecure. I think she understood me.

We were filming at a roller disco, it was an 80s themed party. I dragged Sam outside to the car park and pointed at the waiting taxi.

'Do you want to go home or do you want to go to Dubai?'

'What? What?!' She didn't know what was going on. 'You serious?'

'Yes!' I smiled. I was so pleased with myself.

'When did you plan it?'

'Ages ago.'

'What did you pack?'

'Some bikinis – I didn't pack you any knickers though!'

She laughed.

When we got to Dubai I was sure she'd suss something was going on. But she was just loving being on holiday while everyone else was having crap weather back home. I'd hired a massive private apartment overlooking the whole city.

I waited 'til she was out of earshot and called the boys.

'I'm in Dubai . . . I'm proposing to Sam.'

They were shocked.

'This is massive mate!' Tom said. 'Congratulations, so pleased for you but I can't believe you're doing it!'

I paused.

'What knee do I go down on?'

They were creasing up. But I was being serious. I couldn't work out which one it was. Was it the left or right?

For the next couple of days I walked around the apartment in my swimming trunks (wearing my man-bag), practising what to say. I kept mouthing 'Will you marry me?' in the mirror.

The more I said it the more nervous I became. And the weirder my face looked if I'm honest.

Isn't it funny when you stare at yourself for a long time? I think my mouth grows wider when I look at it.

I'd arranged for us to have a romantic dinner up on the roof of the apartment.

'It's nice here isn't it?' I said.

Sam looked amazing. I couldn't take my eyes off her. But my knees were going up and down like mad things. I thought she must've been able to hear them they were rattling so much.

'This is so nice,' Sam said, taking a sip of champagne. 'You are really lovely to me.'

Sam went off to the loo so I called my dad.

'I'm scared Dad,' I said and immediately burst into tears, which by now you know I do quite a lot! 'How did you do it?'

Dad calmed me down. He loved Sam and was happy I was about to pop the question.

Sam came back from the loo and I knew it was now or never. I started downing champagne.

'You look beautiful,' I said to her with a nervous grin. 'You always look beautiful . . . I love your lips.'

I had my speech prepared on my phone. I couldn't remember it off by heart, so I had to keep looking down.

'Sam, I know we've been through a lot together but no matter what happens you're always there for me – like the lovely little things you do for me, like teaching me to operate the till in Fusey.'

I looked up at her face. My leg was going mental under the table. I started crying.

'Why are you crying?' she asked.

'Because I love you so much.'

'Are they happy tears?' she said. I think she was getting worried.

'Yeah.'

'Good.'

I carried on. My voice was wobbling.

'I brought you out here because Dubai is special and magical like you and . . .'

I got down on one knee. I can't even remember which one it was now. My knees were numb from hitting the table.

'Will you marry me?'

'YES!'

She stood up and kissed me and we both started crying even more. She couldn't wipe the smile off her face. She was the one shaking now.

'I'm really nervous!' she laughed.

It felt amazing.

'I'm officially your fiancée!' she said as we sat back down.

'What am *I* then?' I asked, confused.

'My fiancé.'

'Oh, we're both the same thing?'

She laughed.

'I'm engaged!' She shouted it from the rooftops. She wanted everyone to hear. We were so happy. It couldn't have been more perfect.

We had two engagement parties. One was for TV, which was filmed almost as soon as we'd landed from Dubai. We also had a private one for our closest friends and family a few weeks later.

Funnily enough, just before the party, I'd been in Dubai again. But this time it was to do a PA. My mate Steve had come along with me. We were only supposed to be there for three days but we missed our plane home and ended up there for a week. The day of the party was looming and at one point we thought we couldn't get a flight back. I was crying on the phone to Sam saying, 'I can't get home! I'm stranded!'

We made it in the end. Me and Steve actually cried with happiness in the airport because we were so relieved.

I arrived and Sam was in a bit of a mood because I was late; fair enough to her, I felt really bad. But I looked nice and brown and had on a blue suit I'd had made in Dubai. Sam looked absolutely beautiful too, which I kept telling her, but it didn't seem to make her any happier. I did a big speech telling everyone how much I loved Sam and also talking about my mates and my dad. Just before I got off the microphone I gave a mention to my cousin who had come to the party. He was from my mum's side of the family but his mum and my uncle had split so I'd never met him until tonight. My nan had been talking about him for ages, wanting us to get to know each other, so I thought it was a nice thing to do.

'Oh by the way, I want to welcome my cousin to my family. I hadn't met him before tonight,' I said. I wanted him to feel part of it all.

But, for some reason, Sam wouldn't accept what I was saying.

'He isn't your cousin!' she said in my ear after I came off stage. 'Why are you talking about him?!'

I was confused. He was my half cousin. What was her problem?

At the end of the evening, I took Sam by the hand and said, 'Let's just go home, me and you.' But she wanted to carry on partying. She brought some of her mates back to my flat and they started dancing about, being all loud and having a few drinks. I didn't want everyone there; I just wanted it to be us two. I kept pulling her into the other room.

'Sam, I don't want your mates in my house. I want to go to bed with you,' I pleaded.

'What do you mean you don't want my mates here?' she asked. She was doing it deliberately louder so they could hear her. They carried on dancing. Then she said, 'If you don't like my mates I'll go and party at mine instead. It's shit in your house anyway!' I was really sad because this was supposed to be our night, to celebrate our engagement.

I went into my bedroom and started changing out of my clothes. I stood waiting by the door, frightened about whether she would actually go ahead and leave me on the night of our engagement party. Then I heard her say 'Come on let's go and have a proper party somewhere else'.

She can't leave, I thought.

Not tonight.

I took my trousers off and heard them walk past my room.

BANG! The front door slammed.

'Sam? Sam? Where are you?'

My head was all over the place, I just lost it. I ran out of the door in my pants and tried to catch up with Sam. By now her and her friends were all in the lift.

'Sam! What the fuck are you doing? This is our engagement night and you're leaving me?'

BANG! My door had shut behind me. I didn't have my keys or my phone.

The lift door closed and I heard Sam and her friends calling a cab.

I was left just staring out at her below from the landing. I couldn't believe she'd just left me. I was so upset. Quietly, I went downstairs to the main door of my building and hid round the corner thinking to myself, 'Please don't get in the cab, please don't leave me.'

She wouldn't do this to me would she?

Sam didn't know I was there, watching her and all her mates. Then I saw the cab pull up and she got in the car. I didn't know what I was doing, I was so upset. I jumped into the middle of the road like a nutter.

'STOP! STOP!'

I must've looked like a mental patient. I was in my pants, freezing cold with a stupid look on my face and tears running from my eyes.

'Say sorry to my friends!' she started shouting as she wound down the window. 'Say sorry!'

'Alright I'm sorry everyone, I'm sorry!' I shouted back. I just wanted her to come back inside.

'Please Sam, just come back into the house.'

In the end she got out of the car and her friends left. Then we had to call another cab on her phone so we could go to get my spare keys from my dad's house before finally we went to bed.

The next morning *she* was in a mood with *me*.

'Leave me alone,' she said when I tried to give her a hug.

Oh and that day we were due to appear on ITV's *Mr & Mrs*. She had to go back to hers to get ready. I didn't know how the hell we were going to be able to film the show and look all happy on camera.

We were in the car on the way to her house and just as she was about to go inside I had to say something.

'Can I just bring something up quickly Sam? It's been worrying me'

'What?'

'Why did you have such a fit about my cousin, saying he wasn't my real cousin? Why were you so rude about him?' It had been playing on my mind all night.

She snapped. I've never seen her so mad in my life. She got out and slammed the door.

'Oh my GOD Joey! Shut up about it!'

It was unbelievable. What was her issue with him? Then she flipped even more.

'You know what? Fuck it. Fuck you both. I don't even want to fucking be with you!'

And she walked off.

'You can't dump me now,' I shouted after her.

'I don't want to be with you. It's finished,' she shouted back.

As she closed the door to her mum's house I was sobbing my eyes out. I called my agent Dave. I was in bits. I know in my heart she didn't mean it, but it's the fact she'd even said it.

We were meant to do *Mr & Mrs* in a few hours but I felt like death. I couldn't go anywhere like this. Dave was calm, asking me what had happened. He said it would be really unprofessional not to do the show – they had a whole audience waiting to watch it being filmed. But he also said he'd cancel it if I desperately wanted him to. He wouldn't have made me do something against my will.

We were due there in two hours' time. I was distraught.

Dave spoke to Sam's agent Adam about what to do. Sam was

also telling him she didn't want to do it. But they kept phoning her to try and persuade her.

All of a sudden she said, 'OK I'll do it.'

A car came to pick her up and then came to my house. One of Sam's friends was in the front seat and she was in the back. 'You alright?' she said as I got into the car. I couldn't look her in the eyes.

'Hey listen to this story, right . . .'

She started chatting away as if nothing had happened. What was she doing? I was so hurt I couldn't bear it. I didn't say a word the whole journey. She was chatting in the car to her friend, laughing her head off like everything was normal. It was as if it all meant nothing to her, like I meant nothing.

We got to the TV studios and were taken into the green room. I turned to her mate.

'She doesn't even care,' I said, 'I don't even know if I'm with her.'

He looked at me apologetically.

'I know it's hard, Joey. But just do this tonight and work it out tomorrow.'

Phillip Schofield was announcing our names – 'Welcome Joey Essex and Samantha Faiers! As we walked into the studio I whispered to her unkindly, 'You're fucking mental Sam. There's something seriously wrong with you.'

But we walked out smiling and grinning like we were the happiest couple alive.

In the end, we won the show. Out of the three celebrity pairs we got the most answers right.

In one of the rounds we were separated by a screen and had

to hold up a blue paddle if we thought the answer was me and a pink one for Sam.

Who is the funniest?

Both of us held up blue.

Ding!

Who's the most fashionable?

Blue again.

Ding!

Who's most likely to forget where they park the car?

Blue again.

Ding!

Who would take the longest to hold up a paddle?

Er, what? – I was confused.

Sam held up the blue paddle. I didn't even know what a paddle was.

Ding!

Who has the worst habits?

Blue.

Ding!

Who could last the longest without a fake tan?

Blue again.

Ding!

We got six matches!

In the car on the way home Sam just looked at me.

'What's wrong?' she asked.

I couldn't believe what I was hearing.

'Just forget about it,' I replied.

I was so hurt. As we got into bed that night I was completely baffed and I had to say something.

'You dumped me after our engagement party. How can I ever forget that?'

CHAPTER 26

BIEBER AND BREAKDOWNS

I always thought Justin Bieber was a dude. Whenever I've been to the States the American girls say they think I'm a bit like him (sometimes I think I'm more Bieber than Bieber!). So when I heard he was going to be in the hotel we were staying in, I got a bit excited.

Sam and I were on holiday in Cape Town. I'd arranged to take her on a safari for her birthday in January and we went in the May.

I wasn't stalking Bieber though, I was enjoying every second with Sam. Every day we'd sit for breakfast in our hotel in a normal breakfast-like way. Then one morning we went downstairs and there were thousands of fans camped outside clutching phones that had Justin Bieber's face all over the case. And instead of normal breakfast tables there was a roped-off area with a special big dining table set up.

Wow, I thought. Bieber is in the building.

Sam was as excited about it as I was and said we should see if we could extend our trip so we could watch one of his gigs out there.

I even tweeted Bieber a few times saying hi.

I made sure I did it at night-time so no one would notice.

He didn't reply and I have to admit that's bare long. *Heat* magazine did a funny article afterwards saying, 'Joey's trying to get Justin Bieber to follow him – let's all help!' He still hasn't followed me though.

Everyone says Justin Bieber's gone off the rails but I don't think it's his fault. He's grown up in the public eye and there must be people driving him mad the whole time. If I had that sort of money I'd definitely have a Ferrari. And a monkey.

I got some silly hair braids done on that holiday to make Sam laugh. She kept taking the piss because she used to get them when she was young, in fact we both ended up getting them.

The holiday was just what we needed, we had the best time, always laughing and smiling together. Well, until we had a massive argument about my cousin again.

It was near the end of the trip and we were sitting at the hotel bar drinking cocktails. I kept thinking about what she'd said about my cousin and I wanted to clear it up. It was like it was burning a hole in my head. I just wanted her to say sorry.

'Sam, I know we're on holiday . . . but it's driving me mad. I need you to admit to me that my cousin is my cousin. Please can you do that for me?'

I could tell by her face that she was going to explode.

'OH MY GOD! STOP TALKING ABOUT IT!' she shouted.

'He IS my cousin. What is your problem?' I shouted back.

'He's not, you don't even know him!'

I couldn't understand it. It was so ridiculous. To this day I don't know why it wound her up so much.

'You're a weirdo!' I said. 'What's going on in your head?'

She refused to say sorry. I refused to back down. We had a huge row that night and I told her it was over. We went back to the room and she began making a big deal of trying to find her passport saying she was going straight away. We went home four days later having hardly spoken another word to each other. We were both stubborn and we spoiled what could have been the best holiday ever.

Mmm I'm just eating a digestive. They're so nice. The real ones though, not the fake ones.

A month later we were filming for *TOWIE* again. Series nine opened in Marbella and we were all sent out there for two weeks. I had the worst time ever.

There was a really weird vibe right from the start of the trip. One evening early on, everyone was in one of the bars chatting and drinking when Sam somehow pulled my necklace from around my neck. She accused me of chatting to a girl and was getting jealous. We ended up fighting and I walked off. It was the beginning of the end.

My cousin Charlie and his girlfriend Fern came into the show in this series. We'd always hung about together anyway so it should've made it more fun. But Sam and I just drifted further apart. Fern's one of Sam's best mates and began making digs about me from the start.

One of her digs was that she said I always cried 'crocodile tears'.

I'm sorry but she looks like a swordfish. How can she say I'm like a crocodile?

In one scene Fern's chatting to Billie about me and says, 'I've always thought of 'Mantha having a man that picks up the bill and gives her security . . . but Joey's not like that.'

At least Billie stuck up for me, 'I really like Joey. Samantha loves him and that's the main thing.'

But it wasn't enough.

The producers had put the girls and the guys in different villas and this caused arguments between me and Sam because she was always out with the girls and I was with the boys. I wanted to have Sam to myself for a bit – we'd been filming separately all day and hadn't seen each other – so we arranged to go to dinner on our own.

A couple of hours before we were due to go out I got a phone call. It was Diags and Tom. They said they were in a bar with Sam.

'Send her home and get her to meet me,' I said. I hated it when Sam was drunk and I wanted her to sober up before we went out, so I texted her, 'Sam please come to my villa soon.'

'Yes I'm coming,' came the reply.

About an hour later she still hadn't come back. I was desperately trying to get hold of her but her phone was off. Then my phone rang and Fern's number came up. It was Sam using her phone. 'Jooooey!' she was laughing her head off. I just got wound up.

'Are you coming to dinner?'

'What do you mean?'

She didn't come to mine in the end. Instead she stayed out partying all night and completely missed our date.

I felt like shit.

The stress of rowing all the time was starting to get to me and I was hardly eating at all in Marbella. I was getting really skinny.

'I feel like I'm in a relationship but she's single . . . it's tearing me apart. I don't know what she's doing,' I told Diags one day.

I was crying on camera again and it wasn't good. I loved Sam but the whole thing was making me so unhappy. I didn't know what to do.

Chloe sat me down.

'What do you love about her? You love that she's a womanly mother figure . . . you're too young to even know what love is. You deserve to be happy. You have had a shit life. You are the nicest kid . . . I don't know one person who's had a bad word to say about you apart from her . . . you're funny, kind, generous, it's so fucked up.'

'I know,' I replied. 'But I can't see it like that.'

'I think you can see it. Otherwise you wouldn't be talking about it. I don't know what to say to you because the only person who can do anything about it is you,' Chloe said.

I knew she was right. The boys did too.

'This holiday has opened your eyes. You need to seriously think about what you want . . . it can't be like this . . . you shouldn't have to put up with this,' Tom said to me.

That was it. I was crying again.

'I just wish she had a bit more respect for me,' I said.

I knew what I had to do; I needed to finish it but I couldn't bring myself to. So I set a trap for myself. I told the boys that I was going to end things on the show and I knew if I said it on camera I'd have to go through with it.

They still didn't believe I would.

Sam texted me the next day: 'Come on let's meet for dinner.'

'Too little too late,' I replied.

Then she wrote me a massive long essay of a text demanding to know what I meant.

I went to her villa. I was shitting myself.

The producers wanted to film the scene outside so me and Sam sat on one of the sun loungers by the pool. She started saying she was disappointed that we hadn't spent much time together this holiday. I told her it was because she kept going out. Then she said that she'd only had one big night out and that I'd been out on my own too.

I started sobbing.

I told her I thought she'd been lying and that she'd been going out partying with boys.

'You haven't treated me with respect. You're breaking my heart Sam. I've been ringing you the whole holiday and you haven't even said sorry Sam.'

'I'm sorry,' she said.

'You've been on this holiday like a single girl.'

'I had one mad night!' she shouted. 'The rest of the time I went for dinner and came back home.'

I told her I was upset and that she always seemed to get vicious and angry. Then she said she was more grown up than me. That was it. I took a deep breath.

'This isn't working . . . it's not healthy is it?'

She was shocked and started trying to reason with me.

'But couples argue. If they don't argue it's not healthy!'

By this time, I was sobbing my heart out.

'I think the best thing for me to do is let you go, Sam.'

'But I don't want that,' she said. She looked sad.

'I know you don't, nor do I. I love you so much. I just want you to be happy and I don't make you happy.'

I was in bits; I had tear stains all down my clothes. Then we just hugged and she walked off crying.

I was heartbroken but I knew it was for the best.

About a night afterwards the boys had a party at our villa. I was asleep when a girl crept into my room and took my trainers from by my bed. I was doing a photoshoot the next day at a hotel called Sisu and didn't realise they'd gone missing.

Meanwhile this girl had somehow found out where Sam was eating with her sister Billie, Ricky Rayment and Jess Wright. And the girl caught Ricky on his way in.

'I've got Joey Essex's shoes here, what shall I do with them? Shall I come and give them to Sam or what?' It was so weird! Why would someone do that?

'Hold on a minute!' said Ricky. 'You're going to cause massive arguments if you do that. Let me take the shoes.'

I respected Ricky for doing that. He didn't know what had gone on but was sticking up for me.

Ricky arranged to meet the girl outside in five minutes. But before he could do anything, she suddenly marched over to the table and plonked them on Sam's table.

'Alright Sam – I just wanted to let you know I've got Joey's trainers. I was round his house last night.'

Cheers united for that.

Sam was fuming. She stormed up the stairs to where I was doing the photoshoot and threw the trainers at me.

I didn't have a clue what was going on. My head was spinning. How did Sam have my trainers? And why was she so angry about them? She started ranting about some girl and my villa and I got even more baffed. Oh my God. I was the most confused, frustrated kid in the world.

When we got back to the UK, Sam realised the girl had been lying. She knew I was telling the truth because I didn't text her to say sorry, which would have been like me admitting it. All I texted her was a message saying 'It's for the best' and I wrote her a note asking her not to contact me. I told her I was changing my number and that we needed to stay away from each other.

That morning I had about 48 missed calls and about a million long emails (OK I'm exaggerating but you get the picture). Sam had never been like this in her life. Suddenly she was pouring her heart out telling me how much she loved me and that she wanted to be with me. She said things like, 'I understand that I can get angry. Maybe I am a little bit controlling sometimes but

I don't see it as that and it's frustrating . . . Am I really that bad? . . . It's so unfair.'

But, like I'd already told her, it was too little too late.

My mates had always said to me, 'One day you will go "bam!" and it will click. Something inside will snap and you'll be able to move on.' They were right. Sam had taken me for granted too long and I'd had enough.

The morning after we got home Arg and Tom were at my flat when the buzzer went. I looked through the camera and I could see Sam standing there. She'd never looked so nervous; she was shaky, like she seemed unsure of herself. It's like what had happened had finally hit her. She was fiddling with her hair and texting me saying, 'Joey let me in. Please.'

My mates were advising me to stay strong and not let her in.

I was really torn. But I had to not let her in. I knew if I saw her all the feelings would come back.

Sam had slowly broken my heart into pieces for the last few months of our relationship. I ended up breaking hers in one go.

CHAPTER 27

MOVING ON

Two or three weeks passed. It was the longest period of time I'd ever not seen Sam and no matter how much I tried to stop my feelings, I started to miss her again.

I told the boys I needed to see her.

'Don't fall back into the trap. When you meet her she will be apologising and saying everything under the sun – but you can't change people. She will still be the same,' the boys said. They were just telling me to be careful.

We arranged to meet in the pub. I bought her a toy monkey, I like monkeys.

'I wasn't expecting a present,' she said. She was wearing a black and white outfit and looked so hot. 'It's been a bit of a mad couple of weeks . . . it's been so weird. I've been going out with you for a year and I feel nervous here in front of you.'

'Everyone knows how much I love and want to be with you Sam,' I told her, 'but I can't be going back to how it was . . .'

'I know. We just got to a really bad stage in the relationship,' she said. 'You know I'm stubborn and you knew that from day one.'

I told her that there were 'major things' wrong with our relationship.

'I don't want that anymore,' I said.

'So what are we going to do now?' she asked, getting a bit impatient.

'I want space,' I replied.

Then Billie had a huge fight with Chloe in a nail salon. The fact that Sam had slapped me in Dubai had come out on TV by now but for some reason Chloe was getting the blame for our relationship ending. Billie confronted her.

'I feel like all the comments coming from your side of the family are negative.'

'You're the one who's negative!' Chloe answered.

Billie got really angry.

'Your precious little prince of a cousin – the stuff he's done to my sister! You've got what you wanted now! They're not going to get back together!'

Chloe was being made to look bad on TV and it was my fault for getting her involved in the first place. I should've learnt to deal with my problems myself.

Sam wrote me a letter. In it she wrote that she'd always loved me and wanted me to understand that she only ever had my best interests at heart. She went on to say that it was a shame it had come to this and that she really thought we'd end up together, living our fairy-tale Disney life, but for now she didn't know what the future held and that I should remember I'm my own person and have my own opinions.

She gave me the letter and handed it to me with her engagement ring.

To me the letter wasn't loving; it didn't say anything nice. I didn't know what she was trying to tell me apart from having another dig at Chloe. But at this time nothing would have made me happy.

After I read it I told Sam I didn't want the ring back.

'The ring doesn't mean anything to me Sam. You mean something to me, the ring doesn't. This has been the worst three weeks of my life. I don't want to not be friends. I'll never stop loving you.'

And I walked away.

'That's it,' I told myself. 'I've cried too many tears. It's time to man up. Joey Essex is now one hundred per cent single.'

That summer I kept myself busy. I went to Ibiza on holiday and tried to forget about Sam. I even met a hot Spanish bird. We got papped kissing in the pool at Ocean Club. She was cute, blonde and from Barcelona. We could hardly speak a word to each other – I just kept saying *hola* and *gracias* and she laughed at me a lot. Not that we really needed to do a lot of talking . . . It was good to just have a bit of fun.

Sam unfollowed me on Twitter, to try to make a point I think. She knew the press would pick up on it.

Twitter is such a massive thing when you're in the public eye. Everyone on *TOWIE* had become obsessed with it. People in the show were constantly looking at how many followers they had and compared themselves to everyone else. I don't care about admitting this – and I know it's a bit pathetic – but people think they're more powerful if they have more followers.

In October 2013 I launched my own aftershave and perfume. I'd been working on it for months. Like my hair range, it took ages to get it from the factory to the shelves. They'd send me test samples to sniff and I'd send them back with my comments. I was like a right little scientist.

I knew I wanted the boys' aftershave to be quite fruity and fresh; I didn't want you to be able to tell straight away whether it was for a boy or a girl. I didn't want it all pongy and musky smelling. And I wanted the perfume to be all sweet. I called the boys' Fuscy and the girls' My Girl.

The night before the launch I was driving to my house in my car and I suddenly burst into tears at the wheel. I'd been thinking about how amazing it was that I had my own perfume coming out and how I'd never have imagined this could happen to someone like me. Then I thought about my mum and I knew in my head that she'd had something to do with it. 'She's blatantly done this,' I thought, 'she must've helped me out.' I sometimes talk to my mum when I'm feeling low or thinking about her and this time I started talking to her in the car. Then my sister Frankie called.

'Oh my God, listen to this!' she said, without giving me a chance to speak. 'I've just found the craziest picture of you with Mummy!'

It was like she knew.

'Frank. Before you carry on, can I just tell you something?' I said, trying not to let her know I was crying.

'What, Joe?'

'When do I ever talk to you about Mummy?'

'Never.'

'Don't get upset because I don't want you to be but this is so weird. I've just started crying and I don't ever cry about Mummy.' I told her, 'I was thinking about her and now you've just called me saying you found a picture.'

It was like fate again. Frankie didn't seem shocked at all.

'Things like that do happen, Joe,' she said. 'You shouldn't ever be scared of it. It's a nice thing.'

Frankie has been to talk to a psychiatrist about Mum (or a prediction teller, whatever they're called). She thinks I should go and speak to one too, that it will help me deal with it. But I don't want to.

Just as I've been telling you about my mum I've been half watching a show on TV called Rules of Engagement. *And guess what? One of the couples in it has just been to stay the night in a hotel called:* HOTEL ESSEX. *I told you – Fate!*

The outfit at my perfume launch was Dave's idea. It was a suit that was half black and half pink to reflect the colours of both fragrances. Some websites took the piss out of it but at least it got me press attention! I can always tell when someone's wearing my perfume now. It's such a nice feeling knowing someone likes a smell I've created. It must be nice for them too – like a special little gift from Joey Essex.

I nearly broke a world record for kissing around this time too. I did a kiss-a-thon to promote a new phone tariff for Virgin Media and got 123 girls to kiss me in a minute. After we'd done it I was told the record was 126 and I wanted to do it again. But the man from the Guinness World Records wasn't even there so it wouldn't have made a difference anyway.

But if any girls are reading this and fancy a go at trying it again – let me know!

It was October 2013 and the whole *TOWIE* cast were headed off to Vegas!

This was going to be reem. I was single, I was with my best mates and we were going to score in more ways than one.

The only problem was, Sam was also going and I hadn't seen her for months. I'd tried to fill my time so I could move on from her but it still hurt that we had broken up.

At the start of the trip there were no issues. I did my thing – gambling with the lads, betting Arg $500 I could pull an American bird before him (an easy win to be fair) and we even got to hang out with Mike Tyson (he thought we were Essex gangsters!). We met a couple of girls at the hotel bar – one called Erica and another called . . . Derek. You see all sorts in Vegas.

Sam was doing her thing and spent most of her time partying with Billie, Fern and Jess.

We were staying at the Palms Resort and as I sat by the pool laughing and joking with the lads I felt so happy. I'd been working out, I looked all ripped and was in better shape than I'd ever been – life was good.

Then Tom's phone beeped. It was Sam. She'd sent him a direct message on Twitter:

'Can you get Joey to call me?'

I wasn't sure whether to at first. But it must've been important if she was going through my mates to get to me so I called her.

'You alright?'

She was in a state.

'I don't know who to speak to. You're the only person I can come to when I'm upset. Ricky Rayment started shouting at me last night. We had a big row.'

As it turned out, Ricky had gone out with Sam and the girls – he was dating Jess and they'd all gone to see the Chippendales. Ricky got pissed off because the strippers had dragged Jess on stage in front of everyone.

Sam started joining in when Ricky was rowing with Jess and it obviously hit a nerve. Some things were said that were never shown on TV but it gave Sam an excuse to call me and tell me about it. We chatted for ages and she started telling me she still loved me, I said the same and we said we missed each other. It felt just like old times.

The feelings were coming back. By the next night Sam was sleeping in my room. We snuck about, not telling anyone.

I was falling in love with her again.

We did everything we could to avoid the producers of *TOWIE*. We thought that if they found out about us they'd film it all and that's where the problems would start again.

One day we were coming down in the lift and we got caught. We landed at one of the floors and one of the executive producers got in. Palms Hotel is massive, there are hundreds of rooms in the whole place so it was the worst luck that he ended up walking into our lift!

'Alright guys,' he smiled and looked at us.

I think we were holding hands. Whatever we were doing he could see we were now very much back on speaking terms and I was really scared he was going to say something. But a couple of hours later he took us aside and said, 'I know what's been going on and that you two are under a lot of pressure so I'm not going to reference this in the show.' I thought it was really nice of him but the reality was that the producers knew me and Sam weren't ready to make our relationship official again and unless we were prepared to talk about what we were on camera then they weren't going to cover it. What I didn't know was that Sam had another love interest lined up for this series . . .

Mark Wright's cousin Elliott turned up on the night of Jess Wright's 28th birthday celebrations to surprise her. I was well excited to see Elliott at first – we'd chatted in the summer and I knew he wanted to be on the show. We were shaking hands and saying how great it would be because we'd be able to hang about together and be pals.

The next day I found out he'd snogged Sam.

What a dog.

My head was in a muddle again. What was Sam doing? I knew she loved me so why was she messing about with Elliott? All I could think was that she wanted screen time, however harsh that sounds.

I always remembered her saying to me ages ago, 'Not everyone can just smile and look stupid on telly, Joey!' She'd tell me that sometimes she had no choice but to bring our arguments up on TV. But I wanted to protect her from looking bad and arguments always show you in a nasty light.

But on *TOWIE*, if you wanted camera time, you needed to be doing something interesting. Unless like me you started trying to walk on water, or light your farts through your shorts.

I shouldn't have reminded you of that one. It was with Arg in series three or four and is probably the cringiest scene that ever lived.

Was Sam just playing up to the cameras?

As soon as I realised something might happen between Sam and Elliott I was on the phone to Dave every five minutes. My head was working things out, if Sam gets with Elliott and then we get back together then I could look like a mug and there was no way I was going to get mugged off on TV.

'How do I play it?' I asked Dave. 'If Elliott does this and that and Sam does this then they're going to try and get me to do this . . .'

I'd been in *TOWIE* long enough now to know how things worked. And I knew the producers would just love me and Sam to be at the centre of a love triangle. By bringing Elliott in it was obvious to me that I was meant to be the victim in all this. I was meant to see Sam with him and end up as the sad one crying at the end. But I refused to let it happen, at least in public.

In the end I played the producers at their own game.

The whole situation with Elliott and Sam really played with my head. Every day I sat there listening and watching everything that was going on, and refused to get played by Sam and the producers.

The next night, we were all out together but Sam and Elliott were missing. I went storming up to one of the producers and started quizzing him.

'Where are Sam and Elliott? Are they on a date?'

They wouldn't tell me anything. Of course they wouldn't.

What the fuck was Sam doing? It was really messing with my head now. I got upset in front of Billie and had to walk away. I couldn't let anyone see it had upset me.

I texted Sam and she texted back but she didn't mention a thing about Elliott. I knew she'd been out with him but when I asked what she'd been up to she just said she'd been with the girls.

I was spinning out. Why was she doing this to me? It was like it made her all powerful again and back in control.

I was not going to be screwed over.

I rang up a girl from California, just someone I'd met in Vegas. She answered the phone.

'Oh hiiii Jooooooeeeey! How areee you?'

Her accent was reeeeally American. She was a sort though, or a salty potato* as me and the boys call it.

She was almost a weapon but weapons are usually supermodels like Rosie Huntington-Whiteley or film stars like Angelina Jolie. Weapons are a bit more out of this world. But not aliens.*

'Please do me a favour,' I said to her. 'I need you to come to Vegas. I'll pay for your flight.' She thought I was taking the piss at first but I said I needed her to help me because I was in a bit of trouble.

Sam had been on a date with Elliott and they all thought I was going to find out and be all upset on camera. I know it seems a bit pathetic but I wasn't going to let that happen – I had other ideas. Just as the cameras started rolling my girl arrived in the lift (her flight was delayed and I nearly thought she wasn't going to make it). Jess Wright saw me meet her and say hello and quickly ran over to Sam and whispered in her ear.

Sam was on the balcony about to start her scene and her face froze. She didn't know what to say.

Elliott then told me on camera that Sam had stayed the night at his. I replied to him that she'd also been staying at mine then I walked to where Sam was on the balcony. I knew she'd been thinking I'd be all upset but now she was confused because she also knew something was going on with this girl and couldn't work it out.

'Why did you lie?' I said to Sam as the camera zoomed in on our faces. 'You said you hadn't stayed with him.'

Just at the end of the scene, my American girl grabbed me to go (she only had to do one thing so luckily she didn't muck it up otherwise it would've been a waste of an airfare!). Sam looked upset and started to cry.

And I left the shot.

The producers were pulling me back trying to stop me. But I was pissed off. I wasn't going to be made to look like a sad fool again.

When we got back from Vegas, Sam tried to ring me to 'explain'. But I ignored her. There was a 'Welcome Back to Essex' party for Elliott – he'd been living and working in the Costa Blanca –

and I knew that the minute I set foot in there, the cameras would be waiting to film my facial expression because Sam would be at the bar flirting with Elliott.

And I was right.

I walked inside and Sam was stood with him having a nice drink. I almost laughed to myself, it was so predictable.

I went over to Elliott, smiled and shook his hand.

'You back for good now?' I asked. He'd been running a bar abroad and he said he was back for six months. Then I just walked away.

'You handled that situation very well,' Arg told me afterwards.

Throughout that whole scene I made sure I had a massive great smile on my face. The way it always works is that when there's someone in the 'main action' (in this case Sam and Elliott), there will be about four cameras stuck on the faces of the other people around them, waiting for a facial expression that fits with their storyline. In my case I knew they were waiting for me to look pissed off, unhappy or even a bit bored. I knew that even if my face dropped for a second they would be able to use it to make it look like that was my reaction to what Sam or Elliott were saying. So I just sat there with a stupid grin on my face. I held it for so long that my face ached and I thought my jaw was going to drop off. I was determined though – even if I had been starving hungry or dying for a poo I was going to stay there, all happy. I didn't want to show how I really felt for Sam.

The producers asked me if anything was the matter. I think they thought I was losing it.

The Elliott and Sam storyline was in the show but off camera she still wanted to talk to me and there was still something between us. That's why she looked so torn about what to do. On the one hand she wanted to be with Elliott and move on and on the other she wanted to get with me and I didn't want any of that on camera at all.

After that night, Sam went on a date with Elliott.

Then the producers told us we had to meet up on camera. You're not meant to speak before a scene because they like to keep reactions as fresh and real as possible but I needed to suss out what was happening. I phoned Sam the night before –

'Did you kiss him? Be honest.'

'Yeah.'

I went mad. I would have got back with her but I hated the way Sam was being and felt it was just for the show. Still, we made a plan and I said:

'When we do the scene tomorrow, you tell me you want to make things work and get back with me and I'll agree. OK?'

'OK.'

The cameras were rolling. I went to her house. I was wearing a gold chain and she had gym kit on. Sam told me she felt confused about the situation and that she still had feelings for me.

I confronted her about being with Elliott.

'I still have feelings for you,' she said.

'But you must like him cos you kissed him . . .' I told her.

'I just went with the flow because I was single.'

'Did you kiss him again?'

'Yes . . .' she started getting frustrated.

I'd told her I was going to get back with her on camera and she was obviously wondering what I was playing at. In my heart I wanted to get back together, but my head was saying something different. I couldn't get what she'd done out of my head, even though it was minor.

'Oh for God's sake, Joey. This is nothing to do with Elliott, it's to do with me and you!'

'What do you actually want from this, Sam?'

'Why can't you just grow some balls and say you still love me?' she said as she looked me in the eyes.

I paused.

'I think we just have to accept it's over.' I was so frustrated, our plan went out the window.

Sam was shocked. But she couldn't say anything in front of the producers because then they'd know we'd chatted without their consent. It was her turn to be mugged off on camera now. I wasn't going to let her play me against Elliott.

Once the cameras stopped filming I asked the producer if I could go back inside Sam's house. I said I needed to have a quick word with her as I wanted to check she was OK. As far as they knew, we'd just finished for good so they let me go back in.

'What the hell is going on?' she shouted.

'The reason I just did that to you is because you mugged me off on TV. Every time you do this I will do it back to you. Don't try and play me.'

Then she took me further inside where no one could hear us. She told me she'd just filmed a scene at the gym and her ex-boyfriend from school, Lewis Bloor, had appeared out of nowhere. He was clearly a new character the producers had brought in. It seemed like they were trying to mess with my mind even more! They weren't satisfied with just playing Elliott off against me, they were bringing in another one now!

Sam put her neck on the line to tell me about Lewis. The producers would have killed her if they knew because it would spoil the surprise. Her telling me just made me love her more and showed how much respect we had for each other; my head was doing loops. If you thought I didn't have a brain I had even less of one by now. It was frazzled.

A few weeks later, Sam was being 'auctioned off' for charity and the producers asked me if I wanted to bid for her against Elliott and Lewis. They could fuck off if they thought that was happening. That would be so cringe and I wasn't going head-to-head with Lewis and Elliott when what me and Sam had was more than they would ever understand. In the end I agreed to come in right at the end if it meant I would get the girl.

Elliott started the bidding at £250, Arg went to £500, Lewis said he'd pay £1,000 and then I walked in and shouted '£2,000' and Sam put her hand to her mouth in shock.

'My knight in shining armour!' she said, and I whisked her outside.

As part of the winning bid I took her on another date. This time I recreated the one we had when we first met – I took her back to the dump.

'I thought I'd bring you here to rekindle the passionate side of me . . .' I said, before telling her, 'I've got another surprise . . .'

We got to her house and I'd made a little base camp in her lounge with fairy lights everywhere. I'd made her sandwiches too, only this time they weren't all squashed from my rucksack. She looked at me and her face lit up.

'It's amazing,' she said.

I told her I was so scared of going back to how it was before but that I still loved her and always would. I told her I wanted to take it slow and that we could be 'friends with feelings'.

She started pushing me to make it official again but I was holding back – I was so worried about us falling back into the same pattern.

Anyway, there were other things on my mind and they had something to do with snakes, rats, scorpions and Ant and Dec . . .

JOEY'S FASCINATING FACTS:
#9 50 per cent of koalas have chlamydia (they're not as cute as they look . . .).

CHAPTER 28

JUNGLE JOEY

Things I learnt in the jungle:

- Goat's cheese is no longer the most disgusting food I've ever tasted . . . turkey testicles are
- Crabs don't actually cut your hair
- Submerge means underwater
- Punch line is the end of a joke
- 'confrontate*' and 'glumptious' aren't actual words, they're just Joey Essex words
- water holders in the outback look like man-bags
- Cabbage and lettuce aren't the same thing
- It rains on purpose in a rainforest
- You have to chop vegetables — I thought they just came like that in a packet from Marks and Spencer
- Koalas aren't electric

It was the worst-kept secret of all time. Everyone in Essex seemed to know. I'd walk past an old man on the road—

'You looking forward to the jungle, Joey?'

I'd go into the supermarket and the woman on the till would smile and say, 'You looking forward to the jungle, son?'

I rang Dave in a panic.

'How does everyone know?!!'

I started to get really paranoid – had I been talking in my sleep so loudly that people heard me outside my window? Maybe I had a different walk? Had I suddenly developed a 'I'm going to the jungle to eat some ostrich willy' swagger?

I'd been for a meeting with the producers of *I'm A Celebrity . . . Get Me Out Of Here!* about a year earlier they interviewed a few of us from *TOWIE*. Some other cast members had also been to see them and were talking to everyone about it. But I'd kept my meeting quiet. Dave has taught me to keep stuff to myself until I know it's definitely happening. That way you don't have to 'untell' people. I knew they wouldn't want me in there the year straight after someone else from *TOWIE* anyway and in the end they picked Hugo from *Made In Chelsea* and Helen Flanagan from *Coronation Street* to fit the 'reality TV' category!

Last year, I knew from the start they wanted me. Dave had been confident I would get offered a place in the jungle and he was right, in June 2013 the producers told him they wanted me. Dave told me he would have advised me to do that show for a fiver as it attracts over 12 million viewers and can lead to greater things. He was right too, the launch show got 12.9 million viewers making it the highest-rated TV show of the year, only beaten by Andy Murray winning Wimbledon.

I always thought Andy Murray was a chef. Turns out that was wrong!

Dave signed my contract for a lot more than a fiver though! I had never earned so much money in my life and things were getting very exciting with my career. I was sworn to secrecy about going to Australia and Dave spent a lot of time with me before-hand briefing me on how he thought things might go in the jungle.

He told me he was convinced that I would be voted by the public to do most of the bush tucker trials, but kept telling me not to worry if this happened and that it wouldn't be because I wasn't liked, it would be the opposite – that people wanted to see me and be entertained just like they did with Helen Flanagan the year before.

Dave had also spoken to the producers of *TOWIE* and they'd agreed to leave the door open for my return in case I wanted to come back.

Sam suspected, as did everyone, but I didn't dare tell anyone until our final episode. I couldn't have it getting out.

I said goodbye to Sam on *TOWIE* outside Chloe's birthday party. That was when I told her I was going away.

'I think it will make you and me a lot happier,' I said.

She looked sad.

'It will be easier for me to get over you and move on without seeing you. I'll miss your little face. I'll always love you.'

After we'd shot the scene I asked her to come and sit in my car with me so I could talk to her properly in private. I told her I was going to Australia.

'When are you going?' she asked.

'Two days' time.'

'You're going to get with that Amy girl, aren't you?' she said.

The papers had been guessing who was in the line-up and one of the girls was a model called Amy Willerton, who looked like quite a sort.

'No I'm not,' I assured her.

I honestly didn't think I would. I had my head set on Kendall Jenner from *Keeping Up With The Kardashians*, who I'd also heard they were trying to book!

Imagine me, who looks like a Ken doll going out with someone called Kendall. Jokes.

Sam kept asking me if we were going to get back together when I was out of the jungle.

'Are we still getting married one day?' she smiled.

I told her I didn't know. How could I predict the future?

'Give me a kiss,' she said and tried to kiss me on the lips, but I said 'No we can't' and kissed her on the cheek instead.

I paused and looked her in the eyes.

'Listen Sam, when I'm in the jungle please, please don't sell a story on me will you?'

'What? No, no of course I won't.'

She seemed to me like she was hesitating a bit, like she didn't mean it somehow.

'Please don't Sam. That's all I ask of you. I need to know I can trust you.'

What I didn't realise was that she'd already done one. And it was about to hit the newsstands as I flew out to Australia.

'Joey is in the jungle – but he won't find romance'

The jungle was just what I needed to clear my muddled head from all the shit going on in *TOWIE*.

As soon as I arrived I had my phone taken off me. It felt like losing an arm but after a while it was like I was suddenly free. No Twitter, no texts, no Sam. Just me – Joey Essex of the jungle.

I didn't recognise any of the other contestants apart from Alfonso Ribeiro. I'd watched him as Carlton in *The Fresh Prince of Bel Air*. I'd never heard of Lucy Pargeter from *Emmerdale* and didn't recognise Steve Davis. He was from Essex though so we bonded straight away.

'Could you get any shorter shorts?' laughed Lucy when I rocked up to greet them. 'Probably not,' was the answer to that.

'You're blinding us by your reflection. Your teeth!' Steve joked.

There were only the four of us to begin with. We were on a fancy boat drinking champagne when all of a sudden it started moving. We'd been interviewed on camera a day before we went in and they asked me what sort of person I was. I said I didn't like to 'confrontate' people, which apparently everyone laughed at back home watching it on TV.

But it's true. I don't. I would never confrontate someone on purpose. I wouldn't go out of my way to confrontate someone for no reason.

Ant and Dec pulled up in a speedboat and that's when the show properly began. We were told we had to split into two teams and that the other celebs were on an island waiting to be picked up. Me and Steve were together in the red team and Al and Lucy were the yellow team.

My heart was beating so fast.

We were told it was a race to get one final night of luxury and that the losing team would stay on the island.

'Oh and one last thing,' said Ant with a wink, 'to get there you have to jump out of one of these!'

A helicopter arrived.

Were they serious??!

We were put in jumpsuits and taken up into the sky. I'd already told myself there was no way I could bottle out of anything; I knew my dad would be watching and I didn't want to let anyone down.

But looking out of that helicopter as I was about to be pushed out of it, I wanted to poo my pants. I was screaming my head off like a girl, making all these stupid noises.

Aaa!!!! AAARRGGGHHH! AAAAarrgghh! Aaaarhhh!

It was like Google Earth zooming in on the world. I can't explain the feeling; my brain couldn't work out what was going on. After I got over the fear and I'd jumped and the parachute was out, it was unbelievable. It was the scariest thing I've ever done but the feeling was amazing. Looking back now, it was like an illusion.

Then we had to race to reach each boat on the other side of the island and we were given these water bottle things which I thought were man-bags. We were told we'd get to choose from different celebs on the way so I told Steve that we just needed to pick the fit birds.

We got to Kian from Westlife and the swimmer Rebecca Adlington first. Steve chose Rebecca. Then we met Matthew Wright and sat beside him was Amy Willerton. I was blown away by how pretty she was; she was much better in the flesh than in pictures.

After that we picked Laila Morse from *EastEnders* instead of this dress designer guy called David Emanuel.

I called her Mo the whole time because that's what her name was in *EastEnders*. In the end that's what everyone started calling her. She didn't mind.

In the end, we won the challenge and had one more night of luxury. Woo! At least I didn't have to worry about how I was going to do my hair for one more night.

I was scared of everything before we got into the jungle. Moths were my worst things because they're always flapping about. Now I've spent so much time with them I just say, 'What's happening mate?' whenever I see one.

After a few nights you got pretty used to the rats and snakes crawling about in there but the worst things were these little flying ants. I called them Evil Fairies and they were horrendous. They'd come down from the sky and pretend they were nice little fairy people but then they swarmed around you, like little earwigs, and wouldn't ever leave. They seemed to hate me the most out of everyone. You couldn't get away from them. Even if you went inside your sleeping bag and did the zip right up, they'd still find a little tiny hole and go up your nose. It was like the jungle had another type of weather – and it was raining Evil Fairies.

The first trial we had to do was called 'The Turntable of Terror'. We were all strapped round this circle having to do challenges to see who would win the best camp. We lost ours in the end. It was horrible – lizards were crawling all over my willy! I thought I might lose it at one point.

I remember trying to make eye contact with the camera crew but during a trial they wouldn't talk to you or look at you, which meant you really did feel like you were in it on your own. The only people you could communicate with were Ant and Dec and all they did was smile at you because they knew what was coming! You could always shout *I'm A Celebrity . . . Get Me Out of Here!* but I'd promised myself I would never do that.

My first big jungle achievement was when we managed to light a fire with Rebecca's tampon. It had taken us ages to get it going but then she remembered she had one in her bag. I prayed, 'Dear God, please can you light this fire for us' and he did!

That night it pelted down; it was the biggest storm I'd ever seen in my life. It wasn't normal, it was like it was snowing! It was a good excuse to hug Amy though. I fancied her and I thought I could tell she fancied me, but I knew I wouldn't want to do anything in there with so many people watching. Plus I wanted to get to know her first. I wasn't thinking about anything or anyone else at that point, it was like we were all in our own little bubble.

I was voted to do the first public trial and it was an eating one. I said the worst thing I'd ever eaten was goat's cheese. Surely this wouldn't be as bad as that?

Well it was.

First up was pork chow brains, which was pig brains made to sound like something from a Chinese takeaway menu. Ant told me it would make me clever and to be fair I did need a bit of cleverness.

Matthew was against me from the other camp and he went first. He ate it while I watched and he was gagging all over the shop. Sometimes it was worse watching someone else's facial expression than tasting it yourself. When I asked him what it tasted like he told me to think of chicken liver. I told him I didn't like liver. Ant said I should just think of it as chicken then.

'But it's not liver is it? It's a brain.'

I shoved it in my mouth in one go. It tasted like slimy gut pork, if that makes sense. It was disgusting. Next we had to eat battered sausage except it wasn't a sausage – it was ostrich penis. It even smelt of willy. I didn't think my teeth would be able to chew it. It was rank.

I was eating willy. On the telly.

When they asked me what it tasted like I said it was like a school rubber with wee all over it. And maybe a bit of vinegar and tomato sauce. Afterwards Matthew told me my description was 'spot on'.

Ewwww. Just thinking about it now makes me want to throw

up, it was so dirty. Matthew was making me feel more sick than the food, retching all over the place. I thought he was going to puke on me at one point.

I told him I wasn't going to give up in the hope that he might just stop. But he wouldn't. We both did the whole thing through to the end – camel toe, a scorpion (which I decided tasted a bit like Marmite on toast) and turkey testicles. Five out of five. It was a tie-break.

The decider was that we had to both down something called a 'cock-a-cola' and it was a race to see who could drink it the quickest – it turned out to be a glass full of blended cockroaches. I nailed it by one second. I felt so guilty and bad for Matthew so I told him I wanted to give him some of my food but we weren't allowed.

It was brilliant winning all the food for my camp. I felt like a proper hunter, like a real grown-up. We were all chatting about what everyone did and I asked Rebecca if it really turned purple when you weed in the pool. She said it didn't and that she weed in the pool all the time – I still think that's a lie. I've been too scared to do it all my life. I don't want to be the boy who's known for having the purple wee.

When Amy found out that I couldn't tell the time, she tried to teach me. She was really patient with me and I think I sort of understood it. Usually I don't have much of an attention span but she was a good teacher. And a pretty one. The camp were shocked when I admitted I couldn't blow my nose either. They asked me what was wrong because I kept walking around with tissue stuck up both my nostrils so I admitted it. No one offered to teach me to do that task though!

Seeing the food coming down in the little bag from the sky was like a gift from God. And I'd won it for everyone!

I taught some of the others how to say 'reem' and 'What are YOU sayin'?' I told them that Essex is a pretty easy language to understand – when you say 'Hello' you just say 'Hellllllo'.

I tried to do an Irish accent like Kian's but I just sounded like a pirate.

I kept getting voted to do all the trials for a while after that. Although Dave had told me not to worry if the public chose me to do them I couldn't help getting a bit paranoid about why it was always me. I was up against Matthew a few more times and I started to realise he was a bit of a geek so I didn't feel so sorry for him when I beat him after that. He's a nice enough bloke but he's just a bit of a try-hard. Plus, when he came out of the jungle he did an interview saying that he thought the whole thing had been rigged to be 'The Joey Show' and that it was set up for me to win. He said I was getting special treatment like being given extra towels, which was a lie. I just borrowed Annabel's when she left *and* I'd asked if I was allowed to do it!

One of the trials we did was called 'Up To Your Neck In It', where we had creatures poured on to our heads while we were stood up to our neck in this rice stuff.

Every time I did a trial I just thought, 'What would Dad do?' and I'd know he'd be pushing me to carry on. There were these things called soldier crabs in there that kept nipping at my neck and my hair – I seriously thought I was going to get out of there with a whole new haircut! That worried me more than the cockroaches.

The winner of 'Up To Your Neck In It' was the one who could count the nearest to 60 seconds. I'm sick at counting and I won. I beat Matthew again!

That was a good day in camp. Amy gave me an amazing massage to help ease my neck pain from standing up so long and having all those crabs nipping at me. I pretended my neck was hurting all day long after that. Rebecca said it was like watching porn!

I felt the chemistry between me and Amy but we knew we had millions of people watching – there were cameras everywhere. I didn't want it to happen in that way anyway. I knew I liked her but I felt like it wasn't until we came out that we could do anything. I was conscious that my relationship with Sam had been badly affected by being on TV so I didn't want the same again.

My bandana became like my best mate in the camp. I used it to mould my hair into shape. When I was talking about it one day I swear I heard the camera men laughing in the bushes. There was only one tiny mirror in there, which was weird because you never saw your whole face, so when you came out and looked at your full face again I'd forgotten what I looked like.

There was another trial called 'Submerged', which I found out meant it was underwater. I was starting to learn all sorts of good stuff in the jungle.

About a week in, we had two new camp mates: Vincent Simone from *Strictly Come Dancing* and a woman called Annabel Giles. I had never heard of either of them but they were both lovely. Me and Alfonso had to help get Annabel out of this prison camp she was being held in by completing a crossword puzzle based on questions about her life. We were both as bad at spelling as each other (if you can believe that). But from that I learnt that Annabel had such massive ears she got one trapped in a car once and that there was another singer called Cher other than the one on *X Factor* (Annabel shared a birthday with one of them and that confused me because Cher Lloyd is only about 18 and Annabel was nearer 50).

After that, I was picked to do the live trial. I was fuming because I was exhausted, but at the same time I didn't mind because I knew it was an exciting one to do and it was a good feeling thinking that all the people I knew at home were watching me there and then. I did think there was a dragon on the bridge at one point though. God knows what it was but it looked like a real-life fire-breather. I thought it was part of the trial but I never saw it again. I think the lack of food was messing with my head!

In the live trial, I had to do loads of mad stuff like dance to songs that were being played into headphones while I had creatures poured on my head, get the punch lines to jokes (I didn't know what a punch line was) and sing a chorus of some song called *I Will Survive* when I'd never heard of it. And I had to play the piano while a load of green ants were biting my hands!

During one meal back at camp I was shocked to find out that cabbage and lettuce are different things. I thought lettuce was just cabbage when it was cold but apparently not according to Kian.

Then the bullying started to happen. At first it was just a few little comments, mainly aimed at me and Amy. The women were moaning that Amy wasn't doing much to help out so I tried to do some of her chores. I didn't really see an issue, everyone could do what they wanted as far as I was concerned. But it got really petty and pretty nasty after a while.

I tried to stay out of it as much as I could. If anyone raised a voice or made a comment towards me I'd just put my thumb up and say 'You alright?' and change the subject. But when people found out Amy had smuggled make-up and extra swimming costumes into her bag this whole 'contraband-gate' kicked off. Personally I thought 'good on her' and was laughing my head off in the bush telegraph when they asked about it. But everyone else was getting all worked up about it. What was the point?

We stuck together a lot after that, me and Amy. We'd sit and chat for hours about going to McDonald's together when we got out of there and I told her she could come and visit me in Essex. When Vincent and Annabel came into the camp we needed extra beds so me and Amy bagsied the treehouse, which was like all my childhood dreams come true. At last I had a proper base camp.

'This is creepy sick!' I said to myself.

We were starving most of the time but the food we got each evening was glumptious. We had crocodile sausage one night and emu another night (I thought emu was a cow until someone told me). I even liked the beans and rice, I've bought some since I've been home actually.

We did a memory test at one point when Kian and I were 'camp saviours' – we had to remember as many things going past us as possible in order to win immunity tokens for the others. I got 20 out of 25. It hurt my brain from trying so hard but I proved I could do it if I really wanted to. I was saying to myself, 'Think about your family, think about your career.' I needed to do it so I did.

Me and Kian really bonded in there. I told him about when I worked in the fish market and he was telling me stories about his time in Westlife. Not quite on the same level but there you go.

I saw some amazing creatures in the jungle too. I saw my most favourite frog in the whole world in the bush telegraph – a tree frog. I sat there just staring at it for about ten minutes. It was so green and nice. And I couldn't believe it when I saw a stick insect.

Me and Rebecca were doing this dingo dollar challenge when I saw one of the letters we were sorting out start to move. It was an actual stick! With legs! I think they've actually got brains too – they're living sticks that walk and stuff.

I decided to name it 'Stick'. I still don't know if it's really made out of wood. I also saw a turkey wandering about wearing a gold chain round its neck. At least it looked like that's what it had on. I thought to myself, 'Turkeys are creepy sick out here.'

We had a letter from home, which was a bit emotional. Kian read mine, which was from Frankie:

To my darling baby brother Joey,
I'm your proudest big sis ever.
You seem so independent now and happier than ever.
Mummy will be so proud of you darling.
I know she will always be watching over you.

You're one in a million and I love you so much.
Miss you, love you lots.
Your big sis Frankie xx

I missed my family more than anything. I got to talk to Dad on the phone for a few minutes during one other challenge, who had come to Australia with me and was staying at the hotel, but all he kept telling me was how much he missed the dog at home!

One of the best tasks was when we did a thing called 'Star Wars', where we competed against celebs in the UK. Alfonso had to see if he could spin on the spot more times than Dermot O'Leary, Kian did a soap squirting thing against Peter Andre and I had to take on Stephen Mulhern in a ping-pong pick-up thing. Whoever won got to go into a hot tub with champagne and strawberries. I've never been so pissed on one glass of alcohol in my life!

Annabel was the first to be voted out, then Laila, Matthew and Vincent, Steve, Alfonso and Rebecca.

Then, on day 20, Ant and Dec called out our names:

'AMY AND JOEY, it's time to say your goodbyes.'

Amy had finished fifth and I'd come fourth.

Hearing Ant and Dec say my name was such a strange feeling, like I'd been chosen to meet the world again. It was weird. I was so happy my name was called with Amy's. She'd been my best mate in there and if she'd left before me I would've lost a big part of my jungle experience. We'd spent most of our time together in there and made each other feel comfortable.

It didn't bother me one bit that I hadn't won. All I kept

thinking about was fate – it was fate that me and Amy had been voted out together. There must have been a reason for it.

I had a tingly feeling in my stomach.

In our eviction interview, Ant and Dec kept saying words like 'reem' and 'creepy sick', which made me laugh. They told me afterwards they were shocked that I'd gone and that they thought I'd win. But I didn't care – I could have a shower, I could eat food and I could see my dad.

I got very teary when I finally did see him. I just kept thinking about how he'd brought me up so well, pretty much all by himself. He quit his job for me, he did everything for me and he stood by me. For him to do all that and for me to turn out the way I have – I felt so happy. I felt like he could really be proud of me, like I was taking my own path. On the way back to the hotel I was already filming for the ITV coming out show. They told me they wanted to film me reading the stories that had come out while I was in the jungle, some of which were by Sam. About me. I was in shock and I told them there was no way they could film that.

When I saw myself in the mirror when I got to the hotel it freaked me out. My face was so thin. I'd lost a stone and a half. It was so funny seeing my face again for the first time! I was touching my cheeks. I was like skeleton man!

I called Dave as soon as I could. I sat in my room asking him a million questions about how he thought it had gone and he was so happy. He told me 'It was the Joey Essex Show!' and said he was really proud of how well I'd done. I asked him if any job offers had come in and he laughed down the phone. He told me how ridiculously busy my diary was and that he had signed me up to do my own show for ITV2 – filming would start in Africa in just three weeks' time!

'What?!!' I couldn't believe what I was hearing.

As it turned out no sooner was I back in the UK than I was off having about a million vaccinations (well, nine) getting me ready for my African adventure. If I'd ever needed proof Dave was right to hold out for the correct deal, this was it. My appearance on *I'm A Celebrity . . . Get Me Out Of Here!* has really made me feel like part of the ITV family, and not only have I got my own show now but I've also had invitations to appear on all the best ITV shows including *The Cube*, *Saturday Night Takeaway*, *This Morning*, *Daybreak* and *Loose Women*. The phones at Neon Management are apparently 'red hot'!

As soon as I got settled into my hotel room I just ate and ate and ate. Then I ate some more . . . I had three cakes, a curry, two full English breakfasts, a bacon and egg sandwich . . . it went on and on. I had to ask for tablets in the end because my belly had swollen so much.

We were staying in the Versace hotel, which was amazing. It reminded me a bit of my bedroom at home – all really fancy and over the top. I even bought a Versace dressing gown which cost me £400, a pillow which was £300 and a towel for £180, all as a reminder of staying there.

Amy and I had both gone off with our families and it felt like we'd been split up on purpose because I didn't know what room she was in. By the end of that day I was just saying to people, 'Where's Amy? I want to see her.' But no one would tell me where Amy was. I just had such an urge to find her, it was killing me.

I found out afterwards that she was doing exactly the same thing. Then, as I was sitting there in my room with my dad and his girlfriend Sasha I heard a knock at my door. It was Amy. She burst in –

'I've been trying to find you everywhere!'

She'd blagged one of the security guards and he'd told her where I was.

We spent all that night together with her dad, my dad and Sasha. It felt so normal, like my dad already knew Amy. He and Amy's dad had been hanging out at the hotel while we were in the jungle so they were already mates. While me and Amy were sitting in the corner they were all dancing in the room together! It was really nice.

Eventually everyone else left the room, leaving me and Amy on our own at last. But it wasn't the romantic night people might think. We started to watch a film but before long my belly had swollen up from all the chocolate and dairy I'd been eating since I'd left the jungle. I was so sick that we were both kept up all night with me going up and down to the bathroom. Luckily the second night we spent together went a bit more to plan. As we were talking our faces got really close then we just kissed.

'I've wanted to do that for a little while now,' I said. 'I feel the same. It's so strange,' she replied.

Then we started kissing again! I really fancied her. I thought she was lovely. That night was the first time we slept together.

Then we were sayin' something!

I wouldn't usually have sex with a girl so soon but with Amy it was different. We'd got to know each other in the jungle so it wasn't like it was just a one-night stand that didn't mean anything. I knew her so well that it was almost like we'd be dating for ages. It would've been really odd if one of us had stopped and said, 'No we can't! Let's just get to know each other a bit more.' We'd spent 24 hours a day together! We really fancied each other. It was like nothing I'd ever experienced before.

She was quite a tiger too. One day we were meant to be going to an adventure park with her dad. I went back to the room to get changed and she followed me inside, jumped on me and . . . well, you can use your imagination!

I hadn't found a girl like her in ages.

The *Sun* newspaper bought the rights to do the first newspaper chat with me about my time in the jungle – Dave told me there had been a bidding war over me and everything! Apparently I'd been on the front pages nearly every day back in the UK because people wanted to read about my life. My dad had been interviewed, so had my cousin and my nan. And everyone was quoting what they were calling my 'Joeyisms'.

I did my shoot for the *Sun* holding a koala bear. It was so cuddly and warm. I thought it was a fluffy toy to start with but then I found out koalas are real, not electric.

We met up with all the others before the wrap party and all of a sudden Annabel and Rebecca started on Amy again about the concealer and 'contraband-gate'. Why couldn't they leave it alone? Even Matthew was joining in at one point. I said to him 'You're about 55 years old mate and she's only 21. Leave her alone!' (I knew he was in his forties really but it was like bullying and they were old enough to know better.) He sounded bitter and jealous to me.

When Kian won and everyone cheered him I heard Matthew saying, 'Imagine how Joey feels! Ha ha!'

Whatever he thought, I was proud of Kian. I thought he was amazing.

I told you Matthew was a geek.

At the wrap party I just stayed by Amy's side all night. Her dad thanked me for looking after her and I told him I wouldn't let anyone be horrible to her. I felt very protective. You know I don't like seeing anyone upset.

I had a good dance with Dec's mum that night. She's a right mover! I love Ant and Dec. It feels like I'm proper mates with them now as I've bumped into them a few times at award shows since. They still kept saying, 'We can't believe you didn't win!' but then Dec told me, 'It's always the ones who don't win who do better from the show' and smiled.

There were photographers everywhere that night and people were desperate to talk to me and Amy.

'Are you a couple now?' one journalist asked, sticking a microphone in our faces.

'I'm happy!' was all I could say. And I was.

A few hours before we left to go back to the UK I sent my dad a text:

'Dad, I just want to let you know that I've never been so happy in my life. I feel like I've properly grown up.'

I needed him to know.

I'd learnt how to cope by myself. I genuinely felt like I went in there as a boy and came out a man.

Insects don't even bother me anymore. If I'm alone in my house I'm less scared. I don't care. In your face moths!

CHAPTER 29

MILE HIGHS (AND LOWS)

I knew people doubted my relationship with Amy. Just because we hadn't kissed on camera, people were saying it was a publicity stunt. That confused me. Surely if I *had* snogged her in the jungle that would definitely have looked like I was playing games and wanted to do it for attention?

We were attracted to each other though and what we had at the time was 100 per cent genuine. Amy made me feel like I could do whatever I wanted around her. We talked about anything and everything.

As we all flew home to the UK from the jungle I felt like I was on top of the world. We flew business class on Emirates and we were all so excited to be going back home.

I'd done so many things in the jungle I never thought I'd ever be able to accomplish. Something else I'd never done, but had thought about, was joining the mile high club.

As we were all leaving the Versace hotel a few hours earlier a journalist had shouted to me, 'So are you joining the mile high club then Joey?' and I'd laughed and thought nothing more of it. Amy looked at me and I looked back at Amy. We both grinned. I knew she was thinking the same as me.

We got on the plane and slept for about seven hours. Then Amy nudged me and woke me up. In business class on Emirates there are two toilets with a slate in the middle that you can pull out and join them together. Amy had just discovered this.

We crept out of our seats and both went up different aisles to the toilet entrances. Once we got inside she pulled out the compartment and we stood in there kissing passionately for what seemed like ages.

'We could've had sex three times by now.' I whispered.

When we crept out again I was really para that people were looking at us. I was convinced the people who worked behind the bar knew what we'd been up to; I could see it in their eyes.

We touched down in the UK and it was like my feet never touched the ground. The next few weeks were a whirlwind of cameras, screaming fans, interviews and madness. Dave met me at the airport and drove in the taxi back home with me to Essex.

'There's a lot I need to tell you!' he said.

About three days before I left the jungle I lay on the camp bed looking at the stars.

'I wonder what Sam's been up to?' I thought.

I decided I'd ring her when I got out – there was still so much unfinished business. Even though I was getting closer to Amy I cared about her and wanted to know she was doing OK. When you're apart from someone for so long you forget about the bad times and just remember how special it was. We used to have so much fun together and she knew me better than anyone in the whole world. She was my little princess and we always thought we'd get married.

'What if? . . .' I thought, 'Could things be different? Could it ever work between us again?'

What I didn't know at the time was that while I'd been eating ostrich willy in the jungle she'd been selling stories about me and my willy to the papers back home.

Dave showed me a huge pile of newspapers. He'd kept all the cuttings of everything that had been written about me. Several of them were from Sam. Although I knew about them already this was the first time I'd read them properly and it was still hurtful to see.

'Sam Faiers: Six times a night Joey was a real jungle tiger in bed!'

'Sam Faiers: Baked beans were sauce of our worst row'

'Joey Essex's ex Sam Faiers "heading into I'm a Celebrity jungle"'

The stories went on and on. There were shots of Sam in a bikini against a jungle backdrop, like she was using the fact I was in there to get herself more publicity.

I later found out she'd only done one interview that had been picked up by all the other papers, but at the time I was shocked and I felt sick to my stomach. I was devastated because to me it was the absolute worst thing she could've done.

I started to read the interviews. She was talking about our sex life – 'He was as excited as a tiger in the jungle around me' –

about arguments we'd had and saying crazy stuff about me like my obsession with Justin Bieber had ruined her holiday and that we'd had the worst row ever over a plate of baked beans on toast.

The fact that Sam had sold stories on me when I'd blatantly asked her not to knocked the stuffing out of me. It was like the ultimate betrayal. I felt so used but what I couldn't get my head around was the fact that she was saying in all these interviews that she loved me and wanted me back! She was telling people she wanted us to get married!

I turned on my phone – there were so many texts and messages coming through from people it would've taken me a week to read them all. But there was one message I saw, from Sam's mum.

'Hi Joey, just texting to say you were brilliant in the jungle. Hope you had a lovely time. I'm a bit surprised you haven't been in touch with Sam? . . .'

I didn't text back but I felt like taking a screen grab of one of the newspaper headlines and sending it to her, showing her the reason I'd not been in touch. But at the time it just wasn't worth it, I was too annoyed about what I'd seen.

I could see Sam didn't see what she'd done wrong. She told another magazine, 'He should be grateful – I made him out to be a sex god.'

The trust had gone.

The night I arrived back from Australia Dave took me to the *Sun* Military Awards, or the Millies as they're known. I'd only been back in the UK for a few hours so it was a surreal feeling suddenly being on a red carpet again. I'd managed to squeeze in a quick haircut that afternoon (I needed to do something about my broccoli head) and it was so nice to be able to wear a suit again. I felt fusey, creepy sick and reem all rolled into one.

Amy was at the awards too. She was wearing a long white dress and looked great. We only got a chance to say a few words to each other though because everyone wanted to chat to us, even politicians. I started talking to a tall geezer who Dave told me was called Ed Miliband. He tried to explain who he was and we had a selfie together on my phone. I saw him on TV a few days later and couldn't get over how different he was. He was just shouting and waving bits of paper about saying 'YES! AND I SAY WE DO THIS!' I said to Dave, 'Oh my God he looks like a nutter. Is that what he does for his job? Gets all shouty?'

How can you be that weird and clever? He must have so much passion to be bothered to shout at people like that. It's not even a job is it? It's just being a shouter. I thought he was just a normal person a few days earlier. It would be weird being a politician.

If I had to make the laws here's what I'd do:

LAWS IN JOEY ESSEX LAND:

Respect each other – Respect gives you mates and if you've got respect for people you don't need much else to be honest.

Don't take things from other people – I hate thieves.

Smile as much as possible – Mainly when you go shopping. It would be such a happy world wouldn't it? If you smile it makes you happy, so do avocados.

Everyone must wear socks inside out – I know I've already said this but I hate wearing them the right way. I don't like the seams on my foot so I'd rather it was the other way round and I'd make it illegal to wear them the normal way.

Iron your money – Me and my mates always iron our money. You don't want to take crunched-up £20 notes out to a club do you? They need to look good.

Make sure you keep your teeth white

AND . . .

Make sure you party hard!

Guess what? Ed Miliband invited me to a drinks bash in April. Must have heard about my ideas for how to run the country. VOTE JOEY!

My only magazine interview after the jungle was for *Heat* magazine. It was for their big Christmas issue so I was dressed up in all these Christmassy jumpers and was pretending to be a snow angel. Their photographer's called Nicky Johnston and he's really loud and funny. I was asked all about Amy in the chat and whether we'd snogged and stuff. I told them the truth. They asked me about what I was doing for Christmas and whether I'd have a Nativity under the tree. I was really confused, especially when they told me about the three wise men that visited Jesus. How the hell did they know all this stuff?! They were all laughing their heads off.

I did a TV interview with *This Morning* and Holly Willoughby and Phillip Schofield kept grilling me about whether me and Amy had kissed. Because I'd done my chat with *Heat* I didn't want to say too much – it would ruin the exclusive – so I just laughed and grinned when they asked me. But Holly wouldn't let it go!

I said we were 'close'.

'How close? Tongue close? Lips close?' Holly questioned.

Phillip leant in towards me.

'You answer me right now Joey Essex – have you kissed her?'

I just laughed.

'That's a yes!' said Holly. 'Is she a good kisser?'

I told them me and Amy were meeting up that night and that we were looking forward to a proper date. Then they asked me what the time was and I actually got it right – I said it was quarter past twelve! Amy was a good teacher!

I spoke to Amy in the car on the way back. She'd done an interview with *OK!* and *New!* magazines and she wanted to know what I'd said to *Heat*. I told her I'd told them as much as I thought I should without saying *everything*. She started panicking.

'Oh my God, why Joey? I can't believe you said that!'

She was freaking out.

'What's wrong with that? It's only me! It's not like I'm an embarrassing person for you to have been with is it? I'm not just some random off the street,' I said.

Turns out she'd said the complete opposite in her interview.

I also found out she'd done a newspaper interview saying she didn't fancy me at all and that I was like 'a little brother' to her. What was she doing? She didn't seem to have a clue how to deal with the press. There's one thing you really shouldn't do and that's lie to them. It's all very well giving them just bits of the truth but making a comment like that takes it to a different level, because they will always find out the truth and you will always look worse than if you'd just told the truth in the first place. It's just not a good way to be.

When I read she'd called me her 'little brother' I was like, WTF.

It felt like she was starting to play games and I didn't like what I was seeing. I was with her because I wanted to be, not just for attention. I was starting to get mixed signals and began to wonder whether maybe she wasn't the girl I thought she was.

We were both asked to present an award at the Comedy Awards that evening and once again all the press were gagging to know what was going on. I just smiled and kept tight-lipped but then she started denying everything again. It would then have made what I said in *Heat* look like *I* was the one not telling the truth. She was skitz*!

I introduced her to all my mates from home that night – they threw a welcome back party for me, which we went to before the awards. They thought she was hot and I think they were just pleased to see I'd got Sam out of my system. Amy stayed over at my house that night and the following morning she was papped coming out of my flat. The cat was out of the bag!

Whatever the hell that means. Why would a cat be in a bag in the first place?

That night at the Comedy Awards was one of our last nights together in public. I was ridiculously busy – Dave had booked me doing PAs all around the country and after I'd been in the jungle there were thousands more people there than before. I couldn't believe the screams and the madness caused by just me, Joey Essex, going to say hello.

Things started getting odd with Amy; I just wasn't sure where she was coming from. She wouldn't answer her phone to me all day and then when I'd text her asking what was going on she'd say 'Sorry, I've been having the most amazing time! Loads of meetings!' But something didn't quite add up – she was telling me she was in meetings at one in the morning. Who has meetings at that time? Once she even called me and said she was having a meeting with Graham Norton at 2am! She was either lying or she was just deliberately avoiding me.

A couple of days before Christmas I rang her up to tell her I'd had enough.

'Whatever's going on with me and you, let's put it to bed. I can't do it anymore.'

She suddenly started to beg me to change my mind.

'What? Why Joey? I thought we were friends?'

'That's the whole problem. You know we're more than friends and I can't be bothered with all this anyway.'

I reminded her that she'd turned up at my house a few nights before in the middle of the night! I'd been with my mates chilling and she'd rung at about 11pm saying she was 'just passing'.

She lives in Bristol, how was she 'just passing' Essex?

Then she said she'd be round in half an hour. At the time I said I was with friends so it probably wasn't a good time but she still turned up. If that was just friend behaviour then I was really confused!

Amy still couldn't understand why I wanted to end it and I was getting really annoyed.

'You call me your little brother in the paper but you don't exactly act like that when we're together!'

She kept saying, 'Oh Joey! I didn't think this through. I thought we were friends.'

'So do you have sex with your mates?'

Then I ended the call.

'Leave me alone, you are driving me absolutely insane.'

She texted afterwards saying, 'I didn't mean to stress you out. I'm sorry.'

I blocked her on WhatsApp, Twitter, everything. I'd never blocked anyone in my life but she was driving me mad. The next morning she texted my dad and said, 'Hi Don, just wondering what you're doing today? I've got a meeting in Essex . . .'

I couldn't believe it.

I needed space so I decided not to speak to her for a bit. A few days after Christmas, Amy texted my dad's girlfriend Sasha.

'What's happened with Joey? He's not talking to me anymore.'

So I unblocked her and sent her a little message to say Happy Christmas. Then she started trying to apologise again –

'I'm sorry if I peed you off and dragged you into my ridiculous drama.'

What drama? She was the one making all the drama!

Then she sent me a saucy picture message which read 'Hey lovely'.

My phone beeped again:

'Oh sorry I didn't mean to send you that, it was for my gran. I was trying to teach her how to use WhatsApp – so embarrassing!'

As if it was for her gran. She just wanted to get my attention. Then she sent another message:

'What are you doing tonight anyway?'

I told her I was doing a PA and she texted back saying she missed my bed.

Girls are crazy sometimes.

The original *TOWIE* boys.

One of the most embarrassing scenes I ever did. Me and Arg still talk about it now.

Always pushing the boundaries when it comes to fashion.

If you agree I look like a Ken doll tweet me this picture with #JoeyKenDoll.

Our engagement party. We were so happy.

Me and the boys in Vegas. I always had to stand out, that suit had gold lining and had my name stitched inside.

Best mates since the beginning. Mc, Tom and Diags.

rand Joey. Clothes, perfume, usic, and now a book! Mad.

Never thought I could do this, but I did. My heart was racing so fast.

Joey of the jungle. The most natural I've probably ever looked.

I kept being voted to do the tasks, even the live one – I still smashed it though. I didn't know at the time that it was because people liked watching me.

Me and my good friend Amy. I made those Peter Pan shoes that I'm wearing. Creepy sick.

Looking skinny with Dad and Sasha. They are the most supportive couple ever, thank you both!

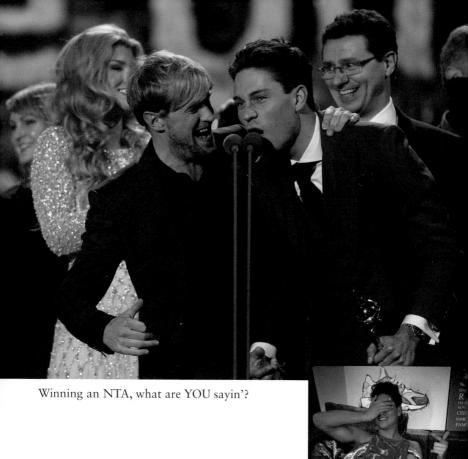

Winning an NTA, what are YOU sayin'?

Losing an NTA, what are you sayin' now? NUTTIN.

I definitely feel a part of the *Celebrity Juice* family now, even if they do mug me off for being thick. I'm cleverer than they think though #streetwise #commonsense.

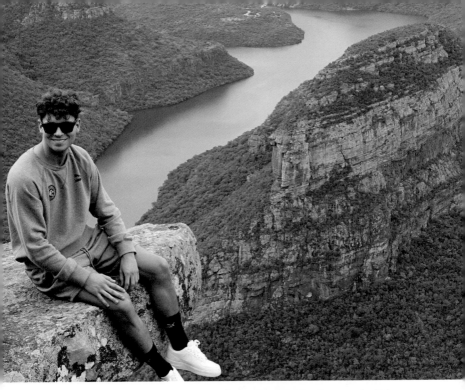

Educating Joey Essex.
The head producer didn't
know I was taking this
picture on the ledge, he
would have killed me.

You haven't lived until
you've taken a selfie
with a Silverback.

Sometimes people say they've done everything they can do,
but for me the sky's the limit.

CHAPTER 30

STILL NOT OVER SAM

Sometimes I wish I could make my own girl. Here's how I'd create Joey Essex's ideal woman from scratch:

- Make-up free (why do girls always worry about their bodies so much? And why do they wear so much make-up? I've watched girls put their make-up on and it just confused the hell out of me — all those eyelashes!)
- Pretty face (no beard)
- Quite slim. It would be nice if her head just about reached my shoulders. I'm just under 6ft so you can work that out for yourself
- Very chatty girl and someone who likes going out and about — definitely not a lazy girl
- Always smiling and happy (a bit like me really, although it would be pretty odd dating a female version of me)

- Brunette
- Dark colour eyes
- Boobs: not too big, just about enough for a handful
- Legs — now that's another story. I love legs. They would need to be slim and toned
- No tattoos (unless it was of a Furby)
- I don't really care about feet (although she'd have to have some)
- Shaved legs! Although I don't care if a girl has a tiny bit of spiky hair on her knee

My mates are always telling me I'm attracted to the wrong girls. For some reason, the ones I date are the sort that like an argument and boss me about. Maybe it's something to do with how I am. Chloe thinks I like having a mother figure who controls me. Personally I think it's that I fancy girls who have confidence. Sometimes they have too much of it that's all!

Just after I stopped seeing Amy, I started seeing a girl called Stephanie. I'd known her from around Essex. I only saw her for a couple of weeks but we were papped in a restaurant – 'Joey and mystery brunette!' the headlines said.

I had to do a press interview to promote some golden dough balls for Pizza Express (I was painted gold for the day, it was jokes) and I was asked about her. I didn't want to start mouthing off about her in the press so I just said 'She was a little sort I met'. The next day I got a text with a screen grab of the interview. It was Stephanie –

'Just a little sort, am I?'

She obviously didn't understand. Why do I attract girls like that? Being in the public eye makes it really difficult to keep things private, and it's hard to make people understand that.

We haven't seen each other since.

While we're on the subject, why do girls always think they're right? I'll admit it when I'm wrong but every girl I've ever met believes she is right even when she's blatantly not. If you saw one of them drop a toothbrush in front of you and said 'You dropped a toothbrush' she'd still say 'No I didn't'.

Sam's birthday is on the 1st January and I'd been thinking about her a lot over Christmas. I really wanted to call her and ask how she was. I wanted to wish her a happy birthday too but I was scared. It had just been announced that she was one of the people going into *Celebrity Big Brother* and I knew if I called her my name would be used as part of her publicity machine. I didn't feel like I could trust her anymore. But I couldn't stop thinking about her either.

We hadn't spoken since I got back from Australia. The only words we'd exchanged were through the newspapers and magazines and that made me sad. I wanted her to know that I was alright and that I didn't hold anything against her and I didn't want her to have her birthday clouded by bad thoughts of me. She thought I hated her because I hadn't made any contact and my mates had told her how mugged off I felt about the kiss and tells.

I'd planned in my head what the conversation would go like – 'Sam – it's Joe.'

'What? What are you doing calling me?'

'I just wanted to ring you up now and say I'm sorry we haven't spoken but after you did those stories about me I just couldn't. I felt hurt. But I want to wish you a happy New Year, I hope you have an amazing birthday and good luck with *Big Brother*. I genuinely want you to do well in it. I want you to do your best in there – do whatever you want to do. And if you meet a guy in there don't think about me, just have fun.'

I meant it too. I loved her that much that I didn't mind if she met someone, as long as they were good to her.

I knew she'd have appreciated a phone call from me too, whatever she was claiming in the papers (she'd stopped saying she wanted to marry me and now she was 'over it'). On the one hand I knew a phone call would make her feel better and give her peace of mind about being in there, but on the other I knew it would get inside her head and maybe ruin her birthday (which was on New Year's Day) and her *Big Brother* experience.

My hand hovered over the phone about a million times. But every time I went to call I had to put her feelings first.

OK, not a million – I'd get finger ache if my hand was hanging about that long. And radiation from the phone probably.

But I couldn't bring myself to call her. I'd lost all trust. I asked my mates what they thought – 'Should I could call her?' They all said the same thing – 'No, she'll just sell what you said to the paper.'

I wished things were different. If only she had never said

anything at all to the papers. The Sam I knew at home, when no one else was around, was such a different person to the one it seemed she'd become – the one who was always in the papers and wanted as much screen time as possible on *TOWIE*. I guessed she'd have earned at least £45,000 on just that one interview while I was in the jungle and I had to try and face the fact that maybe that was more important to her than me.

CHAPTER 31
EDUCATING JOEY ESSEX

I keep thinking I've got malaria. A short while after *I'm A Celebrity . . . Get Me Out Of Here!* I was sent out to Africa to film a new show for ITV2. It was called *Educating Joey Essex*.

I had to have nine injections before I went and also had to take these special tablets to stop me getting malaria. When I got back I had to take them for another month. But I ran out so I thought I was going to die.

I rang the hospital and was told I needed to book an appointment.

'I haven't got time to do that!' I said, 'I've run out already! Thanks a lot. I'm probably going to die now.'

My mates always take the piss out of me because I'm always worrying I've got some illness or another. But googling things on the internet is the worst idea ever though. Once I had a really bad pain in my leg for about a month. I looked it up and it said I had cancer. Every single thing you look up on the internet is

*cancer related. Your fingernail, the hair on your leg, your earlobe.
Everything.*

   I think into things too much.

   I didn't have a clue what was going to happen in Africa or why
they'd even sent me out there to be honest. I thought it was going
to have something to do with monkeys because I'd always gone
on about wanting one when I was on *TOWIE* (and Justin Bieber
had one as a pet. I always thought monkeys would make a cool
pet). Dogs are a bit boring because they can't sit on your shoulder
or watch telly with you on your sofa. I like the idea of having a
monkey who I can teach to make me cups of tea and hand me
my aftershave. Or change the loo roll. Everything was moving so
quickly that I didn't have chance to think about it really.

*I'd also quite like to have a little frog as a mate but that doesn't
mean I'm going to do a show about one.*

On the way there I was upgraded from business class to first
class. Sweet. I was sat right in the nose of the plane which is
apparently the best bit – someone told me it's the one the
Beckhams always ask to be in because it's the most private. People
probably think I always fly first class but I don't. I normally fly
economy. You're only getting from one place to another so what's
the point of spending all that money on a journey that's still
going to take the same amount of time to get there? You still
end up in the same place at the end of it – just a bit skinter if
you've paid six grand for first class. But if you get a free upgrade
then it's *what are YOU sayin'?*

As soon as I arrived in South Africa I had a microphone clipped on to my T-shirt and we started filming. My journey had begun!

I was told to look out for a guy who'd be waiting for me. I didn't know what to expect. In the distance I clocked this geezer wearing a bucket hat.

I had one the same packed in my suitcase. It's a bit like a rain hat. I never expected to see someone like me in South Africa wearing the same thing as me!

This guy was holding a sign saying 'Joey Essex – Welcome to Africa'. He had sunglasses on, Nike trainers and his jeans were rolled up in the same way I wear mine. He was like the Joey Essex of Africa!

'Alright mate?' I said, walking over to him.

'Hi Joey, my name's 1D.'

At first I thought he was named after One Direction but turns out it was spelt more like 'Wandi'.

He kept saying 'sharp sharp sharp' which made me crack up laughing.

I asked him what he did and he told me he had his own shop – he was like the Joey Essex of Africa! How the hell the TV crew had found him I don't know. Apparently he did an advert out there for Nike once so he was pretty well known.

We got into a car and the first place we went to was this neighbourhood in Soweto.

I thought he said we were going to Waitrose.

As we pulled up there were loads of kids all dressed in this sick designer gear – there were loads of them and they were all gathered round the car making these weird faces. I was told they were called 'Boasters' and they're the 'fashion elite' of South Africa. They're known for their love of bling and flashy things and all they care about is showing off their wealth – which means wearing designer clothes in the brightest colours they can find. You'd never think you'd go to a place like that, where people around don't have loads of money, yet they're so obsessed with clothes. All these kids cared about was what they wore.

A *bit like me* . . .

They were looking me up and down really oddly, like they were judging me. In the village there must've been about 300 people and there was a little crew who only cared about clothes. They swarmed round the vehicle and I froze.

'I'm not getting out of this car!' I said.

I was really anxious. I'd only been off the plane about an hour and I'd had no sleep. What was going on? But the camera was filming me so I didn't really have any choice in the end.

As I walked over to these kids they started pointing and laughing at me. They were doing some weird sort of swagger dance. I was way out of my comfort zone and I was getting scared. I thought I was meant to be meeting monkeys not some freaky gangs?

I was told that these kids got money from their parents and then bought these expensive clothes and nutty shoes. To prove they're richer than the other gangs they'd rip their clothes off and put them in the street then they'd go and buy some custard and pour it all over the clothes on the floor.

Well I guess it's no worse than us spraying champagne everywhere.

They did it in front of me and started making these hollering, boasting noises. One of them tried to get me to rip mine off but I'd borrowed my mate Jake's shirt from home and he would've killed me. Imagine if he'd seen me on TV pouring drink over his favourite top.

I had to stamp on theirs though and join in the dance. It was all very strange.

In Soweto we also went to this witchcraft market. There were people on stalls doing all this odd stuff. I saw dead animals and baboon skulls that got crushed into a powder. You were meant to sprinkle it on to your food or rub it into your skin to make you more clever. I told the stall owner I should've visited there a long time ago. It was a bit too late for me.

There was a tree branch that if you crushed it into liquid and rubbed it into your skin would make you lucky. I wanted some of that for myself but I was told there wasn't time.

I believed in all of it. I think if you believe things you can make them come true. It's all in your mind. Wandi kept saying he didn't believe any of it then the next minute he told me a story about having broken his ankle and he rubbed this potion on it. He said it mended it straight away. So why he didn't believe it I don't know.

The next day we went to a shopping centre and I was taken to a sweet shop to meet a lady with a pet monkey. The monkey was called Milo. He had a nappy and a waistcoat on and was going nuts. He was really hyperactive from all the sweets, he lived on them! He even opened the sweet wrappers like a human – these orange and lemon chewy things. It was so weird.

Then the woman said we could take him for a walk. Taking a monkey for a walk isn't like taking a dog for a walk, that's for sure. The woman walked along a bit and Milo jumped on her shoulder. After a while we were walking down the road and I just thought 'They're filming this, it must look pretty boring', so I asked the lady if she'd put Milo on me instead. He lent across me and bit my arm.

Arrrhggghh!!!

Even though it hurt, I wasn't worried at first. Then I noticed one of the producers' faces and I could see he was concerned. But I thought, 'What's the big deal?'

Then he mentioned the 'R' word.

'Don't worry Joey, you won't get rabies or anything.'

That was it. I was in a mad panic then.

'I'm going to get rabies!'

I'd had my rabies jab two days earlier. The first thing the doctor had said when she gave me the jab was 'Just don't get bitten by a monkey', and when I remembered that I started to panic!

I looked at my arm and I was sure I could see the fang piercing. Was it bleeding?

I was going to get rabies!

I didn't actually know what rabies was but I knew it wasn't good. Someone told me it made you foam at the mouth. I thought I'd be running around looking like I'd swallowed some bubble bath. I'd been in Africa for a day and already I was about to die of a foamy mouth disease.

There was a doctor round the corner and after he saw me he told me I'd be fine. I'd been bitten by a monkey on my first day. What a liberty.

After that we saw another guy with a mini monkey in his hand walking past us down the street. He was no bigger than a budgie and made a really weird squeaky sound (the monkey that is, not the man). He had a tiny mouth and was called Coco.

I looked at him.

'Has he had his rabies jabs yet?'

'No,' said the man, 'but don't worry.'

'Allow* *that*,' I thought. I'm not getting bitten by another one thanks.

Wandi took us to his shop. It was quite cool actually. The changing rooms were made of tin. I bought a bucket hat and a T-shirt. I liked him.

That night I was sat having dinner with the crew.

'What time have I got to get up?' I asked. One of the women – who didn't know she was meant to keep it a secret – replied.

'You've got to get up really early!'

Then the producer Phil butted in.

'Nooo he doesn't! He can have a lie-in. You can get up whatever time you want Joey.'

They started looking at each other. I was confused. I got into my room and set my alarm for 8am but before I knew it there was a 'knock, knock' on my door.

What the hell is going on?

'Joeeeey! Joeeeey! Open the door!'

All I heard was this strange high-pitched whiny voice coming from outside my room. Who was it? It sounded like one of the producers on helium. Was it the cleaner? Had a fire alarm gone off without me knowing about it? Hang on . . . was my hair on fire?! I didn't know what was going on.

I looked at the clock and it was only 4am.

I opened the door and saw a funny-looking geezer wearing glasses.

'What the hell? Who are you?'

There was a massive camera in my face with a bright light shining in my eyes.

'Hi Joey, my name's Garland and I'm going to take you on the rest of your trip. You've got to get ready now! We're leaving in five minutes.'

Were they serious? I was all bewildered and the camera crew barged into my room. I was shouting, 'Get out of my room! I can't get ready like this!'

I kept looking at the geezer. He looked a dead ringer for that cartoon cat, Garfield. Only I thought the actual name for the cartoon cat must have been Garland so that's what I called him for the rest of the time. I was chanting, 'I'm going on a massive journey with Garland the Cat!'

I wasn't joking about it being a massive journey either. We got in the truck and travelled for miles until we got to these mountains. I had to eat a crusty worm thing that was covered in termite fat – whatever that was. Apparently that's what they eat in Africa. I just put it in my mouth and chewed it and said 'Mmm, well nice'. I gagged a bit but nothing would ever be as bad as turkey testicles.

That night we went on a sunset safari. It was sick. I saw some well good things – lions, zebras, giraffes, everything but a leopard. I'd seen them before when I went on a safari with Sam but this trip was completely different. The fact that I was by myself and had a camera in my face for most of the time might have had something to do with it . . .

I was having to be all David Attenborough-y and talk to the camera but I wasn't taking it very seriously. At one point we were driving around in the jeep and I kept hanging my head out of the window like a dog, making noises. The driver stopped the car and sicked out at me.

'Joey, didn't I tell you not to mess about? If you do that again I will take you back.'

Then we saw some baboons. Except I kept calling them bamboos.

I always get words mixed up. I can't say spaghetti properly – I call it 'psgetti'. I can't say remember either – I say 'renmeber'.

I saw two baboons shagging. They'd go at it for ten seconds then the bottom one would screech and run off while they were in the middle of it. I was thinking, 'What's going on here? We don't do that at home.' Baboons have got really big red arses. Running off in such a hurry like that probably makes it redder.

At 7pm every night my alarm would go off reminding me I

needed to take my anti-malaria tablets. I was in the middle of doing this little chat to camera and was trying to be all serious and nature-like. I'd gone into a massive long speech about what the animals behind me were doing. It was dark and we didn't want to disturb the animals so I was whispering all seriously and hushed . . .

'Basically there are elephants laying on the ground and they're all having sex. It reminds me a bit of *The Human Centipede* . . .'

As I was in the middle of my sentence my phone beeped. My alarm was going off.

'*Der der der der den*'

You know the sound that everyone has on their alarm? It's really loud and annoying.

'Oh sorry, I've got to take my tablets'.

Everyone was trying not to laugh. I think I must've ruined the sex moment for the elephants.

It seemed like I was being driven around Africa to watch animals' mating habits. The elephants were all over each other. I felt like a right pervert. Garland the Cat kept laughing at me too. There were some funny moments. I saw some zebras crossing the road and shouted, 'Oh look there's a zebra crossing!'

I was very pleased with that one.

Then the next night I was told I had to sleep in the wild. I had to put up my own tent and it took me bare long*. I'd only put up a pop-up tent before. I had no instructions. You'd think they were doing it to me on purpose . . .

One of the production team said, 'Ask us where we're staying tonight.'

'Where are you staying tonight?'

'We're staying in a hotel.'

'NO WAY! If you're staying in a hotel there's no way I'm staying here!'

So I was left in the middle of nowhere (well it was actually called the Kruger National Park) with Garland the Cat. It was without doubt one of the worst night's sleep I've ever had.

I was sweaty, uncomfortable and I couldn't have a shower. And Garland snored his tits off all night. I had to put my earphones on to help me sleep then woke up with some loud rave tune in my head.

A hyena was hanging about around my tent that night too – it was also being really loud. Luckily there was a fence between us but it was pacing up and down all evening, which wasn't exactly comforting.

In the morning I cleaned my teeth in front of an elephant who was hanging about nearby but I wasn't allowed to have a shower. That stressed me out a bit because I hate not having a shower.

Another day I was left to get a bus on my own in this city. People were looking at me all aggressively, probably thinking 'Who are you?'

'I'm Joey Essex,' I tried to tell them.

There was one man who talked to me on the bus. He was called 'Ice Man'. That was his full real name apparently.

We got a plane and flew to some place called Uganda that I was told was in East Africa (I thought it was a different country to start with).

I had to get a boat at 5am. It did mean that I saw the sunrise though, which was amazing. I met a guy called Walter and he told me we were going to Ngamba Island, which I thought meant we were going to an island full of prawns. (Gambas are prawns aren't they?) I don't think he knew what I was on about.

This was a famous island full of chimps and I was introduced to the cleverest chimp in the world called Natasha. She can unlock doors, remember numbers and all sorts. She was well brainy.

I felt quite sorry for her because that place was for chimps who'd lost their parents or had been rescued after their parents had died in the jungle. They'd all been injured or found in a bad way.

Natasha had been found next to her mother who had been trapped in a clamp and died. She'd refused to leave her side but was rescued and taken to this island. It made me feel really sad. Everyone has feelings. This chimp must've known that her mum was dead.

I bought a painting that the chimp had drawn me and also a funny gorilla head that I've got on the wall in my flat.

Then we went to the equator. I learnt that there are three funnel things – one goes one way, one goes the other and the middle goes down.

We met a tribe who were dancing round me like crazy. One of them had a spear and kept trying to throw it at me.

I looked at them all and shouted –

'After me – everyone say "reem!"'

They just stared at me like I was mad.

Then we went off into the jungle or to use its proper name, the Bwindi Impenetrable Forest. I was told this was where the monkeys and gorillas are really wild. So they certainly wouldn't know what reem was.

I met a guy called Augustine. I kept forgetting his name – 'August, Augusty, Afghanistan . . .' Either way, he told me he was going to guide me. He asked if there was anything I needed to know. I asked where I'd go to the loo and he said I had to dig a hole if I needed it.

'Oh so I need to dig a place for my shit?' I laughed. I think I embarrassed him a bit because he was quite shy.

Then I asked him what animals I'd expect to see in the jungle.

'In the jungle you will expect to see the blue monkey, the red tail monkey and the black and huwaite monkey.'

At least that's what I thought he said.

'What's a "black and huwaite" monkey?' I asked.

'Yes the black and huwaite monkey.'

I could hear the camera man sniggering. His head was wobbling up and down because he was trying not to laugh.

What the hell was a 'black and huwaite' monkey?

This conversation went on for ages. Turns out he was trying to say 'black and white'. I thought 'huwaite' was a new word I'd learnt and was cracking up.

When we first got into the jungle we heard some birds singing a really weird tune. I asked what they were and was told that they were special birds that know how to tell the time.

How did they find all these things?! It was like this land had been created especially for Joey Essex!

After three hours we finally got near to the gorillas.

When we saw them for the first time I got shivers. It didn't seem real. We were so close to them but they looked so strange. I thought they were electric. They don't look like actual living things. They're huge too. There was a group of thirteen of them and I was about seven metres away. Any closer than that and I'd been told I'd get punched.

Or eaten . . .

One of them was staring straight at me. To be honest, I don't think it helped that I was wearing a gorilla T-shirt and some strong Versace aftershave.

They were moving and scuffling around and we tried to follow them as quietly as we could. What I didn't realise was that there was a girl one behind me and a boy one waiting for her.

The producer was trying to get me and the gorillas in the same shot so I could say something to camera. But as I was crouching down I suddenly heard a noise on the right.

Out of the corner of my eye I saw a gorilla's head.

OH MY GOD.

It was right by me. I was crapping myself.

What do I do?

One of the crew shouted, 'Freeze! Freeze!' We'd already been told earlier we had to stay really still so we didn't scare them.

'I'm freezing! I'm freezing!' I was shouting.

I felt the gorilla brushing past my back. It was intense.

It was such a mad experience. I still don't think it's even hit me now how lucky I was to be out there watching creatures like that in the wild. Obviously I couldn't resist taking a selfie as a memory while I was in the jungle. When you look at the picture there's a gorilla hiding in the leaves right behind me! He must've been thinking 'What the hell is that weirdo doing?!'

I called my dad straight afterwards and told him all about it. I also told him he looked like one of the gorillas.

JOEY'S FASCINATING FACTS:

#10 The first mobile phones cost £2,000 and their battery life lasted 20 minutes (AND they looked like bricks. Have you ever seen one?)

CHAPTER 32

LIVING THE REEM

The National Television Awards was the first big event I'd been to since being on *I'm A Celebrity . . . Get Me Out Of Here!*. I'd been before when I was with Sam but Dave warned me I'd really notice a difference because so many more people would know who I was this year.

He was right. I have never had so much attention at a big celebrity event.

The problem was, as usual, I didn't know who hardly any of them were.

I never know who famous people are. It's a running joke amongst my friends. Once I was at this festival in London called Lovebox and someone introduced me to this group of girls called All Saints. They were lovely and seemed to know who I was and were hugging me saying 'It's Joey!' I looked at them and said, 'Which branch do you work at?' But they didn't work in All Saints the shop. They were a really big pop group apparently. They were all cracking up laughing.

I never remember people's names, whether they're famous or not. But ever since I was a kid I've created a plan to get round it. Now, whenever someone comes up to me and I don't know their name, I just call them Ashley*.

But the trick is to mumble it so they can hardly understand what you're saying.

'Ashley . . .?'

And Ashley is a name that works for a boy or a girl. So that makes it easier.

Afterwards I'll say to my mates, 'Oh no man, I just Ashley'ed someone off.'

There were definitely a few Ashleys about in the NTAs that night.

I was wearing a green suit that I'd got made for me in Dubai and some shades.

Shades on the red carpet = jokes.

People were coming up to me saying hello and it wasn't just, 'It's that kid from *TOWIE*' anymore, now it was 'It's Joey from the jungle'.

Some smiley woman with gappy teeth came and asked for a picture with me. Someone told me she was the winner of the *X Factor.* I didn't know anything about it, I was in Australia for the entire time!

I also spent a nice little time talking to Laura Whitmore in the ITV box. She was the presenter on ITV2's *I'm A Celebrity . . . Get Me Out Of Here! NOW!* and is extremely hot.

'Do you think she's single?' I asked Dave.

She said she was going on holiday to Thailand the next day and I asked who she was going with.

'My mate,' she replied, so I smiled.

'You're a single lady then?'

Then Dave piped up.

'Joey's single.'

He was like an embarrassing dad. But Laura just laughed. Dave tweeted her afterwards trying to get her to follow me . . . she still hasn't.

I think if we went out together we'd look good, don't you? Hi Laura if you're reading this. I know you usually like indy types but I can be indy. Indy-pendent!

Caroline Flack was there too and I had a picture with her. She's lovely and we always chat when we see each other. There were rumours that we had a bit of a thing once, which was rubbish. I don't fancy her.

A girl from *Corrie* apparently tried to chat me up but I didn't know who she was. I swear Abbey Clancy was giving me the eye too! Though I found out she was married, so probably not. I spoke to her on the phone once when I was on holiday. I'd met someone who knew her and they told me her younger sister liked me so we spoke on the phone for a bit. Random, I know. She was looking at me on the red carpet but at the time I clearly didn't know who she was. I was just staring at her thinking she was a sort. It didn't click until the show started and I saw some girl in the same red dress as she had on going nuts in a dance routine on stage. I said, 'Who's that?!' and Dave said 'That's Abbey Clancy'. Jokes.

Has she had her lips done? They're very pouty. I prefer people who haven't had anything done to themselves. I definitely prefer a girl with natural boobs to boob jobs. I don't know why girls have all this surgery. Some girls in TOWIE *throw 'Botox parties'. That sounds like the least fun party ever.*

As soon as I got inside I saw Keith Lemon. I call him Leigh now because we've become quite good friends since I've been a regular on *Celebrity Juice*. When he talks to me now it's as a mate. He's more normal when he's Leigh and doesn't muck about as much as Keith does. Then someone else will walk over and he'll switch into Lemon mode and be really stupid and jokes. I like the fact I know him as Leigh. He's a really genuine nice bloke and his wife Jill is a good friend to me now . . . she's also quite fit.

Danny Dyer and the girl who plays his daughter on *EastEnders* came over to me and they were saying they always sing 'Truly Glumptious' on set now because of me saying it in the jungle.

There was another girl from *EastEnders* who Dave thought was following me all night. Anyway, she might not have actually been following me – she might've just been going to the toilet.

Spencer Matthews from *Made in Chelsea* was there as well that night. He's proper flash, that boy. He was wobbling about all over the place and trying to get off with some girl in the middle of having his picture taken for *Heat* magazine. I like the *Made in Chelsea* boys and I'm pretty good friends with Jamie

Laing and Ollie Proudlock. Jamie came to Faces nightclub with me in Essex and I got him so drunk he nearly missed his flight to go on holiday the next day. Every time we see each other we say we should do it more often but it never happens.

I'm A Celebrity . . . Get Me Out Of Here! won Best Entertainment Programme. Some of the other camp mates were there too – Kian, Matthew, Rebecca, David, Lucy . . . and Amy. We all went on stage to collect it (I pretended on Twitter that I'd lost the award the next day, but I'd actually given it to one of the producers).

We went backstage to be interviewed in the media room and Matthew Wright immediately started being all annoying. One of the journalists started talking to me and Amy.

'Even though you're not together anymore, are you still friends?'

Matthew piped up.

'Well, you know . . . thirty or forty grand . . . I wouldn't mind getting that every time I went out with a girl and dumped her!' Then laughed ridiculously to himself.

That really wound me up so I asked Dave to get me out of there. Matthew's actually a nice geezer but I didn't know why he was still on about that stuff, and knowing how I felt about Amy when we were in the jungle, it was annoying to think people might think that about me. If I was his age I would never behave in that way. I wouldn't give a shit about what anyone else was doing. 'Very immature,' I thought.

I was actually quite nervous about seeing everyone again. Less so with Amy and Kian, but more the older ones. I loved David Emanuel in the jungle but even he'd said some snide things about me afterwards. I saw an interview he'd done on the red carpet and someone was asking him about me and Amy.

'What did you think of Joey and Amy's relationship? Do you think it was fake?'

He looked at the reporter and said, 'Well you've said it all haven't you? You've said it all.'

Then there was Amy. I thought she was really acting up for the cameras, even her walk didn't look like normal. She had her head flung back with her hands waving around behind her like she was on a catwalk. Either that or she was swatting away imaginary flies. It was jokes seeing her out like this because she'd been so down to earth and normal in the jungle.

Once we were inside the party she started messaging me: 'Where are you?'

I thought I'd wind her up a bit.

'Why do you want to see me so much? Do you miss me?'

'I'll tell you when I see you,' she replied.

We never did see each other again. Me and Tom Pearce went off with two blonde birds that night instead and I had a laugh with the rest of the *TOWIE* cast. Or Richards* as we call them.

We always call girls 'Richards'. Tom told me the other day it's because Richard the Third is slang for 'bird'. Dave then told me it's also slang for 'turd'. So now I'm well confused.

CHAPTER 33

'WHO CREATED THE WORLD?'

I have Google alerts on my phone so I can see if anything's been written about me in the press (or if anyone has been talking about me behind my back!). This is what one said the other day:

'A £5,000 designer wedding dress, a snowy owl and a cardboard cut-out of Joey Essex were some of the bizarre possessions left in hotels in 2013.'

Someone had left a life-sized cardboard cut-out of me in a hotel room in Chelmsford. How funny. When I hear stuff like that it makes me realise how nutty my life has become. I've had so many amazing experiences. I don't want to ever get to a point where I take anything for granted because I know how lucky I am.

I've been asked to appear on all sorts of TV shows – ITV2's *Celebrity Juice* is one of my favourites. They had me on the panel quite a few times and Keith Lemon kept doing special quizzes on me to test my general knowledge. I got most of the answers wrong (every time I do it I always wish I'd revised the night before but I never do). Holly Willoughby told me I had a 'gift' once – she was wetting herself laughing because I said I thought Richard and Judy were the ones who created the world. To be honest, I don't even think I'd recognise Richard or Judy if I bumped into them.

If you didn't see any of the shows – here's how the quizzes went.

JOEY ESSEX QUIZ 1

(Keith tells me people think I'm stupid so this is a chance for me to 'reem-deem' myself . . .)

> *[This is the key: K = Keith J = me]*
> K: What's the capital of France?
> J: Paris
> K: What country borders Wales?
> J: London
> K: What is heavier, a ton of Fearne's bangers or a ton of Holly's?
> [I looked at Holly's and hers looked heavier but I thought it was a trick question . . .]
> J: Fearne.
> K: Joey Essex is not thick – he's just misunderstood.

JOEY ESSEX QUIZ 2

> K: What country does Danish bacon come from?
> J: Germany

The answer was Denmark but why would I know that?

K: How many sides does a square have?

J: Six?

K: Finish off this famous phrase, 'It's raining cats and . . .

J: DOGS!

K: What animal does beef come from?

J: Cows

K: Which country borders Wales?

[He said the last time I answered it I said it was London and that was wrong. I still didn't know the right answer so he told me to guess . . .]

J: Russia?

JOEY ESSEX QUIZ 3

Sam was on the show with me this time and I told Keith I'd been revising a little bit, even though I actually hadn't. Sam said, 'Can I give you a little bit of advice? Think about the questions a bit more.'

K: One of Shakespeare's plays was called *Romeo and Juliet* – but who was Romeo's girlfriend?

J: Romeo? [Sam punched me in the arm and said 'it's Juliet!']

K: How many sides does a rectangle have?

J: Four

K: We've asked you this question twice now and twice you got it wrong . . . so . . . What country borders Wales? Previously you said London and Russia.

J: England.

I got it! Suddenly there were soldiers coming out from behind the studio, glitter falling from the ceiling, trumpets playing and everything! Thank God I did get it right otherwise what would they have done? The trumpet players wouldn't have had a job. Then Keith cut to another screen and said –

'Let's have a look around the world at how people are reacting to Joey getting that answer correct!'

There were shots of people jumping up and down in Leeds and Gatwick airport. It was jokes.

I've never read any Shakespeare. I think it would be well long. The only time I ever talk about Shakespeare usually is when someone's shaking while they're trying to take a picture. Me and Arg just say, 'Oi – do you know who Shakespeare is?' and laugh. So to me, Shakespeare* is just a very shaky, very wobbly hand.

Another time I was on the show and I was asked if I knew who Elton John was. They showed me a picture and I said I thought it was Ozzy Osbourne. Keith also asked if I knew who Ricky Gervais was and I thought he was a singer.

I know who he is now because I shook his hand at the National Television Awards. He looked like he didn't want to know and shook it really quickly then walked off. I recognised what he was doing – I've done it before when someone's come to talk to me and I don't know who they are. He probably thought I was going to be a pest.

Now I have to go 'back to school' on *Celebrity Juice*. I had to answer loads of questions with Helen Flanagan last year and got most of them wrong too. One of them was about the name of Jesus's mum and I said it was Zesus. This year I had to do it against Little Ant and Dec in a *Saturday Night Takeaway* special. Keith told them I'd been kept back a year because I was so stupid. They're so cute. Whenever they see me they always say, 'Joey Essex!' and run up and cuddle me. They're only five and six but are miles cleverer than me.

We were asked about the three little pigs, which was some sort of nursery rhyme I'd never heard of. We had to write down what the second little pig had built his house from.

I thought, 'Well, you can make your house out of bricks and pigs lay in straw' so I guessed it was made from 80 per cent bricks and 20 per cent straw.

It was the wrong answer. The correct one was wood (Little Ant and Dec got it right), but I was very chuffed with myself because it turned out the first little pig had made his house from straw and the third was from bricks. So I was nearly right and mine was a total guess.

I must be able to work out pigs' memories. It was a bit of a stupid question anyway really because pigs can't build, they don't have hands.

Next question –
    'What's the capital of India?'
    I guessed.
    'India?'

I was going to say Pakistan but I didn't know if it was racist or not.

Little Ant and Dec had written 'New Delhi'. Apparently they'd just been learning about the capitals at school . . . Then Keith asked me to tell the time. Both hands were pointing at 12 but I was confused about whether it was am or pm.

I lost the exam.

I'm definitely revising for the next one.

In the most recent series of *Celebrity Juice* Keith has had me dressed as a superhero – I was part of the 'Bangtastic Four' and was up against Rylan Clark from *Big Brother* and *X Factor*, Antony Costa from the band Blue and Abs from the band 5ive.

I'd never met Rylan before then and he's such a lovely bloke. We all had different superpowers – Rylan's was that he could blind people with his teeth. I was called 'The Special One' and my power was that I could think differently to everyone else (that didn't mean I was cleverer than them though . . . so it wasn't really an advantage). Antony was a blue tit or something and Abs's power was that he could make you do sit-ups.

We were put in rounds against each other and had to answer questions really quickly otherwise we would be called out. One of the questions I got massively wrong was when we had to name someone in the Beatles.

Rylan went first and he said 'John' and I didn't know anyone else so I said 'Michael?' and then quickly 'Ashley?' Everyone laughed. I guessed Michael – I thought it was a very 80s name.

Then I found out the Beatles weren't actually from the 80s.

Then we were asked to name an ocean. One of the boys said 'Pacific Ocean' and all I could think of was 'Paris'. Paris Ocean.

That's quite a sick name actually.

I went on *The Cube* recently too. I'm usually quite brave when it comes to putting myself in uncomfortable situations; I'm quite confident so I don't usually get scared of things. But sometimes I worry I won't be able to accomplish something which makes me nervous and I was scared doing *The Cube*. I don't think I'd have minded if it was just for me but I was playing to win money for charity. I couldn't lose.

The first challenge was this box which had loads of balls in it – I had to lift it up so the balls fell out, then pick up all the balls within a certain time. There were twenty balls and I did it straight away. For the next one I was blindfolded and I had to find the biggest ball among a pile. That took three tries.

Talking of balls – people always ask me why I walk along with my hands down my trousers a lot of the time. Well . . . having a willy and balls is annoying! I always have my hands there because it's uncomfortable. Things wiggle around. And it's quite a big area! Imagine a girl having a willy and balls – they'd be really annoyed. They get in the way massively. Also, if you wear really tight boxers sometimes you can lose circulation. I've had jeans that are way too tight. Sometimes I've taken them off in the middle of the street because they hurt so much.

For the third challenge I had to stop these two laser lines perfectly in the middle of these two boxes. It took me aaaages.

I was allowed to ask the audience a couple of questions and all I kept asking was, 'Are my sleeves alright? Should I wear sleeves up or down?' I decided to keep them up.

Phillip Schofield laughed at me.

'In all my years hosting *The Cube*, no one has *ever* asked their family or friends how to wear their sleeves!'

I won £10,000 for my chosen charity called Child Bereavement UK which helps young children who've suffered bereavement. It's a charity I'm really passionate about, given what I've gone through myself.

I'm always being asked to do general knowledge tests and quizzes for people. I think they like seeing me get stuff wrong. I don't do it deliberately, I just don't know as much as other people. Or maybe my superpower really is that I think differently to other people and maybe that's not such a bad thing.

I did an IQ test for *Fabulous* magazine once and they asked me things like, 'Who is the US president?' I knew it was Obama but I didn't know his first name so I closed my eyes and guessed – 'David?' WRONG! Then I was asked what the capital of Spain was and I said it was Tenerife. WRONG AGAIN. Next question was 'What does RSVP stand for?' I thought it was something to do with pets.

I did another interview with *Fabulous* once and ended up getting into a feud with Alex Reid because of it. They'd asked me to play 'snog, marry, avoid'. I avoided Chantelle Houghton who he was dating at the time. I said I thought she got about a bit – well, I thought I'd seen her with a few footballers so I wasn't going to marry her was I?

After he read it he piped up on Twitter demanding an apology.

'@JoeyEssex_thought we were friendly, guess not after ur [sic] salacious defamatory comment in Sun bout @chantellehought. I expect an apology.'

I never apologised. If I ever saw him out I'd just give him a screwface*. He's not with her anymore anyway so I doubt he'd care.

Luckily I haven't fallen out with many other celebrities. Well, apart from a couple of fellas from the band The Wanted. It's probably because I went out with Tom from The Wanted's girlfriend Kelsey Hardwick when I was younger. He wasn't with her at the time but maybe he got a bit jealous.

Then I did an interview with *We Love Pop* magazine and was asked, 'Who do you prefer – The Wanted or One Direction?' I said One Direction obviously! Then Nathan from The Wanted got on Twitter and started mouthing off about me and calling me a nobody. They're not all horrible though. The model one, Siva, is nice. He's the only one who's ever given me the time of day.

A lot of celebs think it's cool to slag off people from *TOWIE*. The rapper Example tried to mug me off once on Twitter. Professor Green once said that he wanted to 'kill *TOWIE* stars'. But whenever I've met him he's always been alright to me. Not that he breaded* me, but we've always just been cool. He couldn't have been nicer to be honest. I met him at a Pixie Lott concert.

Pixie's the sister of one of my mates, Steve. It's weird that I grew up with her being so famous and now I get invited to the same things as her.

I went to a party at Pixie's house once and wanted to go as a dead zebra. I asked Frankie if she'd paint my face with this white stuff I found in the garage and she laughed and told me it was emulsion paint.

CHAPTER 34

THE FAME GAME

CELEB LADIES I FANCY:

Perrie from the band Little Mix — She's fit but she's engaged to Zayn from One Direction.

Selena Gomez — I think she looks like a cool girl and she went out with Justin Bieber so she must be. I don't think he'd be friends with me if I went out with her though so I'd have to think about it.

Laura Whitmore — I'd have to try hard to get her. But I think I'd have to try hard to get all of them to be honest.

Kendall Jenner — Tall, slim and nice lips.

Binky from Made in Chelsea — I know that if you went on a date with her she'd be lovely. She's well down to earth.

Jade from Little Mix — She's little and cute. I've fancied her for quite a while. Her and Perrie are 50/50.

Victoria Beckham — I used to fancy her but she's too
old for me now. So is Kate Moss.
Cheryl Cole — she's probably a bit old for me but she's
still a weapon.

I'm only 23 but I feel like I've done so much, sometimes I feel
more like I'm 43.

Maybe Joey Essex years are like dog years.

I can't imagine getting old, it scares me a bit. I get sad when I
look back at early episodes of *TOWIE* because I look so young
and you know you'll never be that young again.

I'd like to have a Ferrari when I'm older, and a nice mansion (!),
but one thing I can definitely say I've learnt in my 23 years so
far, is that money doesn't bring you happiness in life. When I
was working in the fish market I didn't have a pot to piss in but
I still had my mates around me and always had a laugh and I
was just as happy as I am now. What's that saying again? 'The
grass isn't always greener on the other side . . .' Well it's true. I
realised that when I was in the jungle. Kian, Laila and Steve won
an overnight stay in a luxury hotel halfway through the show
and when Kian came back to camp he said to me, 'You're really
craving food aren't you?' I said 'Yes!' because I was starving.
Then he said the strangest thing –

'When you get out of here, make sure you choose the first
thing you eat really wisely because once you've had one bite the
joy of it will go instantly.'

He was right too. When I got out of there I remember eating

this sausage and it tasted sooo amazing. But when I ate a second one it had become normal. I was over the excitement of it. Worst of all, I just became downright greedy and started eating them for the sake of it. I think that's the same with people who have money.

I have to pinch myself sometimes when I look at everything I've achieved. I've got perfumes, hair products, calendars and a clothing range that's now being stocked in Primark and on the high street. I've even got a CD compilation out called *Joey Essex Presents: Essex Anthems!* I went back to my shop Fusey in Essex the other day and there were loads of kids just screaming at me. I don't have time to go to the shop every day so Tracy keeps it going and also runs the website. Anyway, Fusey is a brand now so I don't need to be there everyday, I go when I've got spare time and I'm so proud of it.

Anyway, if you go to Nike you can't always meet 'Nike' can you?

But most of all, I feel like my job is to smile and be nice to people. PAs are one of my main sources of income so I've got used to smiling on stage *a lot*. PAs are the reason I was able to put down a massive deposit on my house and they help me pay my mortgage every month. All I usually say is 'Reem' and 'What are YOU sayin'?' I must look like a bit of a robot sometimes.

A lot of my job is smiling. And smiling. And smiling. So those white teeth I had done a few years ago came in pretty handy.

Sometimes I think I need to change my smile. Surely people are bored of the same one by now? I think my smile has got bigger over the years. I've smiled so much that my mouth has stretched.

It's definitely wider. And I think my head has changed shape to go with it. My head used to be a lot rounder.

It's weird thinking that just being me, Joey Essex, walking down the street or going to a bar has become a full-time job. When one person asks for a picture, someone else does, then another, then it's 'One more! One more! Can I have one more please?'

That's the thing about being in the public eye – people do think they can come up to you and say anything but it's not the worst thing in the world and I know I'm really lucky. Personally, I'd never go up to someone I didn't know and ask them about some rumour I'd heard about them – even if it was David Beckham! I might smile at him and ask how Posh was but I wouldn't start asking him questions about something I'd read in the papers. It's mental when you think about it.

I can still go out and do everything I want to do – it just takes about a million times longer than it used to. Going to the supermarket can take me about a week sometimes! And even months after I went on *I'm a Celebrity* . . ., I'll get people stopping me on the street –

'You should've won in the jungle son . . . you really should've won you know.'

'Oi, Joey – why didn't you win?'

It's old people, really young kids, girls, blokes and proper grown-up mums and dads. The fact that they all know who I am blows my brain sometimes.

Someone actually dropped their shopping because of me the other day! I was in the shop and this girl came round the corner and when she saw me in front of her she froze in shock. Her mouth was wide open and all her bags flew everywhere – milk, bread – the lot! How crazy is that?!

Tom was with me at the supermarket once and nearly exploded.

'Oh my God man. How can you put up with this? They're bombarding you!'

He's on *TOWIE* so he's recognised too but for me it's another level now.

But if it all ended tomorrow, I'd hate it. Fame is weird – you can't have it both ways. You can't expect to get all the money and glory that comes with it and then have people leave you alone and never ask for a picture. And how can I complain when loads of poor freezing-cold people have queued up or camped outside just to meet me? I went to Liverpool for a calendar signing before Christmas and the organisers said they were so worried about crowds that they had to give out limited wristbands so they could restrict people coming!

Girls will come up to me and say, 'Oh my God I love you' or 'My mum wanted me to tell you that she loves you!' I always say, 'No way! Seriously?'

Which now you're reading this means you know I say that to everyone . . .

You'd think that being famous would make it easy to meet a girl but fame does funny things to people. I can understand why celebrities date other celebrities. Most girls I meet who aren't famous act all weird around me – it's like they can't be themselves.

Want to know what puts me off a girl most? If she pretends she doesn't know who I am when it's obvious she does. I've been in so many situations when a group of girls will come over and a few of them will say, 'Look! It's Joey Essex!' and one of them will look at me and say, 'Who are you?' I'm not being big-headed and saying that everyone must know who I am, but you can just tell. It's like she's trying too hard to play it cool and it really puts me off. All it says to me is that she's automatically a liar. And you know I can't stand liars. The best way a girl can attract me is if she comes up to me and says, 'Hi Joey – you alright?' and not be too interested but just act like a normal person. You know, like 'What you doing now? What you up to?' that sort of thing. I just want to be able to have an ordinary conversation as if we were mates. If the girl then asked, 'Do you fancy going out for a drink sometime?' I'd probably say yes.

I don't mind girls asking me out if they're normal.

And if someone genuinely doesn't know who I am I'd rather they just called me Ashley.

I've got a code language I use with Dave for if it ever gets too much at a PA and I want to get away from someone. I ask him to get me an apple juice*.

A date with Joey Essex:

we'd go to . . . Harry Potter world! I don't even like Harry Potter but I think it would be jokes. And I'd like to run about with wands for a bit.

The first thing I'd say to you . . . would be 'Do you like going on dates?'

The best way to date someone . . . is when you're at a festival or something and they have all their friends who can hang about with your mates. Then you can have a dance together and have fun.

We'll probably drink . . . vodka, lime and soda to keep the reem look. But if we're on a date and I was going for it I might have the cocktail, sex on the beach. Or a purple drink which is one I've made up with vodka, lemonade and this purple stuff you get in Spain. I don't think they make it here. It's a lavender colour.

We'll eat . . . a nice bit of fish, some skate maybe. Apparently there's something you can eat which is actually called a date. Someone asked me if I'd eaten a date before and I thought they were mad. I thought they meant had I eaten a girl.

CHAPTER 35

THE FUTURE

My urge to speak to Sam got stronger after she got out of *Celebrity Big Brother*. She came fifth in the show and there was loads of talk afterwards about her and one of the other house-mates, Ollie Locke from *Made in Chelsea*. I knew she didn't fancy him though. I also knew there was something really wrong with her. She'd hardly spoken in the house and the papers were saying she'd lost over a stone and a half in weight. She was really ill and I was worried.

I missed her.

It felt so wrong not speaking to her. She's so special to me that to see her suffering and not be able to give her a cuddle was killing me. In the end, on Monday February 3rd, I texted her:

I hope you're ok Sam, its Joey. I heard you've been really ill. Get well soon x

She texted back:

Hi, yeah I've been really poorly. Still
haven't had the results from hospital.
Hoping it's not serious. I'm at my mum's
now, resting up all week. Lovely to hear
from you, love Sam x

Then I replied:

I hope everything comes back ok. Get
loads of rest, that will be the best
thing for you, Joey x

She said:

Thanks Joey, yes I will need to get
healthy seeing as I'm going to be number
one aunty [her sister Billie had just
announced she was pregnant]. I heard you
went away to catch a monkey. Good luck
with your show, speak soon x

I replied saying that I wished Greg and Billie good luck and
that my trip to Africa had been good . . . but I hadn't caught a
monkey. She text back with a cute monkey Emoji.

It felt nice having contact with her after all this time. We didn't
text for a few days after that and I started getting concerned that
I hadn't heard back. She'd started filming for the new series of
TOWIE so I asked Tom and Diags if they'd seen her and how
she was. Everyone was saying she looked really unwell and I

couldn't stop thinking about her so I rang her on the morning of 12th February. I was on my way round to see Arg because we were going into London to do some shopping. But before I got there I'd got myself all worked up about calling Sam. My heart was beating so fast just thinking about her.

I bought some sick running gear in Nike. I bought a bright neon-yellow vest and neon trainers. Arg said 'Subtle'.

I was worried about what to say and how she would react. I dialled the number . . . then it went to voicemail.

I didn't leave a message. I waited until I'd left Arg later on and tried again. This time she answered.

'Oh my God! Joey! How are you?'

'Sam, can you talk?'

She told me she was in the car with her nan and phoned me back a few minutes later. She said her nan had heard my voice and was all excited about the thought of us talking again – I'd always got on great with Sam's nan.

It was so good to hear her voice. I told her how worried I was about her and she said she'd been for loads of tests at the doctors and that they thought she might have Crohn's disease. I'd heard of it before because someone we know in Essex has it. I was chatting to her, trying to do everything I could to be positive.

'You'll be alright, I promise.'

We spoke again that night for nearly three hours. I told her I hadn't stopped thinking about her and we admitted that we still loved each other. We spoke about *everything*. There were things we both wanted to get off our chest but now wasn't the time, we were just happy to be talking.

Whenever we start speaking we fall back in love with each other straight away. It's like a chemistry thing, we can't help it.

That's why I have to cut contact otherwise that's it, I've fallen again. I know how dangerous it gets with us.

Everyone around us was speaking again, they'd all made friends – Chloe, Billie, all our friends.

'Everything's healing but it's only because me and you aren't together in the centre of it all, arguing and causing issues between the people around us,' I said.

I still wanted to see her though and told her I wanted to take her to Harry Potter World even though I hadn't ever read a Harry Potter book in my life.

'Why do you want to go there?' she laughed.

'I just want to run about with a wizard's hat on and hold some wands.'

Instead we decided to see each other on Valentine's Day.

That morning she got diagnosed with Crohn's disease. She sent me a message on WhatsApp at 9am from the hospital and she was so upset.

'Everything's going to be fine, I'll look after you,' I assured her.

I bought her a massive bunch of flowers, a little toy dog and loads of chocolates. I'd gone to the petrol station to get the sweets just before I went to her house and the first person I saw in there was her mum Sue. We hugged and I could see her eyes were bubbling up. She nearly started crying, which made me sad. If I was upset about Sam I couldn't imagine how she must've felt.

When Sam and I saw each other it was like love at first sight all over again. We couldn't stop smiling and hugged for about a minute before I even got through the door. I turned round to pick up the flowers from the doorstep and the toy dog was missing. I started freaking out. We began searching for it everywhere; I was running all around her drive but there was no sign of it. I went outside four times that night, I couldn't settle. Sam went to look as well but there was no sign of it. I was convinced I was going to get home that night and see it sitting all weirdly on my bed. When I left a few hours later it was hanging on a bush to the left of the drive. Spooky!

We just sat in her lounge cuddling and watching TV but we both kept moving our faces as if we were going to kiss each other on the lips then hesitating. In the end I said, 'We might as well just do it.'

So we started kissing . . .

It was only a matter of time before we slept together again. As soon as I had a free night she stayed at my flat and then I stayed at hers. We just wanted to be together.

When we see each other it's not like starting all over, it's like we're suddenly back on. Back in love. Like nothing ever happened. No matter what we say, no matter what either of us has done in the past, it all disappears.

But I also know that this is when I get the fear. As soon as we put a label on it and say we're 'girlfriend and boyfriend' it all goes wrong. I don't want to change the way she is or the way I am, we just need to learn to get on with each other. Sam recently said she needs to stop involving her friends too much and that she knows how drunk she used to get and how much it wound me up. I told her I know I can't tell her what to do but at the same time I can't handle it when she behaves that way. I know I need to make changes too, after all I'm controlling, possessive, jealous, high maintenance, moody and I like things my own way. I've also got to make more time to be with her. We need to think about each other's feelings a bit more. We might just be able to make it work this time.

Watching her talk about her illness on *TOWIE* was really hard. It was strange seeing the new series of the show anyway, knowing this was the first time I wasn't going to be in it. But the scene where she's talking about having Crohn's disease with her mum Sue and her sister Billie was really upsetting. They both cried and it broke my heart. I wanted to cuddle the TV screen. What people didn't know at the time was that Sam was sat right next to me. I had a tear in my eye while I watched the show and I held her the whole time.

We tried to keep our relationship a secret from the press as long as we could – until I stupidly instagrammed a picture of me and Sam in bed! You couldn't see our faces, I had my top off and her arm was resting on top of me. It took us ages to get the shot right too!

I was doing an interview for *Heat* magazine the next day and they asked me who it was in the picture. I'd deleted it by then, but it was too late. They'd sussed it. I smiled and said it was nice to know that people wanted us back together because they could tell there was unfinished business between us. I said it was nice to know people like 'Jam' (that's our name when you put Joey and Sam together – in case you think I've started going off on one about the stuff you spread on toast).

Anyway, they didn't need my rubbish photo for evidence. A pap snapped me and Sam together at a restaurant a few days later.

Sam had invited me to a meal for her Billie's fiancé Greg's birthday. I told her I already had plans – I'd arranged to meet Dave and some of the producers from Lime and ITV to talk about solo TV projects – but agreed to go to see Sam afterwards.

My meeting was at Tarantino's restaurant in Brentwood. I ordered the sea bass. I like fish.

. . . well I did until I got a massive great bone caught in my mouth in a restaurant the other day. I took a bite and suddenly had a mad panic and thought I needed to go to hospital. This bone was caught between my back tooth and the inside of my mouth. It took me ages to get it out and I had to go into the toilet with a tooth pick and try and push it out. I honestly thought I was going to have bone sticking out of my cheek for life!

I'd only been in the restaurant for about ten minutes when Gemma, Gemma's mum, Jess Wright and Bobby Cole Norris walked in. When they saw me with the producers they must've thought I was talking about going back to *TOWIE*.

The story turned up in the paper two days later saying 'Joey to return to TOWIE'. But it was a meeting about Educating Joey Essex *and other TV proposals. Papers got it wrong once again.*

It got to about 8.30pm and Sam was texting me asking where I was. She was at another restaurant called Alec's and said they were all waiting for me. She asked what I wanted to eat and said she'd order for me. I couldn't think – I didn't want to tell her I'd already eaten! So I ended up asking for sea bass. Again. I had to have two meals that night. Long*.

As I left Tarantino's I was papped outside. I wouldn't usually have minded that much but I was road-testing my ponytail (it was the 'mun's' first trip out in public and it wasn't ready for any close-ups just yet). The picture ended up online everywhere and in the papers people were saying I was taking hair tips from Harry Styles.

Dave drove me to Alec's. It's a little bit out in the sticks so I felt like it was safe to go there without anyone spotting us. It was nearly 10pm by the time I arrived and I was a bit nervous. I thought it would be full of Sam and Billie's mates and I hadn't seen any of them since we got back together. But when I walked in it was just Sam, her mum Sue, Greg and Billie and they all beamed at me and said how good it was to see me. Billie said she knew there was still so much connection between us and that everyone was happy to see us together – she knows we'll always love each other no matter what.

After about twenty minutes I looked outside – there was a photographer spying through the window. He was taking pictures of us! How long had he been there? I went outside with Sam and confronted him.

'How did you know we were here?'

It was the same photographer who'd papped me outside Tarantino's but there was no way he'd have known we were in Alec's unless someone had told him. And I know we weren't followed.

I started to get suspicious . . .

'Someone inside the restaurant tipped me off,' he said and shrugged as if to say, 'So what?'

Then he started backtracking and telling me all sorts.

I told the pap I didn't want him to sell the pictures. Instead me and Sam said we would do a better set for him a few days later. In truth, I had no intention of doing a set-up for him. I was just fuming he was going to make money out of us. Plus I didn't want everyone in the world knowing we were seeing each other again. Because when people know about our relationship they start interfering and that's when everything goes wrong again, the fact the pap was even there proved how hard it was going to be to keep private, and everyone has always been interested in our business.

As he left, the pap said, 'If you don't stick to your word I'm going to sell the pictures.'

And that's what he did. *Heat* magazine bought the pictures. I didn't want them out there but I was pleased it went to them because I knew they liked me and Sam and would write a good article.

It made the whole front cover – '*Joey & Sam finally go public – friends say "they're attracted to each other like magnets" – intimate new pics!*'

To be fair the pictures were quite nice – and we looked really loved up and happy together.

But a few days later we started bickering again.

I was really worried about things going back to the way they used to be. My head was getting in such a muddle.

If me and Sam were going to work we needed to learn to behave differently. We accept that we're always going to have a few arguments now and then, but we need to move on from what has happened in the past. I said, 'We've got to move on and think about the future.'

So that's what we're trying to do.

But here's the truth.

At this moment in time, even after all the bad times and the things we've said and done to each other we can still look each other in the eye and say 'I love you' and really mean it. I've grown up a lot in these past three years and I know I'm stronger now. You never know what your future holds and what will come across your path. All I know right now is I'm happy, and that's all I can ask for.

CHAPTER 36

AROUND THE WORLD, AROUND THE WOOORLD . . .

For anyone who's already read the hardback version of my book – welcome to a whole new chapter! And for anyone who's reading this as a paperback for the first time, think of yourself as extra special because there are more words in this book than the last one! Actually, if you've bought the hardback *and* you're also reading this one, then you're REALLY the special one. Thank you for being extra reem. You're also better than some of my mates who still haven't properly read this book. Steve says he's saving it for when he goes on holiday so he can read about himself in one go. And Tom Pearce keeps asking me to give him a copy but I told him he needs to buy one in the shop. My dad reckons he's read the book twice . . . but I think it's actually taken him a very looooong time to read it once. He started it in May and he finished by the end of July.

As for Sam? She says she still hasn't read it. I know it wasn't nice for her that I wrote certain stuff about me and Amy but she also understands that everything I've said was true – and being honest is the most important thing to me. At the time of writing this new chapter Sam and I have officially been back together now for four months and it's good between us, it's going well. We're calling ourselves boyfriend and girlfriend but we're still taking it slow. We haven't moved in together yet and I quite like it that way. Sam has asked me to move into her place but I have so much stuff in my flat there just wouldn't be the space for it at her house. It's hard enough only having three bedrooms and a walk in wardrobe when you've got as many clothes (especially Versoooch*) as I have.

Sam tells me the reason she left *TOWIE* was because of me, she felt like it was the only guaranteed way things could work between us. Personally I think she came off the show at just the right time anyway. When she got ill with Crohn's disease it made her think more about her life and what she wanted to do. She had other ambitions like bringing out a perfume (I still got there first though!), plus she didn't want the storylines to all be about her being ill so it was time for her to leave. Sam's a strong person – she hardly ever talks about her illness now – and she's learnt to manage it so it doesn't affect what she can do. The only difference I've noticed is that she has to eat more healthily, and she looks great because of that. It hasn't stopped us going out partying or drinking like I thought it would either – which is a bonus!

I can't pretend it doesn't make a difference to our relationship that our personal lives aren't being played out so much on camera. It means we don't argue as much as we used to, we're able to chill a lot more than we ever could before – I'm doing my thing and she's doing hers. There's no worrying about a scene you have to do the next day or paranoia about which girl or boy is coming out of the woodwork to try and stir things up between you. When we were in *TOWIE* I was constantly second guessing what was going to happen next. If we'd both still been in the show it would definitely have made things harder. Not because *TOWIE* is a curse or anything . . . it's just the way things go on there that's bound to make you have rows! Something's always going to kick off.

I remember talking to my cousin Charlie when he was about to join the show in series nine and he told me that he and Ferne were going to have the best relationship on the show. 'We'll never break up, we're too strong', he said. And now look what's happened! I love him to bits but having to deal with that sudden instant fame takes over your life and there's no way you or your relationships can't be affected by it. It's a different world.

Obviously it hasn't stopped the press saying we're splitting up every five minutes. In July I went to Ibiza with some of the boys for my birthday and as soon as I was out there looking like I was having fun (e.g. at a party in Ocean club spraying champagne in people's faces) it was reported that there were issues because Sam was at home in Essex with her sister Billie and Billie's new daughter Nelly. What they didn't know was that Sam and I already had plans to go on holiday together a couple of weeks later anyway!

After Billie gave birth I held Nelly for about a minute then got a bit scared and said, 'Can you take her back?'. Child birth is weird. I watched that programme One Born Every Minute – it's

JOEY ESSEX

*disgusting. Someone told me Gordon Ramsay refused to watch
the birth of his kids because he doesn't want to think of his
wife's noony in a different way. As disgusting as it is I think I'd
quite like it. I think it would be a mad experience.*

P Diddy was in the club Amnesia when I was out in Ibiza. I didn't
talk to him when I was there but I'm sure he was looking at me
– I think he might have liked my face. Or my style. Apparently
Rihanna was in there too but I didn't see her. She'd definitely
have liked my style. If you want to know about a mad new
celebrity friendship then me and Ed Sheeran have struck up a bit
of mutual loving. He was gigging in Ibiza when I was there and
I sent him a direct message on Twitter asking what he was up
to, and he sent me his number saying we should try to meet up.
We texted each other but never managed to get it together in the
end as he was only there for two days. He seems like a really
nice fella and I like his music so watch this space. I could imagine
the things we'd get up to when we're out – I think we'd do jokes
things like build a rope swing and hang off monkey bars and
take Instagram pictures.

Sam and I still have the odd stupid tiff like any couple but we're
not rowing massively like we used to. When I'm away doing PA's,
or on holiday without her, there are still loads of girls who will
come up and ask for a picture and when they tweet stuff like
'last night with Joey was really fun', it can't be nice for her to
see. But at the end of the day Sam trusts me and I trust her. And
we have to learn to deal with it because neither of us are going
to ignore our fans.

The main thing we argue about is the fact I'm away all the time! Since finishing this book the first time I've been jetting off all over the world for the last two and a half months filming for *Educating Joey Essex* (After the first one I did in Africa it was commissioned for a series of specials by ITV2 because it got over a million viewers, which blew me away – thanks for watching!).

By the way, I've got a mouth full of cheese at the moment, I've just made loads of cheese with crackers and I cut off way too much cheese. Now it's sticking in my teeth.

Educating Joey Essex has been a crazy experience. I've enjoyed every single minute of it, but every time I've got back home it's taken me ages to feel normal again. When I came back from Brazil I went to Lakeside to meet my mates and I just looked around at everyone going about their business shopping and I didn't feel right. I felt like I'd been living in a different world to everyone else and I was properly freaked out. Each time I've come back I don't act the same with my mates for a few days, it's like I've had to get to know them again. I don't know if it's because I've seen more of how other people live and that there are so many people out there who are poorer than us, or that it's just a massive case of jet lag – either way it messes with my little brain.

And for people out there who think the shows I'm doing are piss easy, I can genuinely say that filming them has been the hardest thing in my career. It's not like you have anyone to bounce off like you do in *TOWIE*, you're just thrown into all these strange situations and told to talk to whoever you meet. And sometimes you're knackered and sweaty and your face has gone all swollen – or you're shitting yourself about what's going to happen to you because the producers want you to do something that's out of your comfort zone (like meet some mad gangs or have your hair straightened by a woman in a Brazilian Favela . . !).

I'm going to move the cheese to the other end of the table, there's too much of it. Hang on. . .

The second *Educating Joey Essex* we shot was in Brazil for the World Cup. I loved it in Brazil. The Favela – which is a part of Brazil where all the poor people live – was cool but it was quite sad at the same time. But even though the people living there were really poor you'd never know it because they always have a smile on their faces. They say money doesn't bring you happiness and they're right (whoever 'they' actually are . . ?). I said it before and I still believe it . . . when I used to borrow twenty quid off my dad to go to the local Indian restaurant, I was always really happy. And even though I have money now, it's not like I wake up in the morning and shout 'Yeah! Money!'.

I went to one of the hairdressers in the Favela. I wanted to get a 'Brazilian blow dry' that at home means a treatment that relaxes all the curls in your hair. But as soon as I asked about it I knew they didn't have a clue what I was on about – it's probably just something the hairdressers in the UK make up to sound all continental (although I've only just learnt that word, I thought continental meant a mix of colours). The hairdresser woman then got out one of those plastic caps – just like the one I had on my head when I was a kid that's in the pictures in this book – put it on me and started pulling hair through, she was going to give me highlights! She didn't seem to know what the hell she was doing! I was getting myself into a right pickle . . . I was really worried my hair might end up looking all yellow. You can see from my face I'm not happy at all. In the end I thought, 'I'm here to do a show and there are people watching this – I have to man up and get on with it'. I was sat in the chair for about an hour and a half and you could see the fear in my eyes. I was petrified. I thought 'my hair is going to end up looking like some yellow ironing board!'. I closed my eyes then all of a sudden she pulled out some straighteners. That's all she was going to do all along. Sweet as sweetie pie. After that I'm thinking of getting my hair insured for £1 Million. Joey Essex without REEM hair would be a disaster.

That cheese is doing my head in. It's stinking the flat out and it's staring at me from the end of the coffee table. I've seriously got to stop eating cheese, it's going in the bin.

While I was in Brazil I visited this church thing – a monastery I think it's called. But the men were all like geeks and seemed really weird. None of them had girlfriends and they had rules that meant they aren't allowed to sleep with anyone – which to me is like being barred from life. I would hate to be a monk, that job must be the worst thing ever! I had to try on one of those outfits that they wear, these big dark dressing gown things – they're actually called cassocks, which sounds a bit like a giant sock. I must admit I did look quite good in a cassock, I put my shades on to complete the look. I have to admit that I had a few strops during filming, mainly because you have to film for soooo long. The problem is, if I start fuming about something the cameraman will carry on filming and you can guarantee the producer will leave that bit in the edit. When we shot *Educating Joey Essex* in Patagonia – which is the coldest place in the entire world – I stropped out endless times. And actually, I have to admit it is funny watching it back when I've had a strop on camera, because I can see how serious I am at the time and the fact that no one around me is listening to me winds me up even more! The more I'm saying 'don't film this' the more they just carry on.

I had to do loads of press for *Educating Joey Essex* when the Brazil show came out and one journalist asked me who the members of the England World Cup squad were. I could only name three of them because I only know the boats of football – the ones who are well known, the people who are 'faces'. I don't know the undercover ones. I also told them I thought Patagonia had won the world cup. And Wales. Which was wrong apparently.

The next episode of *Educating Joey Essex* we shot was about me hunting for Aliens near Vegas. I've always thought there was other life out there and now I definitely believe in aliens 100%. I went to a meeting with all these people sat round chatting about their abductions (although I thought they meant adoptions at first). There was an Essexy type woman in the corner (who was actually American), some guy with tattoos, an old lady and an old man, they were all really normal looking but the stuff they were coming out with was mad. I sat there and thought 'What the hell is going on here?'. They were telling all these stories about being abducted by aliens . . . 'Yeah you know, I've been abducted three times this week . . . '. It was so weird.

I actually believe in spirits even more than aliens. I filmed a Halloween show for *Educating Joey Essex* and that was intense! It was shot in Wales and I went to the most haunted place in England and spent the night shitting myself. I also thought I saw the ghost of Michael Jackson recently, but that was for a different show. I was set up by my manager Dave who set me up on a programme called *Tricked* on ITV. It's like *Punk'd* and I didn't have a clue I was being set up. Dave had rung me and told me I was doing photo-shoot for Lotus. He said I'd get paid £20,000 (which obviously I was buzzing about) but when I arrived I was greeted by this guy called Ben Halin – who's a magician but I thought he just worked for Lotus. He took me to this place where the car was and all of a sudden it vanished in front of me! I was spooked right out and didn't know what to do. Then the car reappeared with Michael Jackson driving it. I thought I'd gone back in time and the car had picked up Jacko! That's when the cameras came out and I was told it was all an illusion. And I never did get the 20 grand . . .

I've got a horrible spot on my face and can't stop picking it. I really think I'm getting uglier as I get older.

But of all the trips I've taken for the series visiting Patagonia was the worst. If you ever want to be freezing and wear massive

Puffa coats all the time then go to Patagonia. I was wearing my Ugg boots and they did nothing to keep me warm. Every time I walked outside the door within five minutes my toes would start throbbing and I'd be in more pain than I've ever been in my entire life. I don't know how anyone could live there.

Now I've filmed all the *Educating Joey Essex* shows I'm having loads of meetings about my next project. I got signed by Select models in the UK in May which was reem. I'm on their books as a 'special booking' (I am known as the Special One and I am quite special so I'd rather be in the 'special booking' department than anywhere in the world). The people who work there are all really easy to get on with, they're loud and funny which is perfect for me because they're not stuck up. I love them.

Maybe I'll go into politics. I could do something with my new mate Ed Miliband. I went to a big party of his in the summer and there were loads of important people there – and of course I didn't recognise any of them. The actress Emma Thompson was a guest but I didn't know who she was until someone told me she was Nanny McPhee. Every other person in there was just an Ashley to me. I did make them all do a big selfie though – every time I see Ed now I have to take a selfie! He was doing this massive speech at the party and when he started I happened to be standing next to him, so while he was talking, the whole room was looking across at us – people must've been thinking 'what the hell is Joey Essex doing stood there?' We were so close together I think I was accidentally touching his arm. I felt like he was the Prime Minister and I was about to be introduced as the upcoming Prime Minister. I mouthed to Dave, 'do you think I should be here?!' He just grinned.

Can you smell that cheese? Ughh. I need to go and take the bin out.

Ed Miliband is actually a very nice man, not the shouty one you see on TV. He always asks how I am and how my shows are going. I was meant to go to another of his parties with him and his wife recently too but I was working. Problem is I can't tell him things other than when I see him because I don't have his number. I'm not exactly sure what I'd say to him if I did . . . 'alright Ed? What's up?'. He also invited me to that courthouse where they do all the shouting and waving paper about. What's that called? Parliament? I said I'd probably get bored and want to throw paper aeroplanes about.

I've got loads of plans for what I want to do next but Hollywood isn't one of them. There have been stories in the papers about some 'celebs' wanting to crack America – and then you see them being papped pretending they've been to loads of important meetings. But I know my limits and I know it's important to do as much as I can here before I have some mad illusions that someone across the pond will know who I am. When you start thinking you're too big for your boots that's when it all goes wrong. Not naming any names but there are a few people I could mention.

Oh yeah, since I wrote the first part of this book Diags has finally got a girlfriend – he's dating Fran from TOWIE and is all in love. He's like a little giggly geek. It's so nice to see him happy but he gets himself too locked up in relationships . . . I thought I was bad but he's a million times worse than me. He moves in after knowing someone for about a day. I have got to move out of my flat soon too. I did find an amazing house but someone bought it . . . I can't wait to move, I'll be a lot happier in a nice big house with gates, a pool, a butler, a nightclub, a gym, a slide and a see-saw – I'll be like Willy Wonka and Joey's Creepy Sick Yard. My next plan will be to buy a villa in Ibiza. I've already made an appointment to see some places out there – I want to build a spa. I'm going to call it something flush* like 'Sea-Froo' (which is like see-through but by the sea).

Oh and I've got a new addition to my family – his name is Prince and he's a Bengal cat with the most amazing leopard print fur. I always wanted a Bengal but they're really rare and hard to find. I went to loads of breeders and when I saw Prince I had to have him. At first the man told me he wasn't for sale . . . but I wanted him so badly I wouldn't stop until he let me buy him. The other cats were about 300 quid but because Prince had such an amazing print on him I paid £1,200. He's a proper good cat too (Diags has one called Diago and he's nasty and fat like a rat) but Prince is amazing.

I feed him roast dinner and biscuits, but his poo stinks worse than any poo I've ever smelt. He walks into windows and I talk to him when he's around. Obviously I can't have him at my house every night as I'm away a lot so Tracey looks after him at her house. Problem is he's so cute that she never wants to give him back! I love having a cat because he's quite pimpy* and I can use him as a cat scarf and put him round my neck. So next time you see me walking down the street and you think 'Wow, look at Joey's amazing neck scarf' . . . it will probably be Prince.

Although i'd better not feed him too many more roast dinners because the scarf might turn into a massive leopard print rug.

I don't know what's going on with my hair here! Looks like I have curtains, which I don't.

JOEY'S FASCINATING FACTS:

#11 Pig's brains are more sophisticated than dogs and they are actually cleverer than human 3-year-olds. *I wonder if there's a pig that's cleverer than me . . .?*

EPILOGUE

I was thinking the other day about the sort of things I want to make my goals for the future.

In five years' time I'll be 28 and I'll hopefully have *Joey Essex: The Movie*. It'll be like an hour and a half episode of *TOWIE* but just of me. It might be two hours long actually, I don't think I can get everything in in an hour.

In ten years' time I'll be 33 and living in America. My goal for the age of 33 is that I'd like to be able to breakdance. I'll be married by then too. That's why I'll be able to breakdance because I'll be more secure. You can't breakdance unless you're secure because you need to have someone when you get home making your dinner. Oh and I'll have about five kids.

It makes me feel weird thinking what I'll be doing ten years after that. I'll be 43! Eugh! I won't be able to do anything by then because I'll be so old! I'll have stopped breakdancing because my bones will hurt and I'll have moved to Spain. I really want to learn Spanish. My goal is to be able to talk sentences to waitresses. I'll be chilled and relaxed on the beach and look nice and tanned all the time. My kids will be at a Spanish school and I might change my name so it sounds better out there – Giuseppe or Antonio. Someone just told me they're Italian names but never mind. I'll have a new business – 'Giuseppe's beach club'.

In forty years' time I'll be 63. That's really, really old. By then I'll have told my kids to look after me. They won't need to help me with money though because I'll be a famous fashion designer. I'll be telling people how to dress, I think I'll be good at that. I might live on a yacht in Ibiza when I'm that old. And there will be loads of girls sunbathing on the deck around me. I'll have a long silver beard and hair in a bun. Or a 'mun'. I don't think I'll go bald – I hope I don't anyway. That would freak me right out. I'd have to wear a different wig every day.

Now you've read my book you've hopefully learnt some stuff about how to live like me. It's all about being as reem as you can. But just in case you don't get what I mean, I've come up with a few Rules of Reem. And just to make them extra reem all the rules begin with R. So I'll leave you with these.

I hope you remember them.

The Rules of Reem (beginning with R)

Read

Only this book. I've never read a whole book in my life but I'm definitely reading this one the whole way through. Be prepared to learn about a very different way of life. Don't worry about history books or any of that nonsense.

Race

A reem person should always come at least first or second in a race. If you don't, then don't tell anyone because it doesn't count in your collection of trophies.

Run

Run away from people who tell you off. But only from between the ages of 11 and 16, that's the running age. When you're older you can't run away from things. You have to face up to them. Otherwise it's against the rule of reem.

Romance

If you're reem you're a romantic person. Always buy small gifts for your girlfriend – like knickers or bras. It's good to buy little gifts for each other. A reem girl can give something little to a boy for a present too. Like a toy frog or something. I sometimes buy mugs – if I've gone to a country like Dubai or Disneyland. I know girls like getting flowers but they go after a week. A mug is better than flowers, it's much more thoughtful. Flowers are usually bought for arguments or Valentine's.

Radical

That's the American version of reem. Or 'rad' for short. In America they probably say 'That outfit is radical' when they mean reem.

Randall

Don't be a randall. A randall is a snitch. I used to watch a cartoon called *Recess* and there was a character called Randall in it. A snitch is someone who gets themselves involved in other people's stuff, which gets them into trouble they don't need to get into.

Room service
The reemest way to get food! Even better than a posh restaurant. If you want room service you just need to lean over and pick up the phone. It's just a phone call away.

Ring
Personally, rings hurt my fingers. But rings are good to buy for a girl – maybe a promise ring when you're young and an engagement ring when you're older. Boys should only wear a ring when they're getting married. Not before.

Royal
This sounds like loyal, which is important for someone who's reem. Always be loyal. The royals are also reem – they seem like a good laugh to go out with. The party royal is the most reem though because he goes to Vegas. What's his name again?

Raphael
I'm just saying random things beginning with R now . . .

Ralfie
Anything called Ralfie is reem. That's my dad's dog's name. Dogs are pretty reem anyway, they just hang about eating and sleeping. They don't need to try and be reem – they just are.

Reply

You should always reply to texts. Always. Reem people are not rude. The only time you might not reply is if you're in a business meeting.

Wrong

I know it's not spelt with an R but it sounds like it is. It's always important to admit you're wrong if you're reem. Otherwise you're a liar. And reem people don't lie. E.g. If someone comes to your house and you've bought a lasagne – you should never lie and say you cooked it. Why would you bother pretending you've made it when you can go to Marks and Spencer and buy a sick one that they've made?

Rainbow

Rainbows are reem. They're colourful and remind me of holiday. They're sick.

Robot

That's the ultimate thing to have for someone who's reem. I'd love to have a robot even more than a monkey. They're servants and don't even mind.

Rabies

Don't get it. No one reem gets rabies because it means they'll end up foaming from the mouth and look like they've had a bubble bath.

Relief

It's a relief when you get things finished. Just like this book. I usually say 'It's in the bag' when I've achieved something. And this book is now 'In the bag'. I hope you've enjoyed it.

Stay reem.

Love Joey x

Things I've Learnt Doing This Book

Richard and Judy didn't actually create the world

Elton John isn't Ozzy Osbourne

Wales doesn't border London or Russia

The prime minister isn't called Gordon Ramsay and there isn't a prime minister of Essex

Koalas aren't electric

Cabbage and lettuce aren't the same thing

Stick insects are like actual sticks with brains

Submerged means you're underwater

A punch line is the end of a joke

Charles Dickens is not in the royal family. He wrote books

Blue is not the name of the royal baby, that's George

Guy Fawkes didn't die on the cross. He tried to blow up Parliament

Jesus's mum is called Mary not Zesus

Michael was not in the Beatles

The plural of mouse is mice not mouses

A square has four sides not six

Blow-drying and hair-drying are the same thing

Parliament is where politicians work and doesn't have the flag up when people are in – that's Buckingham Palace

OCD means obsessive compulsive disorder not over controlled dilemma

'Mutton dressed as lamb' doesn't mean you look like a lamb, it means you're dressing too young for your age

Vanessa Feltz is not the woman who does the voiceover for *TOWIE*

Paris is not the name of an ocean

Ricky Gervais isn't a singer

David is not Obama's first name

Tenerife is not the capital of Spain

RSVP is not something to do with pets

BAFTA means British Academy of Film and Television Awards

MP is Member of Parliament (although I still think it should be MOP)

Manifesto isn't men having a party

Joey Dictionary

Abalooleelalelin – Absolutely disgusting

Agg – Aggravating, annoying

Allow – No thanks, e.g. 'I won't allow that'

Apple juice – Used to get out of awkward conversations. 'Give me an apple juice' means 'Get this person away from me'

Ashley – Something to call people if you don't know their name

Baffed – Confused (baffled)

Bait – Annoying or out of order

Bare jokes – Very funny

Bare long – Extra long

Bean – Idiot

Blurt – Run fast

Boat – A cool and suave individual who is usually wealthy

Breading – To creep or brown-nose around someone

Capri Sun – Silly, stupid

Cheese and onion – A dirty-looking girl who is not very pretty

Confrontate – To stand up to someone

Creasin' – Funny, e.g. 'I was creasin' up'

Downer – Feeling low or fed up

Flush – Perfect, really fresh and clean

Fusey – A bit like a street version of **reem**; a way to describe an extra-cool and unique dress sense

Glumptious – Tasty

Jokes – Funny

Laggin – Pissed, drunk

Latex – Later (e.g: 'I'll see you latex')

Long – Annoying or too much effort. 'Do you want to go for a run tonight?' 'No, that's long'

Lotion – Drip

Lunchbox – Something no one gives a shit about

Melt – Someone who's a bit wet

Mug – Idiot, make a fool of. E.g. 'Don't mug me off'

Muggy – Bad-mouthing/out of order

Murders – Trouble or big arguments

Naughty – Can be good or bad

Nit – Not. E.g. 'Oh my god that girl's well fit – NIIIT!'

Noony – Vagina

Para – Paranoid

Pesto Pasta – A pest (Arg's new nickname because he keeps pestering me to come out)

Pied – To be dumped or made to look an idiot in some way

Pimpy – Pimp like, to look cool

Prawn cocktail – A good-looking girl. Also known as a **salty potato** or a **sort**

Reem – Brilliant, good, cool, fashionable (See also: *Creepy sick*)

Roogst – Shag. 'Did you roogst her last night?'

Richard – Slang for Richard the Third. Meaning bird

Salty Potato – (See also: Prawn Cocktail)

Say say – Also used to describe the feeling of something good. Usually used along with '**What what**' and '**Do do**', e.g. 'I pulled a right salty potato last night. Say say what what do do!'

Screwface – An angry expression used when you don't like someone

Seen – OK, standard, alright

Shakespeare – A term used to describe someone with a very shaky or wobbly hand

Sick/creepy sick – Good, brilliant (See also: Reem)

Sicked out – Had a fit or got angry

Skeen – Sweet, good

Skitz – A bit mad, nuts

Slush Puppy – An idiot

Sort – (See also: Prawn Cocktail)

Super boat – Extra cool and suave. Better than a 'boat'

Techers – Technique

Topping – To 'top' something or to have something better than someone else

Turbs – To get out of somewhere quickly like Turbo Man. E.g. 'I was gone again like turbs'

Turner – 'Turn up for the books'. Can mean good or bad. E.g. 'I went out last night and this girl didn't want to get with me – what a turner.' Or 'I just won £200 – what a turner!'

Versooch – Versace

Weapon – An extra-good-looking girl, usually a model or a film star

What are YOU sayin'? – A way to express excitement about something you've done. E.g. 'I just bought a Ferrari – what are YOU sayin'?'

Zeypenning – What's happening? (e.g: 'hey Diags; zeypenning?)

Acknowledgements

Firstly I'd like to thank Lucie Cave for helping me turn my life into words you can read and enjoy. I don't know why she's called a ghostwriter, she's not actually a ghost, she's a real person! Anyway, she's sat in my flat and drank the cups of coffee I've made her and I don't think ghosts like coffee. A big thank you too to my editor, Briony Gowlett, and all of the brilliant team at Hodder & Stoughton, including Liz Caraffi, Veronique Norton, Bea Long and Sophie Camp. I also want to thank my manager, Dave Read of Neon management, and literary agent Amanda Preston of LBA, for all their support and encouragement and getting me the deal to write my own book (I still can't believe it!). Finally, thank you to all my family and friends for always believing in me and being there for me. You are all reem!

Picture Credits

The author and publisher would like to thank the following copyright-holders for permission to reproduce images in this book:

Alamy/Wenn: 23; © Camera Press London: 20 (Ray Burmiston); Corbis UK/Splash News: 16, 26; FremantleMedia: 37; Getty Images: 42 (WireImage); PA Photos: 19, 35; Rex Features: 27, 29; Rex Features/ITV: 17, 18, 21, 22, 24, 25, 30, 31, 32, 33, 34; Wenn: 28

All other images are care of the author.

The author and publishers have made all reasonable efforts to contact copyright-holders for permission, and apologise for any omissions or errors in the form of credits given. Corrections may be made to future printings.

What are YOU Saying?

WE ASKED FANS FOR MESSAGES TO JOEY AND HERE'S WHAT THEY HAD TO SAY. . .

@rickardzz I'm a big fan cos you're the main man, you're like a dream always looking reem. I love your charm so I got you tattooed on my arm

@LeahEssexFaiers LOOK REEM SMELL REEM BE REEM REEM

@alice_essex Joey Essex is everything you could ask for in an idol, so proud

@arianneM_x Joey Essex, if you were a potato in a field, you'd be the saltiest

@_sophiejohnsonx I love you so much Joey and I'm proud of you!! Next time you go to Africa make sure you don't get bitten by a monkey x

@rachelmagee Congratulations on your new book, can't wait to read it, love you

@erinmccarthyxx I can't stress how much I love @JoeyEssex_

he's such a legend! I got his CD, now gotta wait till May to get his book. #buzzing

@Towie_Officials All fans are so proud of Joey! You've come so far! Don't Stop Being Reem ;) What are you saying!

@LucyAmdur I love u Joey

@phoebejones_x I love you so much, you're my idol and I hope my dream comes true to see you one day, stay reem love you forever

@megaanlaura so proud of how far you've come joey, this book is going to be so amazing! P.s. Try not to get bitten by any more monkeys ;)

@Toni_Sharland can't believe how well you're doing man! Proud of you! Keep it REEM bro

@Chloe_Williams8 all us fans are so proud of you, love you loads <3

@RosieJenkins_ yo yo yo my name is Joe! I will always love you JOEY!! You are amazing! :))

@Lucy_Alford14 I love you even though you can't blow your nose, tell the time and think that Richard&Judy created the world. #teamjoey

@darcylouiseeX Joey there are not enough characters on here to express how much ily! <3 Your so adoreable and cutee! Ilysm <3

@EmilyJe27 yo yo my name is Emily! I'm a huge fan of yours and love you soo make me a fusey girl and pop my message in your book

@Emmaloves youxox So proud of you Joey for everything you've achieved and I know you're going to go so so far

@jess2000hsm you are beautiful and reem, make me smile so

much xxx educating Joey is the best thing in the world. Love you xxx

@JillieB_Xx Fuseys, ankle watches, creepy sick, reem, Joey Essex has invented more things than you ever will. What are you sayin? Say nuttin

@LiamOfficial1 you're the best inspiration ever keep going never look down WE LOVE YOU

@kaays_henry I hope I meet Joey one day, and give him a kiss and a cuddle and say.. I LOVE YOU!!

@jennychandler99 I love you so much, you're actually the funniest person to watch on tv <3

@adjoka99 This book will need its own dictionary of Joey-isms. So proud of you Joey. Well done. STAY REEM. BE REEM.

@Bradley_jay9 so proud of you bud, you've come on so far in life, I'm a celeb was hilarious, your hair is sick! Love you joey

@jade29belieber Joey is such a nice person, he is really funny as well, his jokes are amazing!!

@EILajOneS100 I have been a fan from when you first appeared on TOWIE 2011 and I am still a fan to this day in 2014 and I will always be a fan

@hannahmounseyxo you started off just being on TV, you have become the face of Essex, you've come so far. You're reem, lots of love

@MrsEssex_Reem I love Joey Essex so much I would do anything to meet him he is my idol he is so perfect omg though he is hot!

@monicataylor_12 the boy was taken out of essex, but essex will never be taken out of the boy (literally because it's his surname)

@charloxoxox wot are you sayin charl? Im saying that joey is the most reemest man on earth, and being forever totally reem, love charl x

@Rebecca_McC90 Joey Essex is Reem. That's the score, you know the score, what you gonna say. NUTTIN

@Michelle4uxxx 'Yo yo yo ma name is Joe' 'What are you saying?' 'REEM' that's why we love you, because of the amazing looks, hair and personality

@lozza2015 I love you so much. You are so cute and amazing!!! <3 you xxx love laura xx

@Becks_xxxx So proud of you joey , you've made us all so proud and we will continue to support you throughout everything love you joey! <3

@BandOverload_ #LookingReem love you Joey, you've come soo far, and you're amazing! Love you soo much <3

@tia_ashton When someone makes up a word like reem and people say he's dumb.. as if.. Joey Essex is proper smart so #whatyougonnasay

@LouWottonX So so proud of you Joey, you have made us fans so proud and will continue to support you throughout everything love you Joey!

@HawaMalik1 Joey I love you so much omg ;), you're so funny, and so cute, I wish you came back to towie L xxx

@kristenbrannanx you are the most hilarious person ever I love you

@Beckyleigh_x Joey started the 'reem' word now everyone uses it

@SophiaNeale Joey is perfect, his awkward smile, his laugh and his cluelessness never fails to make me smile, this book will be the same.

@megannicolexxx I love you joey I know your mum is looking down on you and is very proud of you and so are all your fans

@HisGirlKyraa Joey Essex Is Just Too Reem!! I Love Him So Much!! Stay Reem And Keep Dreaming! Live Life To The Fullest! From Kyra xx

@_jesslovesjoey the only person who wears shoes too small and can't tell the time but this is why we love him

@yea_im_meg Joey I love you so much! What you saying? You're soo. . . REEM! I love you man! You're creepy sick especially your show love you man <3

@alysha_browne Joey Essex is doing so well! Fusey, His T.V show, Hair products, Perfumes, calendars and now his book!

@chloenoble4 You're anyones checklist! You've created words of your own, your hair styles have been reem, dress sense is perfecto longggg!

@laramacphersonx No matter how bad my day gets I know for a fact if I watch 15 mins of Joey Essex I'll be smiling! #HappyDay

@Morgan_24_ your mum will be so proud up there, you should be proud too, all of your fans are here for you

@lornaellen you are very inspirational and show that people can succeed by just being themselves #yoyomynameisjoe

@rubyBenfieldXxx look reem! Smell reem! Be reem! REEM!!

@SophieEssex_ Yo yo yo your name is Joe, you're so reem even tho you can be slow, your fusey reem hair is done with the blow, just remember Joe, Many fans love you loads <3

@tia_ashton Slinkin around just #beingreem what you gonna say.. reem on mate #yhhhhhhh I love you

@ellenamyxx Hi Joey, I love you so much I can't believe I went on Facetime with you once! You're so funny, lovely and REEM!

@Animallover88 You made a book we all should read and take a look! the words you use are really sick and not to mention super slick

@shanshan_beer This book is going to be absolute jokes, what you saying? It's so long waiting for it to come out man

@howesjordan1993 mate you're one of the coolest guys I've seen on TV you're loved by so many people and myself. Hope to meet you sometime.

@MelanieMuir2 you have started off a trend of fuseys Mr Joey Essex, feel proud and the fact that Essex is actually your surname is fab

@jolieprincess3 Joey what r u saying about putting me in your book you're not a Capri sun, and it won't be long if I meet you, you are amazing

@Claire_Caoilin Joey makes me smile everyday he is such an inspiration I hope to get as far as he has when I'm older love Caoilin

@holly_moses This sentence is extremely reem but not as half as reem as everything else in this book

@Leeshyylou He might not be 'educated' but he's educated his fans, to love, to laugh, and to live. Elisha Thompson Bedford

@Big_Ray_LTFC I could say me and Joey Essex have a lot in common for example we are not idiots and we are not twins but we are both funny

@livmccarthy3 Joey's book comes out 4 days before my bday, it would be the BEST present if my message was in it – Yo yo yo yeh my idols name is Joe, he's the king of Reem since 1990

What are YOU Sayin.. He will only confrontate you if there's a purpose, he thought Richard&Judy created the world, he could have a dictionary called Joeyisms and he walks on water. There is only ONE Joey Essex and I'm proud to say he's my idol and inspiration. I can't wait to read Being Reem, I know it will be a top seller because of his amazing story. I'm so proud of you Joey love you lots

@TaliaEssex you're the nicest person I have ever met and you're so funny!!! You're one reem man!! Xx

@backofthebuswot *inserts I will always love you by Whitney Houston

@AntoniaHollowa8 Joey is so sweet, kind and funny – everything you need to be Reem! Such a genuine guy, Joey should be the definition of Reem

@livfaiers_ look reem smell reem be reem. If it wasn't for Joey Essex reem, creepy sick, fusey wouldn't be in this world

@welljel1 Every single one of his fans are so proud with everything he has achieved, most perfect person ever x

@casey_osman so many of your sayings have become well known. The other day I called my dad and he answered saying 'wot are you sayin? Nuttin'

@michaelealiston I love you Joey you are amazing one of your biggest fans stay reem

@daydreaminbcjde perfection at its finest @JoeyEssex

@Eden_T2012 I just love Joey for purely being Joey

@jazessex Joey Essex to us fans is the most funniest, nicest, caring, bright teethed creepysick Essex boy

@miarichards1 Good luck for the future and your book is going to be sick! Love from siouxsie xx

@hannaaah_1 Joey Essex is creepy sick and my love for him is reem so what are you sayin?! Xo

@chloe_williams8 So proud of you Joey for everything, can't wait to read your book! Stay Reem Joe! Love you

@chloestevensss He thought that Richard and Judy created the world, He's never learnt how to blow his nose, He's sick at counting, He walks on water, he thought Russia bordered Wales; He made up the words fusey and REEM! There's only one Joey essex, he's amazing and an inspiration! And this is why we love him! Love you Joey